The Trinitarian Dharma

American Society of Missiology Monograph Series

Chair of Series Editorial Committee, James R. Krabill

The ASM Monograph Series provides a forum for publishing quality dissertations and studies in the field of missiology. Collaborating with Pickwick Publications—a division of Wipf and Stock Publishers of Eugene, Oregon—the American Society of Missiology selects high quality dissertations and other monographic studies that offer research materials in mission studies for scholars, mission and church leaders, and the academic community at large. The ASM seeks scholarly work for publication in the series that throws light on issues confronting Christian world mission in its cultural, social, historical, biblical, and theological dimensions.

Missiology is an academic field that brings together scholars whose professional training ranges from doctoral-level preparation in areas such as Scripture, history and sociology of religions, anthropology, theology, international relations, interreligious interchange, mission history, inculturation, and church law. The American Society of Missiology, which sponsors this series, is an ecumenical body drawing members from Independent and Ecumenical Protestant, Catholic, Orthodox, and other traditions. Members of the ASM are united by their commitment to reflect on and do scholarly work relating to both mission history and the present-day mission of the church. The ASM Monograph Series aims to publish works of exceptional merit on specialized topics, with particular attention given to work by younger scholars, the dissemination and publication of which is difficult under the economic pressures of standard publishing models.

Persons seeking information about the ASM or the guidelines for having their dissertations considered for publication in the ASM Monograph Series should consult the Society's website—www.asmweb.org.

Members of the ASM Monograph Committee who approved this book are:

Susan Maros, Affiliate Assistant Professor of Christian Leadership
Fuller Theological Seminary

Sue Russell, Professor of Mission and Contextual Studies
Asbury Theological Seminary

RECENTLY PUBLISHED IN THE ASM MONOGRAPH SERIES

George Shakwelele, *Explaining the Practice of Elevating an Ancestor for Veneration*

Peter T. Lee, *Hybridizing Mission: Intercultural Social Dynamics among Christian Workers on Multicultural Teams in North Africa*

The Trinitarian Dharma

Contributing to the Mosaic of Global Christianity

Pabitra Mani Bhandari

American Society of Missiology Monograph Series 74

☙PICKWICK *Publications* · Eugene, Oregon

THE TRINITARIAN DHARMA
Contributing to the Mosaic of Global Christianity

American Society of Missiology Monograph Series 74

Copyright © 2025 Pabitra Mani Bhandari. All rights reserved. Except for brief quotations in critical publications or reviews, no part of this book may be reproduced in any manner without prior written permission from the publisher. Write: Permissions, Wipf and Stock Publishers, 199 W. 8th Ave., Suite 3, Eugene, OR 97401.

Pickwick Publications
An Imprint of Wipf and Stock Publishers
199 W. 8th Ave., Suite 3
Eugene, OR 97401

www.wipfandstock.com

PAPERBACK ISBN: 978-1-6667-6370-6
HARDCOVER ISBN: 978-1-6667-6371-3
EBOOK ISBN: 978-1-6667-6372-0

Cataloguing-in-Publication data:

Names: Bhandari, Pabitra Mani, author.

Title: The Trinitarian dharma : contributing to the mosaic of global Christianity / Pabitra Mani Bhandari.

Description: Eugene, OR: Pickwick Publications, 2025. | American Society of Missiology Monograph Series 74. | Includes bibliographical references.

Identifiers: ISBN 978-1-6667-6370-6 (paperback). | ISBN 978-1-6667-6371-3 (hardcover). | ISBN 978-1-6667-6372-0 (ebook).

Subjects: LCSH: Christianity and other religions. | Theology—Doctrinal | Trinity. | Nepal. | Christianity and culture.

Classification: BR118 B24 2025 (print). | BR118 (ebook).

VERSION NUMBER 02/21/25

Dedicated to

Adherents of Christian Dharma in the Himalayas

Contents

List of Illustrations | viii
Preface | ix
Acknowledgments | xiii

1. Introduction | 1
2. Dharma: The Social Foundation | 21
3. The Crossroads of Faith: Exploring the Confluence of Christianity and Dharma | 45
4. Apostles' Creed to Social Trinity: Navigating the Trinitarian Journey | 62
5. Building Bridges: The Social Trinity as the Cornerstone of Constructive Theology | 88
6. In Action: Unveiling The Social Trinity in Contextual Engagement | 103
7. Dharma And the Social Trinity: A Transformative Encounter | 128
8. Dharma Unveiled: The Trinitarian Praxis of a Global Church | 154
9. Bridging Nepali *Dharma* and the Social Trinity for the Transformation of the Church | 162

Glossary | 165
Appendix—Timeline of Political and Religious Development in Nepal | 171
Bibliography | 175

Illustrations

Figure 1—Distribution of Population by Religion in Nepal, 1951–2001 Censuses | 57

Figure 2—Relationship of Action to Theology in Dharma | 132

Figure 3—Flow of Theology and Praxis in Social Trinity | 133

Figure 4—Cooperation between Dharma and Theology in the context of Nepal | 135

Figure 5—Proposed Relation between Dharma, Trinity, and Nepali Church | 151

Preface

As I set out to explore Christian teachings, my intellectual journey naturally led me through the corridors of Western Christian theologies. From church history courses to broader educational pursuits, the narrative was predominantly Western-centric—a logical consequence of the West's integral role in spreading Christianity across the globe. For a significant stretch, Christianity and the West were virtually synonymous.

Yet, the tides have shifted. We find ourselves in an era where Christianity has carved out its narrative on the global stage, no longer tethered solely to Western influences. The story of global Christianity unfolds with unique characteristics, diverging from the well-trodden path of Western Churches. It has evolved into a force with distinctive traits, some of which are entirely new and unfamiliar to the Western Christian experience. Within the pages of this book, I aim to shed light on the nuanced struggles of global Christians as they navigate multi-religious landscapes, traverse non-Western cultures, and grapple with social challenges distinct from those faced in the West. The responses to these challenges have given rise to a mosaic of new global theologies, each a testament to the dynamic nature of faith in a changing world.

This work doesn't claim to be the definitive account but stands as one voice among many contributing to the ongoing conversation about the diverse nature of global Christianity. It acknowledges that any attempt to encapsulate the essence of Christianity within a singular definition is futile. The dynamism of global Christianity constantly shapes new characteristics in response to the diverse challenges posed by unique contexts.

Preface

It's crucial to recognize that nothing evolves in isolation. While global Christianity charts its unique course, it remains intricately connected to the currents of Western thought. Relationships are fostered, and an ongoing dialogue is maintained, revealing a symbiotic connection that shapes the contours of global Christian development.

Theological contemplation grapples with reconciling the persons of the Son, Jesus Christ, and the Holy Spirit within the framework of Jewish monotheism. This struggle birthed the doctrine of the Trinity—a distinctly Christian conceptualization of the monotheistic essence of three divine persons. The ambiguity surrounding this concept necessitates an ongoing process of redefinition. On the global stage, the exploration of the Trinity goes beyond its original definition, inviting new perspectives and interpretations. This book, in particular, seeks to transplant the core tenets of the Christian idea of God into the culturally rich context of Nepal. In this intricate process, the Trinity becomes not only relevant to the specific context but also enriches our understanding of the Divine through the lens of a unique cultural tapestry.

I present this book as an exemplar of theology unfolding on the global stage—a convergence where the nuances of a specific context and the timeless truths of the Trinity engage in a symbiotic dance, mutually informing and transforming one another. May this exploration serve as an inviting gateway, encouraging readers to delve deeper into the rich diversity of global Christian thought and celebrating the vibrant tapestry that is the Trinitarian Dharma.

IN THIS BOOK

Christianity in Nepal faces the imperative to define its identity and mission amidst the prevailing political and social pressures. To effectively navigate this challenging context, Nepali Christianity must cultivate an indigenous contextual theology that resonates with Nepali society. This study endeavors to facilitate a constructive dialogue between Nepali dharma and the concept of the social Trinity, establishing the groundwork for a Nepali contextual theology. Initially, the research delves into the understanding of dharma within the Nepali context. Subsequently, it posits that social trinitarianism serves as a fitting platform to initiate a constructive discourse between Christianity and Nepali dharma. Finally, the study presents a constructive dialogue between Nepali dharma and social Trinity, offering guidance to the Nepali church in engaging with society and addressing prevalent social issues.

Nepali dharma, representing the practical religiosity of the Nepali people, serves as the bedrock for family, community, and the entire nation of Nepal. Nepali culture and dharma are inseparable, with dharma providing a collective identity for the people while also delineating individual responsibilities toward family, society, and the nation. The creative engagement of Nepali Christianity with Nepali dharma is indispensable for establishing a meaningful connection with Nepali society, as a superficial relationship falls short of the desired outcome. However, the intricacies of Nepali dharma, entwined with social issues such as the caste system, women's suffering, and poverty, necessitate a thoughtful approach. The indigenization of Christianity within the framework of Nepali dharma must concurrently address these social challenges, rendering any Nepali contextual theology relevant to addressing societal issues like the caste system, women's suffering, and poverty.

Social Trinity emerges as a theological gateway for Nepali Christianity to embark on a constructive dialogue with Nepali dharma. Rooted in the community of three divine persons, the perichoretic relationship of God, and trinitarian openness to human history, social trinitarianism offers a model for Nepali Christianity to formulate a theology tailored to the Nepali community and foster a connection with Nepali society reflective of divine perichoresis. While Nepali dharma necessitates the transformation of Nepali Christianity into a practical religiosity, the openness of social trinitarianism provides the means to integrate it into the fabric of Nepali Christian life. Dharma, when embraced as part of the Trinity, mirrors communion, equality, and mutual surrender. This trinitarian praxis positions the Nepali church on a distinctive trinitarian mission, addressing the challenges faced by women, low-caste individuals, and poverty within society.

—Pabitra Mani Bhandari

Acknowledgments

I WOULD LIKE TO express my profound gratitude to God the Almighty for granting me the opportunity to pursue my PhD studies at the Global Institute of Theology (GIT), Yonsei University, and for guiding me through the successful completion of this academic journey.

My heartfelt thanks go to Prof. Jun Hyun-Shik for his invaluable supervision and guidance in my research. I am indebted to GIT director Prof. Dr. Samuel Pang for his unwavering support from the inception of my project. Special appreciation is extended to Prof. Han Sung Kim (ACTS) and Seung Hyun Chung (Juan International University) for graciously accepting the role of readers for my dissertation. I am grateful for the concern and assistance provided by Prof. Chammah J. Kaunda and the encouragement and support offered by other faculty members of UGST whose commitment to GIT students, including myself, has been commendable. To my friends from around the globe at GIT, your camaraderie has been a source of strength and inspiration.

My deepest appreciation extends to my family and the members of Juan Church Nepali ministries, who have been my pillars of support. My parents (Nagendra M. Bhandari and Yuddha Maya Bhandari) have been my prayer warriors, interceding with God on my behalf. I am indebted to my wife, Eunice Bhandari, for her unwavering encouragement and support, ensuring that I did not overlook any important dates in my schedule. The smiles of my children, Rhoda and Enoch, brightened my heart and made them invaluable study companions during the dissertation writing phase. The sincere members of Nepal Juan church provided

Acknowledgments

me with a home away from home, offering Nepali food and unwavering understanding of my conflicting schedules. Their prayers and support were instrumental in my journey.

Lastly, I extend my gratitude to the Monograph publishing arm of the American Society of Mission for their significant role in transforming my dissertation into this book, with their thorough reviews and valuable suggestions. This journey has been a testament to God's provision, and I am sincerely thankful for the collective support that has brought my study to fruition.

1

Introduction

BACKGROUND AND STATEMENT OF THE PROBLEM

THIS STUDY ENDEAVORS TO facilitate a dialogue between the social Trinity and the concept of *dharma*, aiming to construct a contextual theology for Nepal within the trinitarian praxis model. The initiation of Nepali contextual theology involves a comprehensive examination of the role, characteristics, and meaning of *dharma* in Nepali society. Rather than delving into the intricate definitions and theories within Hindu-Buddhist scriptures and teachings, this research focuses on discerning the implications of *dharma* on the formation of identity, values, and the overarching social system of Nepal. This understanding serves as the contextual bedrock for the formulation of Nepali contextual theology. Additionally, the trinitarian model provides a framework through which the Nepali church can embody and fulfill its transformative mission.

Contextualizing Christianity within the framework of Nepali *dharma* holds immense significance, given the prevailing perception of Christianity as a foreign religion in Nepal. The first decade of the twenty-first century marked a pivotal period for the nation, witnessing a political upheaval that culminated in the abolition of the 240-year-old monarchy and the transition from a Hindu Kingdom to a secular republic. This transformative era not only reshaped the political landscape but also interrupted the religious

The Trinitarian Dharma

practices associated with the monarchy, where the King was revered as an incarnation of Vishnu, the Hindu God.[1]

As Nepal embraced its identity as a federal republic without a monarchical office, the Christian community, perennially under threat, found a sense of relief. The conducive political environment fostered remarkable growth for Christianity in the country.[2] However, this period of respite was short-lived, as the newly formed communist government, aligning with the Hindu majority, passed a restrictive bill in August 2017, curbing Christian activities in Nepal.[3] Subsequently, Nepali Christians once again found themselves on the defensive, facing accusations of proselytizing and experiencing arrests.[4]

The Nepali Church confronts a dual challenge stemming from these conflicting forces and the evolving socio-political landscape. First, Nepali people are suspicious that Christianity's spread eventually will facilitate Nepal's long-term subordination to Western interests.[5] Nepali Christianity is over-dependent on foreign aid for its projects gives credibility to the claim that Christianity is an arm of the western empire.[6] For the majority of Nepali people, Christianity is a *bidesi dharma*, or foreign religion that damages its culture and way of life because for them, "Hinduism [is] the bedrock of Nepali identity,"[7] and converting to Christianity is losing one's *dharma* (religion one's dignity and identity of being Nepali).[8] Christianity in Nepal has the task of proving that they are not part of an empire, and their interest lies in Nepali society alone. Sometimes Christians are blamed for luring underprivileged Nepali people to Christianity in return for economic or material benefits.[9] Unfortunately, when Nepal was declared a secular state, some Christians took it as if it were their

---

1. Mocko, *Demoting Vishnu: Ritual, Politics*, 1–4.

2. Central Bureau of Statistics, *Population Monograph of Nepal*, 22.

3. Ochab, "Nepal's Protection of Religious Freedom on Downward Spiral," para 10. Shellnutt, "Nepal Criminalizes Christian Conversion and Evangelism," lines 1–5.

4. Wagner, "A Rumour of Empire," 147. Wagner reports bomb explosions at two churches in Jhapa, a Southern district bordering India.

5. Wagner, "A Rumour of Empire," 148.

6. Khatry, "Church and mission relationship in Nepal," 301–5.

7. Wagner, "A Rumour of Empire," 162.

8. Letizia, "Shaping Secularism in Nepal," 81.

9. Fricke, "Tamang Conversions: Culture, Politics and the Christian," 58. Fricke found out that material and economic advantage was one of reasons for Tamang people's conversion to Christianity.

Introduction

victory, which brought an immediate accusation to Christianity.[10] Nepali people characterize conversion to Christianity as a change of culture. For example, people are eager to change their Hindu or indigenous Nepali names to biblical or western names, and the western style of marriage ceremony in the church is considered the authentic biblical wedding.[11] Since Christianity in Nepal is a minority group in a Hindu majority country with many social problems such as the caste system, discrimination against women, unemployment, poverty, decades-long political instability, and war, it cannot limit its transformation cultural aspects alone.[12] In the present condition, Nepali Christianity faces multiple challenges. The foremost challenge is, how can the Nepali church make itself part of the larger Nepali society. What sort of cultural and religious aspect of Nepali society does the Nepali church have to reflect on to be part of the Nepali community? Politically, Nepali Christianity has a task to resolve its role in society and find how the Nepali church can witness God's love, justice, and salvation or liberation in the community.

Dharma, which is commonly translated into English as "religion," means righteousness, and in Nepali society, it is a way or duty of life.[13] *Dharma*, as a primary value system, defines the functions and characteristics of Nepali culture. It explains an appropriate lifestyle, as harmony in "the philosophical, social and environmental" spheres. *Dharma* is observed by being involved in religious rituals and social activities and fulfilling responsibilities. The rituals and social activities are part of religious festivals and ceremonies determined according to an individual's status in society.[14] Since *dharma* is the center of belief, practices, and Nepal's social system, Christianity cannot avoid dealing with it. So far, the Nepali church's position is counter-cultural toward *dharma*. As a religion, Christianity has positioned itself as a separate *dharma* or a distinct way of life in Nepal. Nepali Christianity finds itself in a dilemma that "accepting the old ways [Nepali *dharma*] upsets the church and rejecting them upsets the family and her/his wider social milieu."[15] Nepali Christians' exclusivism and inadaptability to adopt

---

10. Sharma, *Christian Identity and Funerary Rites*, 132.
11. Bharati, "Conversion is the Confusion," para. 4–5.
12. Sapkota, *Ten Years of Upheaval*, 45.
13. Majupuria, *Religions in Nepal*, 6.
14. Ingles, "Religious Beliefs and Rituals in Nepal," 209.
15. Sharma, *Christian Identity and Funerary Rites*, 21.

The Trinitarian Dharma

local culture aroused anger in the Nepali people.[16] If Christianity cannot be part of Nepali *dharma*, it will always remain a foreign entity in Nepal. As a result, the Nepali church does not possess the quality to be accepted by Nepali society and fails to be a transformative force.

This study advocates for a "trinitarian praxis" as the foundation of Nepali Christian theology, aiming to break away from its inward focus and actively engage with Nepali society. The relational and communal perspective of the "social Trinity" is employed as a crucial tool for contextualizing Christianity within the framework of Nepali *dharma*. According to the social Trinity, God reveals Himself in the economy of salvation through Jesus Christ, where all three persons of the Trinity are active during the incarnation of Jesus. The unity of God is manifested in their communion and love relationship, as evidenced in the economy of salvation. Humans, particularly within the church, become integral components of this intertrinitarian communion of God. Consequently, both the church and individuals derive their identity and mission within society.

In this context, the trinitarian God actively participates in the ongoing history of Nepali *dharma* through the Nepali church, making the church an essential part of God's trinitarian mission in the world. The Trinity serves as the wisdom for the Nepali church to engage in self-reflection and contribute to the transformation of society. The trinitarian praxis of Nepali *dharma* is centered on incarnating the trinitarian life within the cultural context of Nepal.

RESEARCH QUESTIONS

This research focuses on the issue of contextualization of Christianity in the Nepali context. It employs trinitarian praxis based on the social Trinity to examine how reinterpretations of the Trinity could overcome the abstract metaphysical speculation to establish the Trinity as a resource for constructing Nepali Christian *dharma*. This study follows the following research questions to complete this constructive project:

1. Are there resources in Nepali *dharma* drawn to constructively dialogue with the social Trinity to make Christianity relevant to Nepali culture?

---

16. Zharkevich, "When Gods Return to their Homeland in the Himalayas," 107. Christianity is disliked by the local people is due to their exclusivism and intolerance to local culture, or their traditional *Dharma*.

Introduction

2. How can social Trinity be brought into dialogue with Nepali *dharma* to contextualize Christianity as Nepal *dharma* to enrich Nepal Church's missional identity?

3. How has Nepali society been using *dharma* to establish relationships with outsiders such as Christianity?

4. Viewing through *dharma*, how does Nepali Christianity appear to the eyes of the whole Nepali community?

5. In what ways can trinitarian praxis contribute to the process of contextualization of Nepali Christianity?

RESEARCH METHODOLOGY

Since this study attempts to construct an indigenous Nepali theology by establishing a constructive dialogue between the concept of the *dharma* of Nepali society and the social Trinity, it seeks an inclusive vision. It prefers locality, particularity, and difference over universality and globality by allowing diverse and even conflicting and opposing opinions to be part of the discourse. This is an "authentically inviting and dialogical" which honors the "otherness of the other."[17] This study employs the synthetic model of contextualization of Christian theology, as stated by Stephen B. Bevans, to layout the conversation path between *dharma* and the social Trinity.[18] The synthetic model emphasizes the interaction of the Christian faith and experience and culture and social location. As a cultural element, Nepali *dharma* can interact with the social Trinity to develop Nepali indigenous theology.[19]

The synthetic model speaks of a dialectical process that gives equal value to culture and traditional theology. While employing a synthetic model in the Nepali context, *dharma* is considered a worthy partner for theological dialogue.[20] Simultaneously, it justifies the study of the social Trinity, a predominantly western theological subject, for the Nepali context. Though there is a grave danger of producing a weak theology faithful to neither side, the social Trinity and the *dharma*, this study attempts to be loyal to both. As David Thang Moe, a theologian from Myanmar, proposes a synthetic model to establish a dialogue between Myanmar's non-dual

---

17. Kärkkäinen, *Constructive Christian Theology*, Intro, para. 6.
18. Bevans, *Models of Contextual Theology*, 88–102.
19. Bevans, *Models of Contextual Theology*, 88.
20. Bevans, *Models of Contextual Theology*, 90–91.

The Trinitarian Dharma

spirit concept and with Trinity, he states, "Cultures host the gospel and localize its meaning, but the gospel transforms cultures. A dialectical act of cultural appreciation and cultural appropriation plays a crucial role in the dynamic process of critical contextualization."[21] In Nepal's context, *dharma* hosts the social Trinity and localizes it, while the social Trinity acts as a transformative force in society. This study proposes a synthetic model of contextualization to lead Nepali Christianity to fulfill its dual tasks, inculturation of Christian faith, and transformation of the society.

This study takes three steps to establish a synthetic model dialogue between Nepali *dharma* and the social Trinity. First, it analyzes the historical development of religion in Nepal to layout Nepal's present religious context. For this purpose, this study examines the resources, documents, and ethnographic studies on Nepali culture, society, and religion to determine the role of *dharma* in Nepali society. The in-depth research of *dharma* provides a platform on which a contextual social trinitarian theology can be developed. Secondly, it does an analytical study of the social Trinity by analyzing the historical development of the doctrine and analyzing various aspects of the social Trinity, arguing for its appropriateness for the Nepali context. The social Trinity is evaluated in light of other contextual and non-western theological developments to see if it is implementable in a context very foreign to Christianity. Lastly, the *dharma* and the social Trinity are made conversation partners to contribute to the theological formation. This study especially attempts to establish Nepali *dharma* as a foundation to build a trinitarian theology for the Nepali context while the social Trinity will challenge Nepali *dharma* for social transformation.[22]

LITERATURE REVIEW

Nepal has been the most Hindu country in the world; however, most studies on Hinduism have always been centered on the Hinduism of India. Many scholars assume that Hinduism in Nepal or other parts of the world is the same.[23] Since this study aims to propose a trinitarian contextual theology grounded in the experience of *dharma* in Nepali society, it cannot focus on

---

21. Moe, "Conceptualizing and Contextualizing with and," 153–72.

22. Tracy, *Plurality and Ambiguity* 19. Here David Tracy speaks of the theological formation in dialogical way and role of the conversation partners, which is similar to synthetic model chosen in this study.

23. World Factbook indicates that 81% of Nepali population is Hindu which is highest in the World. Central Intelligence Agency, "Nepal," *World Fact book*; Nov. 11,.

Introduction

such an orbital understanding of the Hindu religion. It is crucial to establish a dialogue with the *dharma* in Nepali people's lives to construct Nepali Indigenous theology. This study deals with works on Nepali Hinduism, especially those who have studied Hinduism in Nepali people's lives. This research examines the previous contextual studies on Nepal and establishes each work's contribution toward this research. Doing so reveals the gaps in the existing research as a justification for the proposed task. This literature review is organized thematically under Nepali Religion and culture, the Theology of Nepali Christianity, and the social Trinity.

Nepali Dharma *and Culture*

The majority of the scholarship on Nepal's religions provides general characteristics of Nepali Hinduism for Western readers. These works can be a great reference point for observing the uniqueness of Nepali society. *Religions in Nepal,* A work of Trilok Chandra Majupuria and Rohit Kumar Majupuria, is an example. Rather than giving the uniqueness of Nepali society, they wrote from the perspective of Hinduism as a tolerant and embracing religion. They took famous Hindu epics such as *Ramayana* and *Mahabharata* rather than the local myths, rituals, and deities as the source for understanding Nepali Hinduism.[24] They put Buddhism, Jainism, Sikhism, and other indigenous practices under the fold of Nepali Hinduism. Majpurias ignore Indigenous people's struggle to find their own identity apart from what is given by the Hindu universal claim.[25] Unlike, Majpurias, GL Rai Zimmdar has written from a Nepali indigenous perspective. He has utilized local myths, legends, and other related sources to note the arrival of Hinduism in Nepal and strives to give an account of Nepali society before its Hinduization.[26]

Scholars have paid attention to Nepal's specific religious context and observed various festivals of Nepal in particular. While some festivals have their origin in Hindu scriptures such as *Ramayana* or *Mahabharatha*, most originated locally and have local significance. Through their research on Nepal's religious festivals, foreign observers and Nepali writers attempted to show such distinct characteristics of the Nepali religious context, especially Hinduism. Mary M. Anderson was fascinated by the number of festivals and the fashion of their celebration. Anderson produced a classic

---

24. Majpurias, *Religions in Nepal,* 72–89.
25. Majpurias, *Religions in Nepal,* 89.
26. Zimmdar, *Pre-Brahminic Nepal,* 9.

The Trinitarian Dharma

collection on the Nepali festival, *The Festivals of Nepal,* by following the Nepali calendar and connecting it to Nepali life.[27] Unlike Mary Anderson, who recorded Nepali festivals following the Nepali indigenous calendar, Trilok Chandra Majupuria and S.P. Gupta opted to follow the Gregorian calendar and tried to provide meanings of the observance of the rituals related to each festival.[28] Hemanta K. Jha shows the syncretistic nature involved in the celebration and festival rituals where Hindu and Buddhist traditions are fused and celebrated together. He also pinpoints the origins of the festivals in respective historical or mythical heritage[29] Jim Goodman groups Nepali festivals according to seasons and attempts to connect them to Nepali people's daily activities. Rather than seeking the sources of the celebrations in the scriptures, Goodman finds their origin in people's myths and legends.[30] Dhurba Krishna Deep describes the deities related to the festival as well.[31] The works on the celebrations of Nepali religion show the interrelatedness of faith and people's everyday lives. Though such works are mostly descriptive, they provide valuable information regarding religiosity and the community-centeredness of Nepali life.

Many writers have attempted to show the Nepali religious context's uniqueness by showing the legends and beliefs in society behind Nepali people's practices and beliefs. These legends and myths are important for Nepali social and religious identity. Dhurba K. Deep listed several deities worshiped by Nepali people and the stories and meanings behind such beliefs. Deep's account provides the significance of such stories for Nepali people.[32] William P. Forbes and V.K.Chaube dug out the information in two indigenous Nepali scriptures, *Himavatkhanda* and *Nepala-Mahatmayan,* initially written in Sanskrit, a language spoken in ancient Nepal and many parts of India. Forbes and Chaube's work points out Hinduism's value for Nepali people by showing the religious and scriptural significance of mountains, valleys, and places where they live.[33] Desmond Doig and Dubby Bhagat's book digs into Nepali legends and relates the tales to temples, religious

27. Anderson, *The Festivals of Nepal,* 15–16.
28. Majpuria and. Gupta, *Nepal: The Land of Festivals,* 7–26.
29. Jha, *Hindu-Buddhist Festivals of Nepal,* 10–12.
30. Goodman, *Guide to Enjoying Nepali Festivals,* 1–7.
31. Deep, *The Nepal Festivals,* xi-xii.
32. Deep, *Popular Deities,* 13–170.
33. Forbes and Chaube, *The Glory of Nepal,* 269–80.

sites, Nepali festivals, and history.[34] Jan Kaji Shrestha also provides the non-written legends and myths among commoners about their beliefs.[35] The works on the sources of Nepali religious beliefs and practices show that their spiritual way or *dharma* is interconnected to their place, customs, and people. They show that Nepali *dharma* is inseparable from Nepali life and the land. However, being descriptive, these works are limited because they do not reflect people's perspectives.

Anthropologists have begun to study the Nepali religion in Nepali people's lives by focusing on a specific place, people group, or some particular aspect of religion. Sherry B. Ortner researched among *Sherpa* people group of Nepal who mostly follow Buddhism. He demonstrates the structure of *Sherpa* culture and its tension and relationship with the religion. He also points out that, in Nepal, religious affairs are intermingled with political affairs, even on the ground level.[36] David H. Holmberg, one of the pioneer ethnographers to study the Nepali people group, observed Tamang, a Buddhist people group. Based on their indigenous myths and traditions, their belief and rituals are far from what orthodox Buddhists or Hindus identify with. He points out that while rituals and practices among these people seem contradictory and opposing, they act toward fulfilling their social life.[37]

A native Nepali anthropologist, Bal Gopal Shrestha, did extensive research on his people, *Newar*. His study focuses on the town of Sankhu, a traditional *Newar* colony. He points out that Hinduism and Buddhism coexist in *Newar* people's lives and the unique social system of *Guthi*, a social association related to religious activities and social works in society. These *Guthis* are associated with their identity and economy. However, they are divided among the castes within society.[38] Shrestha points out that through the performance of festivals and rituals in the *Guthi* community, people form relationships with their deities and people. Gregory Price Grieve, another anthropologist who researched the *Newar* people, studied God's concept in them. Grieve discovered that among *Newar* people worshiping does not depend on the concept and meaning of God, but rather the function of

---

34. Doig and Bhagat, *Down History's Narrow Lanes*, 1–4.
35. Manandhar, *Myths and Legends of Nepal*, 1–10.
36. Ortner, *High Religion*, 3–11.
37. Holmberg, *Order in Paradox*, 3–4.
38. Shrestha, *The Sacred Town of Sankhu*, 2.

The Trinitarian Dharma

worship in society determines the meaning of God. Religions and rituals ensure that everyone is part of the community.[39]

Nepal's unique Hindu scripture and tradition of Swosthani Barta Katha has been the subject of ethnographic study. In 1985, Linda Louise Iltis researched the practice of this uniquely Nepali tradition of reciting a narrative of Goddesses and a month-long ritual among Nepali women, who are mostly not the main actors in Nepali *dharma*.[40] While Iltis focuses on women's issues through the Swosthani text and tradition, Jessica Vantine Birknenholtz researched it for the political, historical, and social significance and development of a new localized Hindu identity. Birkenholtz's research deals with the issue from the perspective of political transitions in Nepal.[41] Both Iltis and Birkenholtz's research shows that Hinduism in Nepal is localized and integrated into people's daily lives.

Anne Taylor Mocko did extensive research on Nepali belief in the Monarch as a Hindu god in the backdrop of Nepali political change that transfigured the country from a constitutional monarchy to a secular republic. Mocko discovered that even when the monarchy is gone, the rituals and ceremonies continue with the country's newly elected president.[42] Similarly, Nawaraj Chaulagain researched Nepali Hinduism, focusing on its Monarchy. Chaulagain examines the Hindu teachings and philosophy to extract the concept of kingship and connect it to society's social structure.[43] Lal Dosa Rai goes to a more philosophical description of Nepali *dharma* where he seeks to demonstrate how the concept of Nepal's *dharma* meets the societal need for a human right concept in society. From a non-Western perspective, *dharma* is the foundation of human rights in Nepali society, and the author shows how it relates to ethics, politics, and all aspects of culture.[44]

This review of the works mentioned above shows that most works on the Nepali religion are devoted to general and widespread practices. However, anthropologists who were more specific in their study discovered that Nepal's unique religious field is more practically oriented. Various Nepali societies have devised their own social way of functioning. It is hard to separate

39. Grieve, *Retheorizing Religion in Nepal*, 137.
40. Iltis, "The Swasthani Vrata, 1–10.
41. Birkenholtz, *Reciting the Goddess*, 4–8.
42. Mocko, *Demoting Vishnu*, 3–7.
43. Chaulagain, "Hindu Kingship," 1–2.
44. Rai, *Human Rights in the Hindu-Buddhist Tradition*, 51.

Introduction

Nepal's politics and the daily lives of people from their religion or *dharma*. Though many of these studies bring the universal concept of Hinduism to describe the Nepali religion, the original ethnographic studies are valuable for this research to make a clear picture of the Nepali context to develop a contextual theology. It requires an exceptional effort from Nepali Christian scholars to do theology and mission in Nepal. What has been done from the side of Nepali theologians needs to be reviewed as well.

Theology of Nepali Christianity

The Nepali church leaders have realized that the church cannot avoid responding to the challenges put forth by society and have devised their own responses to the challenges. Differentiating Christianity from Hinduism, answering cultural ambiguities, and raising political voices are some of the ways the Nepali church has responded to their society. This section exemplifies three Nepali church efforts to respond to their theology, which demands Nepal's comprehensive political theology.

First, the missionaries published their experience with Nepal and Nepali cultures. Thomas Hale, May Cundy, and David E. Watters wrote several books on their experience of Nepal, Nepali culture, and newly planted churches in Nepal. Such missionary accounts glance at Nepali ordinary life through their eyes and how the gospel reached this Himalayan Hindu country. Secondly, some non-Nepali authors produced academic writing on Nepali Christianity, documenting the establishment and growth of the Nepali Church.[45] Cindy Perry researched the Nepali Church history and published two monographs. In contrast, she showed that the beginning and development of Nepali Christianity happened at the hands of the native Nepali-speaking community converted outside of the Nepali border.[46]

Johnathan Lindell and Valerie M. Inchley contributed with their account of the expansion of Nepali Christianity. While Johnathan's account gives a more descriptive history of Nepali Christianity, rather than following historicity and dates, Inchley connects the growth of the Christian

---

45. Hale, *Don't Let the Goats Eat the Loquat Trees*; *Living Stones of the Himalayas*; *Light dawn in Nepal*; Cundy, *Better than the Witch Doctor*; Watters, *At the Foot of the Snows*. These are a few examples of the writings from the missionaries who have ventured into Nepal.

46. Perry, *A Bibliographical History of the Church in Nepal*; and Perry, *Nepalis Around the World*. Perry's books are considered first books on Nepal church history.

population in Nepal with the Nepali diaspora community.⁴⁷ Though most of these works concentrate on the issues related to Nepali church growth, Norma Kehrberg dealt with conversion and its social implications. Kehrberg mentions a great need to contextualize Christianity to integrate the Christian message in Nepal's social, cultural, and historical context.⁴⁸ Rajendra K. Rongong, a prominent Nepali Christian leader, provides more inside stories of Nepali churches lacking from non-Nepali authors' accounts and focuses on the suffering and persecution faced by Nepali Christians.⁴⁹

Lately, Nepali Christians themselves have begun reflecting on Christianity from their point of view. Mangal Man Maharjan, one of the first Nepali Christian scholars, tried to show the differences between Christian and Hindu doctrines. He hoped to offer the truth of Christianity, showing the differences between the two religions in various topics. He acknowledges that he did not attempt to give a detailed interpretation of Hindu and Christian scriptures.⁵⁰ Maharjan speaks of Hinduism and Christianity's comparative study in Nepal, but he heavily depends on Western scholars' understanding of both Hinduism and Christianity to show the differences. He does not detail Hindu beliefs in Nepal, nor tries to state the faith of Nepali Christians. Maharjan sees a genuine need for such comparison but hardly speaks of anything from the Nepali Christian perspective.

Many Nepali Christians have sought higher studies in theology in recent years and have researched various theological topics. Ramesh Khatry obtained his doctoral degree in the New Testament from Oxford University, but he did not relate his research to Nepal's contextual issues.⁵¹ However, in 2007, Khatry wrote an article titled "Christology for Everestland" for a South Asian journal *Dharma Deepika*. The title is quite deceiving because rather than bringing Nepal's experience of Hinduism and challenges to formulate a Christology, Khatry blindly proposes Jesus as the King metaphor for Nepali people.⁵² King is not a liberating factor in the society, and the kingship was removed from the country by the uprising of the Nepali people.

47. Lindell, *Nepal and the Gospel of God*; Inchley, *The Nepali Diaspora*, 547–54.
48. Kehrberg, *The Cross in the Land of the Khukuri*, 63.
49. Rongong, *Early Churches in Nepal*, 147–51.
50. Maharjan, *Comparative Study of Hinduism and Christianity*, 13.
51. Khatry, "Authenticity of the Parable of the Wheat and the Tares and Its Interpretation."
52. Khatry, "Christology for Everest Land," 7–23.

Introduction

Lok Mani Bhandari did theological research for his doctoral study in which he provides his recipe for church growth in Nepal. However, Bhandari fails to make contextual elements the subject of a theological enterprise and instead seeks to confront the traditional Nepali belief with the tools of charismatic movements of the West.⁵³ In 2014, Manoj Shrestha published his dissertation on practical theology. Shrestha seeks to supplement the growth of Christianity in Nepal with a practical approach to teaching the Bible. While giving helpful suggestions for preaching, the genuine theological challenges posed by society are ignored.⁵⁴

In 2012, Bal Krishna Sharma published his book titled *Christian Identity and Funerary Rites in Nepal*, in which Sharma deals with the issue of the Christian identity of Nepali Christians in the subject of funeral rites. Nepali Christians were struggling with the funeral issue of whether to cremate the deceased believer's body or not. He wisely proposes the cremation as a viable option. Even Sharma gave a practical discussion of a grave theological subject of the Christian identity in Nepal.⁵⁵

In 2019, Olak Bahadur Sunuwar published his research in which he pinpointed Nepali society's problem where injustice toward lower caste people, women, and Christians exists, and he observed the fault lies in Hindu philosophy. Christian concepts of social justice are the proposed solution. Rather than giving a Nepali version of Christian social justice, Sunuwar looked toward the tiny Nepali Christian community to prove Christians are a just society.⁵⁶

Since 2013, the Nepal Research Centre at the Asian Center for Theological Studies, South Korea, has published an annual theological journal, *Nepali Christian Journal*. Many Nepali emerging scholars who are master's and doctoral level students in various theological schools have published their opinions. The articles are useful to understand the real context of Nepal and the challenges faced by Christianity. However, none of the papers attempt to formulate indigenous theology from the Nepali point of view. The journal contains articles that show the need for contextual theology in Nepal and a different paradigm of Christian missions.⁵⁷ Nepali scholars are

---

53. Bhandari, "The Role of Power Encounter in the Growth of Christianity in Nepal," 1999.

54. M. Shrestha, "Contextual Expository Preaching."

55. Sharma, *Christian Identity and Funerary Rites in Nepal*, 195–201.

56. Sunuwar, "Social Crisis and the Alien God," 2019, ii.

57. Kim, "From Nepal Mission to Mission Nepal," 75–94. Kirchheiner, "The

The Trinitarian Dharma

still engaged in practical and theological issues without particularly making Nepali culture a theological subject. The online journal *Voice of Bhakti was* published from 2002 to 2005, and most of the writers were non-Nepali scholars based in Nepal and did not give a detailed view from the insiders of the Nepali church. The purpose of publishing *Voice of Bhakti* was to clarify "what it means to be bhakta (devotee) of Christ among Nepali People." They have touched on some essential issues and devoted some unique problems to these issues: the caste system of Nepal, Hinduism in Nepal, and Christian attitude and relationship to some festivals and cultures of Nepal. They have pointed out the genuine need for the Nepali church to articulate the cultural issues theologically. They have given them some suggestions regarding those for Nepali Churches and the Christian community.[58]

All the examples mentioned above show that the church in Nepal is trying to respond and be effective in society; however, the lack of a theological proposition hinders the process. The church in Nepal is searching for a theology that can lead to the following things: first, the theology should define the Nepali Christian identity; the theology can consider Biblical history and their cultural heritage to give them their new identity. The theology should transform the church itself as an effective witness of Christ in society to be a transforming agent of the Nepali community. Lastly, theology should be able to address the needs of society in light of the gospel. If the church should be involved politically, the theology also gives the scope and limitation of the politics of the Nepali church. If they should be involved in society, they need theology to articulate the goal and method of their social involvement.

The Social Trinity

Though Trinity has emerged as "a touchstone of truth, a non-negotiable article" of Christian doctrine, it has often become a subject of theological controversy. There always have been efforts to make it reasonable for a human mind to grasp the concept of three and one at the same time.[59] Such an attempt to rationalize God is detached from human experience and life. However, we cannot separate God from our life.[60] Recently, there

---

Challenge of Tika," 95.

58. Richard, "H-Scale for Hindu Contextualization"; M. Johnson, "Lifting the Yoke," 2004.

59. Sproul, *What Is the Trinity*, 1–3.

60. Gutiérrez and Shaull, *Liberation and Change*, 82.

Introduction

have been many attempts to overcome such abstract and nonrepresentational nature of God. This study examines newer interpretations of the Trinity that seek to overcome the abstract metaphysical speculation to establish the Trinity as the model of our spirituality and church life. Researcher turns to theologians known for their distinct non-traditional interpretation of the Trinity like Jürgen Moltmann, Leonardo Boff, and John Sobrino, and feminist theologians such as Anne E. Carr and Catherine Mowry LaCugna. Since the whole idea of a relational, communal Trinity began with Eastern Orthodox theologies, the works of Eastern Orthodox theologians Dumitru Stanioloae and Aristotle Papanikolaou are reviewed. The researcher visits the assessment from prominent theologians like Miroslav Volf, Stanley Grenz, and Ted Peters.

While Karl Barth made God's revelation the only criterion to know the mystery of the Trinity and rescued it from human reasoning, Jürgen Moltmann made human history part of God's history. He says, "We cannot say of God who he is of himself and in himself; we can only say who he is for us in the history of Christ which reaches us in our history."[61] To establish a connection between human history and God, Moltmann interprets the cross as "a Trinity event of love in the suffering and death of Jesus."[62] By doing this, Moltmann rescues the Trinity from its self-containment in heaven and opens the trinitarian eschatological process for men and women on earth.[63] In the event of the Trinity, Jesus leads people into the relationship with the Father as the children of God and to the anticipation of the Kingdom of the Spirit.[64] The kingdom of the Spirit is historical and experienced here in the Son's fellowship, and It presupposes "the kingdom of the Father" (creation) and "the kingdom of the Son" (incarnation) and points in its way toward the eschatological kingdom of glory.[65] Trinity becomes God's involvement in human history, which allows men and women to participate in history as they are in their eschatological journey to the kingdom of God.

Leonardo Boff speaks Trinity in terms of communion where the Father begets the Son with the Holy Spirit; the Son reveals the Father in light of the Holy Spirit, and the Holy Spirit reveals the Father in the Wisdom

---

61. Moltmann, *The Crucified God*, 238.
62. Moltmann, *The Crucified God*, 249.
63. Moltmann, *The Crucified God*, 249.
64. Moltmann, *Trinity and the Kingdom*, 210.
65. Moltmann, *Trinity and the Kingdom*, 212.

The Trinitarian Dharma

of the Son.[66] With such communion and communication, the Trinity relates outward to human history. Boff goes one step further than Jürgen Moltmann and makes some concrete implications of the trinitarian communion. He takes the plural unity of three divine persons to criticize the dominating nature of capitalism. Similarly, Boff criticizes socialism that does not accept the differences among people. He gets a clue from Moltmann to make Trinity a source of inspiration for fellowship, equality of opportunity, and generosity. The Trinity is also put forth as a basis to build a messianic community. At the same, it criticizes the monarchial structure of the institutional church.[67]

John Sobrino, a Jesuit Catholic priest and a theologian, speaks similarly to Moltmann and Boff that God reveals his way through history. Jesus calls his followers to address God *abba* as he did. The invitation of people into God's family includes their involvement and availability for the Kingdom of God's work. God reigns the world through and with the people, liberating and transforming society. The gift of the Kingdom of God becomes the task for the people.[68] For Sobrino, grace, and praxis converge in the construction of the kingdom of God. Praxis without the Spirit is a grave danger. Sobrino speaks in terms of the Kingdom of God rather than the Trinity that the building of God's Kingdom is a trinitarian act that is done in participation by God's people.[69]

Pioneering feminist theologian Anne Carr speaks of God in terms of the incarnation of Jesus Christ, unlike Boff and Moltmann, for her, it is a symbolic idea. Even then, she does not spare, making God part of human history. The metaphorical concept of God's incarnation in Christ indicates that God and the creation of the world are "irrevocably united, joined, made one in God's self-gift to humankind and so to the world."[70] Like Jürgen Moltmann, Carr puts God in the eschatological orientation; in a way, it shows that the current dilemma is a temporary one. Though she speaks of the Trinity as the mystery of God, she saves The Trinity from metaphysical and abstract interpretation. God is on the side of the poor, oppressed, marginal, and outcasts of society. For her, The Trinity as the symbol of God's image

---

66. Boff, *Trinity and Society*, 146–48
67. Boff, *Trinity and Society*, 153–54.
68. Sobrino, *No salvation outside the Poor*, 78–79.
69. Sobrino, *No salvation outside the Poor*, 91–93.
70. Carr, *Transforming Grace*, 149.

Introduction

provides women with an image and concept of God worthy of imitation because it includes both the suffering and final vindication.[71]

Catherine Mowry LaCugna, another prominent feminist theologian, has given her valuable contribution to the area of trinitarian life in her book *God for Us: The Trinity and Christian Life*. For her, "God's economy is the wellspring of trinitarian faith," and the Trinity is not an abstract idea or theological principle.[72] The economy, which speaks of God's salvation work, is shared between God and his creatures. Unsurprisingly, the meeting between God and creatures at a commonplace of God's economy is practically relevant for Christian living. LaCugna refuges to reduce Trinity into a set of principles for the solutions to the current world problem. Instead, the Trinity provides a theological framework for "seeing two hands of God at work in our salvation," and it is "unavoidably bound up with the praxis of Christian faith, with the form of life appropriate to God's economy."[73]

Dumitru Staniloae, an Orthodox Priest and theologian, sees The Trinity as a divine community. God is a single God when three divine persons are in a relationship that each includes the other two. "The divine essence is only divine when hypostasized in three persons because these three have a value and a relationship between them that deserves and is capable of absolute love."[74] For Staniolae, the trinitarian relationship is the destiny of all human beings; however, our union with God differs from the trinitarian divine relationship. He states that The Trinity is a model to be followed, and the incarnation of Christ is the point of departure. The Trinity is to be participated according to the standard set by itself. The relationship with God is not possible without the Holy Spirit's work, which is the real binding force within a trinitarian relationship. The spirit gives us birth into real life in God and sustains us in it, and this is growth in holiness. By imitating the incarnation of Christ with the help of the Spirit, we become like The Trinity that we value others as ourselves. Staniolae makes our relationship with God essentially integrated into our relationship with the world.[75] In his book *Being with God*, Aristotle Papanikolaou compares two prominent orthodox theologians of the past century, Vladimir Lossky and John Zizioulas. Both theologians share the realism of divine-human communion. According to

71. Carr, *Transforming Grace*, 156.
72. LaCugna, *God for Us*, 377.
73. LaCugna, *God for Us*, 380–81.
74. Staniloae, *The Holy Trinity*, 17.
75. Staniloae, *The Holy Trinity*, 66.

The Trinitarian Dharma

Papanikolaou, the Christian faith is communion with God the Father, in the person of Christ, by the power of the Holy Spirit.[76]

To implement trinitarian praxis in Nepal, I add more practical implications of the social Trinity that help lay the foundation for the transformative spirituality needed in the context. First, I take trinitarian ecclesiology in Miroslav Volf. He seeks to establish the harmony of the church in the binding of the Holy Spirit. Volf grounds all the church members' rights and responsibilities in their trinitarian life or mission.[77] Secondly, I invite Stanley Grenz, who has connected the social Trinity with anthropology. Grenz discusses the concept of "*imago Dei,* created in God's image" and links it to Christ, who is the ultimate revealed image of God and the new humanity in him. In Christ, *imago Dei* is an eschatological goal and present reality of human beings. "Moreover, the already-not yet the character of the relationship of the new humanity to the *imago Dei* leads to an ethical imperative for life in the believing community."[78] Lastly, I use Ted Peters, who refuses to use the Trinity as a symbol to use as a "model for human society"; instead chooses "the character of the Kingdom of God."[79] However, he similarly uses the Kingdom of God as we intended to use The Trinity. In its eschatological projection, the Trinity embodies the Kingdom of God that Ted Peters speaks for.

All of the above examples show that the Nepali church is trying to respond and be effective in society, but the lack of a theological proposition hinders the process. The Church in Nepal needs to construct its theology for the following things: first, the theology should define the Nepali Christian identity; the theology can consider Biblical history and cultural heritage to give them their new identity. Secondly, Nepali theology needs to be the cause of self-transformation to transform society. Lastly, theology should address the needs of the community, taking into account the gospel. Nepali contextual theology provides the scope and limitation of the social involvement of the Nepali church. This research proceeds with the conviction that meeting between the openness of the social Trinity in the Nepali religious and social context is the departure point for the long process of making Nepali contextual theology.

---

76. Papanikolaou, *Being with God*, 161.

77. Volf, *After Our Likeness*, 220.

78. Grenz, *The Social God and the Relational Self*, 224.

79. Peters, *God as Trinity*, 184–85.

Introduction

CHAPTER OVERVIEW

Chapter 1 furnishes the research background, statement of the problem, research questions, research methodology, and literature survey on Nepali religion and culture, Christianity in Nepal, and social Trinity. Chapter 2 deals with the meaning of *dharma* in the Nepali context by analyzing the religious development in Nepal and establishing the basic concepts of Nepali *dharma*. Nepali *dharma* is analyzed to be a communitarian religious practice in Nepal, which implies social and individual religious life. Chapter 3 focuses on how the social problems of Nepal are related to *dharma*. The caste system, women's issues, and poverty are related to *dharma* and its struggle for meaningful liberation from each crisis. It also shows the place and relationship of the Nepali Church with Nepali *dharma*. Nepali Christians are a suffering minority who are isolated from various social aspects in Nepal. Chapters two and three make the Nepali context readily available for dialogue with the social Trinity in later chapters.

Chapters 4, 5, and 6 deal with the development and characteristics of the social Trinity. Chapter 4 shows how The Trinity's story became an abstract theology, irrelevant to Christian living. In the twentieth century, the development of the social Trinity reestablished the trinitarian theology in the center of Christian living. Chapter 5 argues that the social Trinity can be utilized as a foundation for Nepal's constructive theology. Religious diversity and egalitarianism, the openness of triune God, and trinitarian involvement in history make it a suitable platform to establish a contextual theological dialogue. Chapter 6 argues for the suitableness of Social trinitarianism for the Nepali context by relating social trinitarianism with various liberation and contextual theologies worldwide.

Chapter 7 puts Nepali *dharma* and social Trinity at the same table for a constructive dialogue. The social Trinity is placed alongside the practical religiosity and community concept in Nepali *dharma*. The social Trinity also brought attention to social issues such as the caste system, women's suffering, and poverty. Chapter 8 argues that *dharma* can be a platform for the Nepali church to be involved in Nepali society. At the same time, The social Trinity assists Nepali Christians in creating their new identity and community politics. Perichoresis can be made a tool for liberation from the caste system and the suffering of women, while Nepali Christians can imitate intra-divine trinitarian love to be in solidarity with Nepali people. Chapter 9 concludes this study by giving a summary and implications for

The Trinitarian Dharma

further studies. It argues that this research can be considered the first step for the Nepali church's huge contextual task.

2

Dharma: The Social Foundation

THIS CHAPTER ANALYZES NEPAL'S religious context from historical and religious perspectives, providing a contextual platform to construct Nepali contextual theology. Firstly, it delves into the historical development of Nepal's present religious state, shaped by various political events. Consequently, Nepali religion has evolved into an amalgamation of multiple belief systems, including Hinduism, Buddhism, and folk religious practices like shamanism and animism, collectively known as Nepali *dharma*. Secondly, the chapter explores the essential characteristics of Nepali *dharma*, portraying it as a practical religiosity, community consciousness, and a manifestation of Nepali people's social participation. The chapter establishes a foundation for subsequent sections that analyze the suitability of the Social Trinity in addressing the specific needs of the Nepali Church.

HISTORY OF NEPAL AND INSTALLMENT OF HINDUISM IN SOCIETY

Nepal's present socio-religious context is the result of the process over the last two thousand years, during which a form of a religious system, commonly understood to be Hinduism, has become an integral part of the society. Even though Nepal's religion is known as Hinduism, the Nepali religion is a conglomeration of various beliefs and practices combined throughout the centuries.[1] An analysis of Nepal's history provides

---

1. Vaidya et al., *Social History of Nepal*, 1.

The Trinitarian Dharma

a clearer understanding of contemporary Nepali society in which Nepali Christians are striving to find their place.

The Early Introduction of Hinduism into Nepali Society

In its ancient history, Nepal has been a place where various people groups came to take refuge, but it remained isolated from the rest of the world for the most recent history.[2] Therefore, Nepali society is a mosaic of various cultures, but it remains unexploited by modern developments. Due to Nepal's reclusion from the rest of the world between the 17th and the first half of the 20th century, there were no changes in the religious atmosphere.[3] Because of its unique social development, the Nepali religion is different from Hinduism in India or elsewhere.[4]

Among the three main divisions of Nepali people, Mongoloid, Aryan, and pre-Aryan indigenous people, Mongoloid people are considered the earliest settlers of Nepal, while Aryans are the most recent arrivals.[5] Scholars believe that the Hindu element entered the land with the recent appearances of the Aryan people from the southern lands, of present-day India. Two thousand five hundred years ago, present-day Nepal did not have a strong, politically centralized nation, but various people groups ruled the tiny principalities.[6] Cattle herdsmen known as *Gopala* (cow herding people) and *Mahispala* (water-buffalo herding people) ruled Nepal, and *Kirat*, an indigenous people group, currently living in the eastern mountainous region, were the rulers of present-day Kathmandu valley.[7] During the early historical period of Nepal, the society was mostly

---

2. Vaidya, and Bajracharya, *Nepal: The People and the Culture*, 1.

3. Wright, *Nepal*, 110. Wright mentions the Sakya Buddha's visit to Nepal and his disciple's settlement in Nepal preaching their religion. Wright also records Ashoka the Great's visit to Nepal and his daughter's settlement in the present-day Kathmandu Valley. Wright cites archeological evidence to support his statements. These migrations took place before 232 BC. These are the examples of influx of people to ancient Nepal.

4. Bista, *Anthropology of Nepal*, 83. Bista argues that though there are similarities between certain social systems of Nepal and Hindu society of India, Nepali society due to its political and social history contain grave difference. His prime examples are similarities and differences between caste systems in Nepal and India. In India caste system was developed along its social-economic development, but Nepali caste system was the result of political decision.

5. Vaidya, and Bajracharya, *Nepal: The People and the Culture*, 3.

6. Savada, ed., "Ancient Nepal, 500 B.C.–A.D. 700," in *Nepal and Bhutan: Country Studies*, para. 1–5.

7. Acharya, *Nepal Culture Shift*, 4. Northey and Morris, *The Gurkhas*, 9–11.

Dharma: The Social Foundation

indigenous cultures having more Buddhist influence than Hindu.[8] However, in the 4th century C.E, the Lichhavi people's arrivals, an Aryan ruling class from India, infused Hindu deities in Nepali religious systems, and the non-Hindu, non-Arian people, were made subject to Hinduism and Hindu social structures such as caste systems.[9]

Many immigrants from present-day India began to settle in the Himalayan land and intensified the Sanskritization of society.[10] The flow of people into Nepal from India brought the indigenous animistic practices face-to-face with a different culture and religion and brought other significant changes to ancient Nepal's autonomous principalities. At that time, the land belonged to a clan rather than a person, and there was no systematic taxation system. However, it was soon changed by the arrival of immigrants, who introduced the idea that the King holds the ultimate ownership of the land and has the authority to raise taxation.[11] In his book *Nepal*, Nagendra Kr. Singh traces Nepal's militant races, such as *Magars* and *Gurungs*, and writes that the migrants were more talented than the locals, making them indispensable to the government. Later, they deposed the local kings and established their regal line.[12] When they rose to power, they began to transform society according to the Hindu belief system. The immigrants overtook the kingship of the indigenous people, but they were not displaced from the land. Instead, they were made to abide by the rules set up by the newcomers. Vulnerable indigenous groups lived in a group and tried their best to preserve their language and culture to some extent till today.[13]

Nepal, previously a non-Hindu community, was forced to establish Hindu social systems. The caste system was introduced as early as AD 465 and formalized during Jaisthiti Malla's reign in the Kathmandu Valley in

---

8. Dowman, *Power Places of Central Tibet*, 16, 41–45. It is illustrated by the fact that Nepal and Tibet had various cultural exchanges during this period. Queen Bhrikuti of Tibet was princess of Nepal who brough various Buddhist deities to the land. Buddhism of Nepal played significant role in the development of Tibetan alphabet and advancement of the Buddhism in Tibet.

9. "Nepal Prehistory and Early History," in *Encyclopedia: Britannica*, para. 1–7.

10. Sanskritization is a process in which complex values and culture system of indigenous people group were assimilated into the values and system of high-class Hindus in Nepal. Whelpton, *A History of Nepal*, 10.

11. Whelpton, *A History of Nepal*, 26.

12. Singh, *Nepal*, 1–5. Singh writes that those who once were rulers in various parts of present-day India were then forced to be refugees in Nepal but eventually transformed themselves into rulers and brought in the changes.

13. Vaidya, and Bajracharya, *Nepal: The People and the Culture*, 7–8.

The Trinitarian Dharma

AD 1382.[14] People, who did not know anything or had nothing to do with Hinduism and the caste system, were forced to adapt to and abide by it. Despite being dismissed by the law, the caste system prevails in all areas of Nepali people's life, today.[15] Although the people had their own indigenous identities and culture, political and social change was inevitable.

Formation of Present-day Nepal and Further Solidification of Hinduism

Before the formation of the present-day nation, in the eighteenth century, the name "Nepal" meant the Valley of Kathmandu. By then, there were many principalities ruled by various rulers. These land fragmentations were reminiscent of earlier four major kingdoms such as the *Khasa* Empire, *Malla* kingdoms of Kathmandu Valley,[16] *Kirat* land in the Eastern part of present-day Nepal,[17] and Mithila kingdom of the southern plain area of Nepal, which included parts of Bihar of Present-day India.[18] Historians believe that it came into existence before AD 1000. However, around the beginning of the fifteenth century, the land was divided into many small principalities.[19]

In his *Advance History of Nepal*, Tulshi Ram Vaidya writes that by the end of the 15th century, there were as many as fifty-four such principalities within present-day Nepal territory.[20] According to Vaidya's details, there were constant quarrels and fighting between these principalities. For example, three brothers ruled three different principalities in the Kathmandu Valley, and they were frequently in conflict with each other.[21] Although they were founded on the same Hindu principles, namely the caste system, and shared similar languages, there was no unity. Nepal was fragmented into small principalities and became vulnerable to any invasion. The East

---

14. Bista, *Fatalism and Development*, 35.

15. Vaidya et al., *Social History of Nepal*, 22. Serchan, *Democracy, Pluralism and Change*, 11.

16. Singh, *Nepal: Refugee to a Ruler*, 37. Whelpton, *A History of Nepal*, 22. Khasha empire occupied the land between Kathmandu Valley and Kashmir of Present-day India.

17. Chemjong, *History of Kirat People*, 93.

18. Acharya, *Nepal Culture Shift*, 3. By the eighteenth century, Mithila was severely weakened by invasion of Shamsud-din Ilyas, Muslim ruler of Bengal, in 1349. But this civilization remained influential in Nepali society till today.

19. Whelpton, *A History of Nepal*, 23.

20. Vaidya, *Advanced History of Nepal*, 4.

21. Vaidya, *Advanced History of Nepal*, 8.

Dharma: The Social Foundation

India Company of the British Empire increased its power in the neighboring country, India. Nepal would be an easy target for the imperial power if it planned to extend its border to the Himalayan Mountains.[22] These fragmented states were culturally bound with a similar religious system but politically fragmented within. The unification and formation of modern Nepal marked the political homogenization of Nepal's spiritual and cultural spectrum through Hinduization.[23]

King Prithvi Narayan Shah, who ascended to the throne of a small, tiny state country called Gorkha in 1743, realized Nepal's vulnerability being situated between the two powerful forces China on the north and Britain on the south. Both China and Britain were actively seeking to expand their borders toward the Himalayas.[24] When King Prithvi Narayan Shah ruled Gorkha and saw the fragmented principalities, he envisioned a chance to unify them into a stronger nation.[25] Upon realizing such a threat from both sides, especially from the British side, who were looking for a shorter route from India to Tibet through Nepal, King Prithvi devised a plan to unite the small principalities into a unified country that could defend its sovereignty.

Under the leadership of King Prithvi Narayan Shah, Gorkha began to extend its borders. Jonathan Lindell, who has traced the early development of Christianity in Nepal, describes King Prithvi Narayan Shah as a person of far-sighted vision and gifted with qualities of leadership. Lindell states that the King's efforts gave Nepal shape and its people security.[26] However, the unification was not a treaty they decided to come together; King Prithvi Narayan Shah began to conquest the neighboring countries. Leaders of indigenous ethnic groups ruled many of these neighboring countries. Such a conquest would be an invasion by a Hindu king. Nepal's unified nation developed into a robust Hindu government that vigorously enforced Hindu values, such as caste systems and rituals in the society.

The formation of the nation also coincided with making Nepal a Hindu state. For example, some Capuchin missionaries were in the Kathmandu valley before the country's unification and enjoyed the former rulers' warm hospitality. The newer rulers cast the missionaries out of

---

22. Lindell, *Nepal and the Gospel of God*, 33.
23. Kharel, *A Brief History of Nepal*, 41; Birkenholtz, *Reciting the Goddess*, 130.
24. Whelpton, *A History of Nepal*, 36.
25. Kaphle, "Prithvi Narayan Shah and Post-Colonial Resistance," 138.
26. Lindell, *Nepal and the Gospel of God*, 35.

The Trinitarian Dharma

the country and closed the Nepal border to all foreigners.[27] In post-unification Nepal, Hindu priests, the highest caste Brahmans, traditionally non-rulers, got the political role of being advisors to the Kings and rulers. The Hindu priest legitimatized the kingship, and in return, the priest received their political and social status to dominate over the people who traditionally did not practice the caste system.[28] Hindu priests translated Sanskrit texts, especially *Puranas*, into Nepali which served as sources for their higher status in the society, the divine appointment of the kingships, and the exaltation of Hindu deities in Nepal.[29]

What followed the country's unification was the further expansion of the country, mainly by Bahadur Shah, the second son of King Prithvi Narayan Shah.[30] During the 1790s, Nepal's territory extended from Bhutan in the east to Kashmir in the west and Tibet in the north to the British provinces in the south of modern-day India.[31] However, in 1814, war broke out between the East India Company and Nepal. Because of their superior knowledge of the landscape, the Nepali army had an advantage over the British force, which greatly outnumbered Nepali. The war ended with a treaty signed in Sugauli, Bihar, India, in December 1815. Though Nepal was able to preserve its sovereignty against the British's imperial aspirations, it was squeezed to its present shape losing most of its *Terai*, the southern plain region of Nepal, and some in the west and the east to the British power. As a result, its ambition of further territorial expansion came to an end.[32] The country's Sanskritization or Hinduziation continued even when the state's expansion ceased in the late 18th century. The British power's inability to penetrate Nepal prevented the introduction of Christianity in the land that was spreading in other British territories.

King Prithvi Narayan Shah's farsighted vision and skill helped the tiny principalities unite into present-day Nepal, and the courage and bravery of the Nepali soldiers protected national sovereignty from the hands of the British. However, this period was full of internal disputes of the ruling

27. Kafle, "Prithvi Narayan Shah and Postcolonial Resistance," 137.
28. Whelpton, *A History of Nepal*, 50–51.
29. Birkenholtz, *Reciting the Goddess*, 134. Birkenholts especially argues that *Swasthani Vartha Katha*, a Sanskrit text translated into Nepali during the Medieval age, played a significant role in Hinduization of Nepal.
30. Whelpton, *A History of Nepal*, 35–37; Vansittart, *Notes on Nepal*, 38; Bajracharya, *Bahadur Shah, the Regent of Nepal*, 61.
31. Vansittart, *Notes on Nepal*, 38.
32. Whelpton, *A History of Nepal*, 42.

Dharma: The Social Foundation

family.³³ Revealing the chaotic condition of Nepal, Parajulee summarizes his survey of transitional politics between 1775 and 1846 by saying, "None of the *Mukhtiyars* [prime ministers] between 1769 and 1846 died a natural death; their lives ended abruptly either by the assassin's bullets or sword or by their hand."³⁴ This way kings of the royal house of the shah thought only about themselves, their power, and status, and they neglected ordinary people's welfare. Nevertheless, the pattern of war among shah kings halted when Jung Bahadur Rana, an influential person in the military who was used as a weapon by the royals to eliminate their enemies, took his opportunity and imprisoned the royal families. This was when the Rana dynasty's dark rule began in Nepal, and it lasted for 105 years.³⁵ This section of Nepali History marks further solidification of Hinduism in Nepal.

During the *Rana* period, Nepal's foreign relations extended to the British rulers, and the *Rana* rulers introduced modernity. However, for internal affairs, they continued with the traditional approach. Hinduism was crucial for their rules and they did not terminate the Shah dynasty. Instead, Shah Kings retained their kingship throughout the *Rana* regime though *Ranas* were the actual rulers, who confined Shah Kings to their palace with no influence over the political affairs.³⁶ The *Ranas* were the self-proclaimed rulers of Nepal, and they wanted to legitimize their regime by a diplomatic relationship with the British super-power in the south.³⁷ They isolated the country, depriving Nepali people of the sort of development enjoyed by the rest of the world.³⁸

From the time of the country's unification to Rana's monopoly rule in Nepal, the ruling side needed the means to legitimatize their control, and they used religion, especially Hinduism, for their benefit. Hinduism, which gives legitimacy to Kingship, was promoted at the cost of other indigenous beliefs. However, there never was an attempt to persuade people to Hindu teachings. Rulers, especially Prithvi Narayan Shah, simply declared Nepal

---

33. Vansittart, *Notes on Nepal*, 35; Bajracharya, *Bahadur Shah*, 21–24.

34. Parajulee, *The Democratic Transition of Nepal*, 29.

35. Vaidya, "The Kot Massacre: A Critical Assessment," 7.

36. Kharel, *Brief History of Nepal*, 108–9. Jang Bahadur Rana used then King Surendra to consolidate his power. Rather than going after king's life, Jang instead created matrimonial alliances with the Royal family. He gave his daughter to the king's son, and his second son got married with the king's daughter.

37. Upreti, *Nepal: Transition to Democratic Republican State*, 13.

38. Manandhar, "British Residents at the Court of Nepal," 17; Parajulee, *Challenge to democracy in Nepal*, 33.

The Trinitarian Dharma

to be the pure Hindu Kingdom.[39] *Rana* rulers knew that Hinduism legitimatized the kingship, and even though they were more powerful than the kings, they never sought to declare themselves as kings; instead, Rana rulers worked as if they were the protector of the kingship.

The *Ranas* made Hinduism the state religion and manipulated its caste system to control the people. In the process, they used the high-caste people to carry out their will.[40] The declaration of Hinduism as a state religion was not the result of religious zeal. Instead, it attempted to legitimatize *Rana's* unlawful rule in the country and continue their dynasty among themselves.[41] Nepal remained a Hindu nation until the new constitution of Nepal declared it a secular government in 2006.[42] Hinduism became overwhelmingly powerful in Nepal because both the Shah kings and the *Rana* rulers used religious frameworks to retain their influence in areas where the state was weak. The government gave Brahmans the roles of leaders who would work according to the state policies.[43] Hindu priests received a position to legitimize the systems and an authority to implement those policies in society. Thereby, Hinduism became the de facto religion of Nepal.

During this period, the political bodies used the Hindu religious and social system for political reasons, but in the end, the people of Nepal internalized the Hindu system and integrated it into their own beliefs and practices. For example, though the caste system is new to Nepali indigenous society, the Nepali indigenous community adopted the caste system to rank themselves in society. Mongoloid people group did not speak against the caste system but boasted their superiority over lower-caste people.[44] This way, Hindu practices, and the religious system became a collective identity of Nepal society.

RELIGIOUS SOLIDITY AMID POLITICAL UPHEAVAL IN NEPAL

The twentieth century marked several significant political changes in Nepal. While some of the changes were for democracy and Nepali people

---

39. Birkenholtz, *Reciting the Goddess*, 132.

40. Brown, *The Challenge to Democracy in Nepal*, 2. Brown terms the imposition of the Hindu religion on the non-hindu people as "hinduisation."

41. Kharel, *Brief History of Nepal*, 116–17.

42. Government of Nepal, *Interim Constitution of Nepal 2063*, 1.

43. Wheapton, *A History of Nepal*, 52.

44. Bhattarai, *Historical Dictionary of Nepal*, 12.

Dharma: The Social Foundation

had the freedom to choose their ruler, others simply handed the power back to the Kings, the Hindu divine ruler. Changes were confined to politics because they could bring very little difference to religious matters. After all, Hinduism controlled various aspects of society for centuries. Previously, religion was used as a political tool by rulers; however, presently, religion is separated from politics, but its influence in society has not diminished. On the social level, *dharma* as a form of Nepali religion had become an essential part of Nepali life.

The changes resulted from the Nepali people's desire to bring freedom to Nepal when Nepali people saw changes hovering over neighboring India and the rest of the world and witnessed India's anti-British movement. People were inspired to establish a similar campaign against the *Rana* regime in Nepal. After the World Wars, the Nepali soldiers recruited by the British as *Gurkha* soldiers returned home with Western ideas of freedom.[45] As a result, Nepali people in India established many different anti-*Rana* parties and organizations such as the Gorkha League(1921), *Praja Parishad* (People Conference)[46](1936), Nepali Congress(1942), and the Communist Party of Nepal(1949).[47] People's knowledge and desires for freedom and the formation of different Nepali organizations in India developed into Nepal's full anti-*Rana* movement. Even King Tribhuwan participated in the effort to free Nepal from the hands of *Rana* Autocracy. Initially, *Rana* rulers pursued to contain the uprising, and they used various tactics to protect their ruling power.[48] However, they were eventually forced to come to the negotiating table.[49] For the first time in Nepal's history, Nepali people could participate in a democratic process to choose their rulers.[50]

This transitional period brought some tension between the monarch and the political parties. The king, who regained political power after the 1950s people's revolution against the *Ranas,* wanted to exercise executive control over government affairs. However, the political parties who dethroned the *Ranas* desired to keep the power to themselves.[51] Even though it was a tense time, the government held the parliamentary elections, and the

45. Parajulee, *Democratic Transition of Nepal*, 37.
46. Brown, *The Challenge to Democracy in Nepal*, 16.
47. Parajulee, *Democratic Transition of Nepal* 16.
48. Parajulee, *Democratic Transition of Nepal*, 39.
49. Brown, *The Challenge to Democracy in Nepal*, 16.
50. Khadka, "Crisis in Nepal's Partyless Panchayat System," 430.
51. Parajulee, *Democratic Transition of Nepal*, 42–45.

The Trinitarian Dharma

Nepali Congress received the highest number of seats in the parliament.[52] On 26 December 1960, King Mahindra dissolved parliament and took national affairs into his own hands.[53] King cited the elected government's failure to maintain law and order and corruption and encouragement of anti-national elements to dismiss the parliamentary system.[54] It was the end of the first, brief experiment in Nepali democracy and the beginning of another struggle by the Nepali people against autocracy and oppression.

This period also shows one of the most critical changes in Nepal's religious history, that foreign missionaries received permission to enter Nepal to be involved in development works, though they were not allowed to conduct any religious activities. With the political change, Nepali-speaking people from India entered Nepal with the Gospel and began evangelizing the Nepali people.[55] Since the authority was in the King's hand, who was the official protector of Nepal's *dharma*, Christians were persecuted. Many were imprisoned, while others were expelled from the country.[56] The ruling system was effortlessly intended to protect the Nepali religious system from outside influences such as Christianity.[57]

Not only persecuting the Christians, but the government also proactively prioritized Hindu festivals, rituals, and activities over other beliefs such as Buddhism and the folk religions of Nepal. By prioritizing Hindu religious events as part of the national calendar while giving less attention to other folk practices, people were made to observe and be part of the Hindu religious system.[58] Hindu values and systems were syncretized in all aspects of Nepali religious life. The Nepali religious system gave a collective identity as *dharma* under Hinduism's universality, and Nepali people incorporated Hindu elements in their folk practices.[59]

---

52. Parajulee, *Democratic Transition of Nepal*, 46.
53. Khadka, "Crisis in Nepal's Partyless Panchayat System," 434.
54. Whelpton, *A History of Nepal*, 98.
55. Rongong, *Early Churches in Nepal*, 43–45.
56. Rongong, *Early Churches in Nepal*, 101–12.
57. Serchan, *Democracy, Pluralism and Change*, 57–61.
58. Serchan, *Democracy, Pluralism and Change*, 61.
59. Dastider, *Religious Minorities in Nepal*, 46–47.

Dharma: The Social Foundation

CONTINUATION OF OLD RELIGIOUS SYSTEM IN A NEW POLITICAL ENVIRONMENT

The multiparty democracy, which began on 16 April 1990, resulted from the struggle of people of all classes, professions, and parties uniting in a peaceful movement against the autocratic Panchayat monarchy system.[60] All parties celebrated when King Birendra announced the dissolution of all panchayat bodies, allowing the multiparty system to exist. However, the events that followed the announcement of a multiparty system did not meet the people's needs for security, development, and economic prosperity. As a result, it was another unsuccessful system.

Not all parties were satisfied with the declaration because they believed that the constitution was insufficiently democratic. Many opposed how the constitution gave emergency powers to the king and made him the supreme commander of the Royal Nepal Army.[61] Those representatives of the Dalits (the low-caste people in Nepal) sought a secular republic to find freedom from high-caste Hindu elites.[62] Those representing Terai sought proper representation of Terai[63] in the country's politico-administrative structure.[64] To various groups, the new parties and their representatives proved to be incapable of running the government. The political parties conducted an almost constant power struggle. As a result, governments frequently changed. For example, in the year 1998 alone, Nepal had three different prime ministers.[65] Maoists took advantage of the political parties' disappointing performance and the people's dissatisfaction. They lured the dissatisfied and those wanting to be included in central power by advocating the struggle for an ethnically autonomous and regional government.[66]

The year 2006 brought a dramatic change in Nepali politics and marked the year of humiliation for the royals and the establishment of a secular

---

60. Khadka "Democracy and Development in Nepal," 47.

61. Upreti, *Nepal*, 36.

62. Upreti, *Maoists in Nepal*, 36.

63. *Terai*, one of the four geographical zones of Nepal, is a southernmost narrow belt of flat land that borders India. The other three are Chure (600 ft. to 3,000 ft. above sea level), Mahabharat parbat (mountainous region, hill region up to an elevation of 10,000 ft.), and Himal (alpine region above 10,000 ft. above sea level).

64. Upreti, *Maoists in Nepal*, 36.

65. Acharya, editor, *Nepal Political Review*, 45.

66. Whelpton, *A History of Nepal*, 233.

The Trinitarian Dharma

republic in Nepal.[67] The enmity between the political parties and the Maoists ended with a twelve-point agreement, signed in India.[68] This situation isolated the king, who continued to act as the country's supreme authority and was determined to oppress the public uprising by imposing curfews and restrictions.[69] The Nepali people saw that the way out was to establish democracy without a King in Nepal. As a result, presently, Nepal is a multi-party republic country, without a Kingship that headed the nation culturally and politically for many centuries. Being an absolute authority of the Hindu Kingdom, the King's role was more than political and included many Hindu rituals that the King performed at the state level. Such practices gave the King divine authority over people and earned their loyalty.

The political change also brought a significant impact on religious affairs. The Constitution of Nepal 2063 (2007) declared that Nepal is a secular state that altered Nepal's official position as a Hindu country.[70] Though the country's official religion is no longer Hinduism, it is naïve to anticipate Nepali politics without religious affairs. It is essential to note the roles Hinduism plays in the secular state of Nepal. At present, there was no king to promote the religion for their political gain, but Nepalis who lived centuries under the collective identity as Hindus were not comfortable with the idea of a secular nation.[71] As the protector of their *dharma*, the demand for a Hinduization of the country is associated with the reinstating of the monarchy. Though it is not part of political affairs, *dharma* remains at the center of Nepali people's life.[72]

The declaration of secularism in Nepal resulted from the demands of minority people who sought to be independent of Hinduism and recognized at the state level.[73] People called for an end to Hinduism's primacy to ensure their equal rights in the country. Some view that such change made religion a personal choice rather than a hierarchical encompassing order that ignored public and private affairs of life.[74] Though it was the political process that

---

67. Gellner, "Nepal and Bhutan in 2006," 80–86.
68. Hutt, "Nepal and Bhutan in 2005," 122.
69. Gellner, "Nepal and Bhutan in 2006," 82–83.
70. Government of Nepal, *Interim Constitution of Nepal 2063 (2007)*, 1.
71. Mazumdar, "Demand for Restoring Nepal's Hindu Identity, 1–5.
72. Letizia, "Ideas of Secularism in Contemporary Nepal," 71.
73. Letizia, "Ideas of Secularism" 42.
74. Gellner and Letizia, "Introduction: Religion and Identities in Post-Panchayat Nepal," 5.

Dharma: The Social Foundation

gave them Hinduism, religion became part of their lives, and now people cannot imagine themselves apart from their *dharma*.[75]

There have been concerns about the country's secularism and demands to rename it to the official Hindu nation. Many Nepali people welcomed the country without a King, but many demanded to restore Hinduism as a national religion.[76] The majority of the people are for a Hindu state. However, this sentiment is led by high-class Hindu majority people who previously enjoyed their privileges in society.[77] The proponents of the Hindu state in Nepal always argue that there is still space for other religions in the Hindu country Nepal.[78] Nepali politics took back steps regarding religious freedom to earn the favor of Hindu adherents. Though the Nepal constitution 2015 did not retract secularism from its definition but added an explanatory note to define secularism. It is interpreted as follows "For this article, "secular" means protection of religion and culture being practiced since ancient times and religious and cultural freedom."[79] In 2018, parliament passed an ordination that prohibits religious conversion. The primary purpose of the ordination is to contain the spread of Christianity in the country.[80] Ever since the passing of the ordination, many Christians have been accused of proselytizing their beliefs and persecuted.[81]

The Hindu majority of people plan to contain Christianity's growth and restrain their activities in the country. Though the King, the Hindu guardian of the country, was removed from office, the Hindu legacies associated with the King and his politics continued. In Nepal's new political scenario, the Kingship is replaced by the office of the president, whose social legitimacy was not religious but political, being elected by the people.[82] Despite not being a symbol of Hindu divinity, the president has begun his duty like that of a king especially fulfilling the Hindu ritual of the former king. Except for those who had enjoyed special political

---

75. Birkenholtz, *Reciting Goddesses*, 154–55.
76. Carvalho, "Nepali Party Wants to Refound the Hindu State," para. 2.
77. Gellner and Letizia, "Hinduism in the Secular Republic of Nepal," 283–85.
78. Gellner and Chiara Letizia, "Hinduism in the Secular Republic," 288.
79. Government of Nepal, *The Constitution of Nepal 2015*, 11.
80. Ochab, "Nepal's Protection of Religious Freedom on Downward Spiral," para. 3.
81. Shellnutt, "Nepal Criminalizes Christian Conversion and Evangelism," para. 1–2. Shepherd, "Nepal Enacts Legislation Punishing Proselytizing with Prison Sentence," para. 2.
82. Gellner and Letizia, "Hinduism in the Secular Republic of Nepal," 295.

The Trinitarian Dharma

favor from the King, Nepali people never missed the King and his divine authority for their day-to-day religious functions.[83] However, the non-divine president may not have the power to instate any Hindu rituals as former kings with divine entitlement did. The presence and participation of tradition by the president as the head of the state mark these Hindu rituals as national heritage, and Hinduism is made and accepted as Nepal and Nepali people's national identity.[84]

Though the new constitution refrains from using the word Hinduism and does not promise to be on its side, it is evident that the government body tends to lean toward the Hindu majority. It instead seeks to protect the so-called Sanatana-*dharma*. A renowned journalist and political analyst from Nepal puts this as follows: "On the contrary, it will specifically obligate the state to protect Sanatana *Dharma*. This seems to be a declaration of a Hindu State by stealth. After all, the term Hindu is merely a Western invention for the group of faiths that were once collectively known as Sanatana *Dharma*."[85] Nepal's secular constitution is so inclined to protect the Sanatana *Dharma*[86] but does not call it Hinduism as commonly called. *Understanding Nepal's society is incomplete without understanding Sanatana Dharma*, protected by the state and accepted by society.

DHARMA AS THE FOUNDATION OF RELIGIONS IN NEPAL

Since Nepal is the country where most of its population claims to be Hindus, it is wrongly assumed that Nepal's religion is the same as Hinduism in India. Religion in Nepal is unique because it has developed its characteristics and traits differently from India.[87] Nepali Religion did not go through the influences of other religions such as Islam and Christianity. Due to its isolation from outside influence throughout its history, the Nepali religion retained an ancient practice of the region, and it was not influenced by the newer developments in Hinduism that happened in India.[88] Certain practices and

---

83. Mocko, *Demoting Vishnu*, 173–76.
84. Gellner and Letizia, "Hinduism in the Secular Republic of Nepal," 296.
85. CK Lal, "Nepal Has Become a Hindu State Through the Backdoor," para. 3.
86. "Sanatana *dharma* is a term created in 19th-century India as a more meaningful synonym for Hinduism. It is sometimes taken to mean the ancient truth behind all religions." Jones and Ryan, "Sanatana *Dharma*," 380.
87. Panta, "Religion, Society and State in Nepal," 50.
88. Dunham and Luhan, "Nepal's Virgin Goddesses," para 4. The article reports about a yearly ritual in Nepal in which a virgin girl (Kumari) is worshiped as a goddess. The

Dharma: The Social Foundation

symbols are especially emphasized and worshiped differently than in India. For example, animal sacrifices are standard practices of Nepali Hinduism, whereas it is not common in India. Nepali religion cannot be explained by the non-violence teachings of Hinduism in India.[89]

Nepal is also a place where uncensored syncretism takes place between religions and faiths. For general people, there is hardly any distinction between Hinduism, Buddhism, or any folk religion.[90] However, Islam and Christianity are not much assimilated because they tend to keep themselves from syncretizing. Therefore, understanding religion in Nepal demands our understanding of *dharma* because the term Hinduism is narrow, and derives its identity and experience independent of other faiths. In his book Religions in Nepal, Trilok Chandra Majpuria explains *dharma* that does not speak about religion; instead, it represents "a way of life, including the socio-cultural life."[91] Since *dharma* has multiple meanings, it can denote a specific religion such as Hinduism, Buddhism, or Islam. For Nepali people, "it means rituals and religious merit, what one gains through rituals and other prescribed action."[92] In other words, the Nepali context is a dharmic society, a society that recognizes *dharma* as a law of life and is guided by it.[93]

Dharma: *Practical Religiosity of Nepali People*

Since *dharma*, which includes morality, righteousness, and duty, is considered one of life's goals, Nepali people seek to achieve it by practicing morality and fulfilling their responsibility in society.[94] Nepali people do not define their religion based on doctrines or teachings. We can see people indiscriminately adoring both Hindu and Buddhist deities. Though they accept philosophical Hinduism, it makes very little difference in their actual

---

ancient practice of Kumari worship is alive in Nepal, which is believed to be 2300 years 2300-year-old practice to the late Vedic period.

89. Forbes, "Dashain," para. 1–12.

90. Shastri, "Hinduism and Buddhism in Nepal," 49. Kumari worship is a prime example of how syncretism is a common practice of Nepali religions. Worship of a virgin girl as a kumara is considered a Hindu practice while the girl who is worshiped is taken from a Buddhist family.

91. T. C. Majpuria and R. K. Majpuria, *Religions of Nepal*, 47.

92. Gellner, *The Anthropology of Buddhism and Hinduism*, 93. Jones and Ryan, "Dharma," 130–31.

93. Rai, *Human Rights in the Hindu-Buddhist Tradition*, 72.

94. Regmi, *Dimensions of Nepali Society and Culture*, 116.

The Trinitarian Dharma

religious life. A Nepali can profess to be Hindu and Buddhist at the same time, not by following the doctrines of both religions, but by participating in the rituals from both sides.[95] The multi-religiosity of Nepali people is exemplified by Sunil K. Yadav, a chaplain of Rush University Medical Centre, Chicago when he confesses his religious belonging as follows.

> Today, when I have to, I identify as a Hindu-Buddhist. I practice both Hinduism and Buddhism as it is practiced by many in Nepal. And no! It is not a practice of two religions, Hinduism, and Buddhism; instead, it is a practice that holds up multiplicity at its core: the elements of "Hinduism," "Buddhism" and other local beliefs. And these beliefs exist as one in an organic way.[96]

However, one should not assume that there is no teaching in Nepal's religion; Nepali religiosity is expressed in more practical ways than creeds and doctrine. Nepali people are less interested in their religion's doctrinal aspect, but they keep rituals and participate in them.[97] It is the uniqueness of their *dharma* that makes their belief more practical-oriented. The practice of *dharma* is not limited to the religious function, but the whole life is directed by the rituals and festivals that people enthusiastically take part in.[98] Participation in religious ceremonies and undertaking social activities such as festivals are essential for Nepali people to observe their *dharma*. Through such involvement, deities are worshiped, and every function of life such as birth, marriage, and death involves ritual makes human-divine connections.[99]

The life-cycle rituals mark life transitions such as birth, adulthood, marriage, and death. Such traditions also keep the connection between the divine and history.[100] In Nepal, it is *dharma* to get married because it is considered a religious sacrament and "spiritual bond" rather than just a reunion of two individuals as Rishikeshab Raj Regmi, a social anthropologist in Nepal, writes:

---

95. Jha, *Customs and Etiquette of Nepal*, 39.
96. Yadav, "Hi! I Am a Hindu Buddhist and More . . . !" para. 2.
97. Kehrberg, *The Cross and the Land of the Khukuri*, 65–66.
98. Jha, *Customs and Etiquette of Nepal*, 38. Jha provides examples of rituals related to birth, marriage and death. These rituals are more family-oriented ritual, but they are not independent of religion.
99. Ingles, "Religious Beliefs and Rituals in Nepal," 209.
100. Michaels, *Homo Ritualis*, 181.

Dharma: The Social Foundation

Hindu marriage binds the wife and husband to perform *dharma* to procreate and to fulfill other duties concerning physical, social, and spiritual requirements. Marriage is the foundation of Grihastha Ashrama. Procreation is necessary to pay one's debt to parents as well as the ancestors of the family. Because of this man can attain Moksha. Marriage for Hindus is considered a sacramental union.[101]

This way, Nepali people fulfill their *dharma* by practicing the rituals involved in the marriage ceremony.

A funeral is another part of life in which the fulfillment of *dharma* takes place. Nepali people consider death a path to the afterlife, and relatives take an important role after the soul's departure. It is the *dharma* of the dead's relatives to perform appropriate rituals that ensure the well-being of the soul of the dead in his/her afterlife. Therefore, Nepal's 13-day-long funeral ceremony is part of *dharma* that Nepali people do not avoid.[102] The performing *dharma* for dead parents does not end at the funeral but is repeated every year on special occasions to ensure the deceased ancestors' safety. However, these rituals are not the same everywhere in Nepal. Though they vary differently among a people group, such rites are essential everywhere. These are a substantial part of one's *dharma* in Nepal, which goes beyond the worship of deities[103] Besides the *dharma* performed through the rituals associated with life events, birth, marriage, and death, other religious events occur in Nepal, in which Nepali people are bound as a society.

Nepali people follow the old religious calendar, which outlines the special days for them to remember and participate. These festivals are centuries old and bear their own religious or social significance. Though some are non-religious originations, it is part of *dharma*, and people celebrate these festivals and participate in the rituals that these festivals require of them.[104] During celebrations, Nepali people remember their deities and their deeds as told in Hindu epics or their legends and worship them. By participating in the rituals involved, Nepali people establish their connection to the particular deities.[105] These festivals are dedicated to certain

---

101. Regmi, *Dimensions of Nepali Society and Culture*, 90.
102. Acharya, "Thirteen Days of Mourning," para. 1.
103. Ghimire, "Death Rites and Rituals," para. 5.
104. Anderson, *The Festivals of Nepal*, 41–42.
105. Jha, *Hindu Buddhist Festivals of Nepal*, 10.

The Trinitarian Dharma

religious functions and provide social opportunities for people to develop a bond and create their collective identity as Nepali people.[106]

Festivals are other factors of Nepali *dharma* that connect people into one body. In fulfilling religious duties, these festivals mostly unite people and renew their identity as Nepali people. One such community event is seen during the *Machhindranath rath* festival (chariot) in Patan, a city within Kathmandu Valley. The festival itself requires lots of resources and time for preparation. A hand-built 60 to 70-foot-high wooden chariot is made ready to be pulled by volunteer devotees around the city.[107] Thousands of people join the event and make this vast festival a success. Swati Pujari, who researched this particular festival, concludes that this festival brings the people of Patan city together and strengthens the collective identity of Patan. Since the festival itself is centuries old, people of the present are connected to the past.[108] Pujari's research shows that most people involved in the festival were for their religious cause, in other words, as part of their *dharma*.[109]

Dashain is the most auspicious festival in Nepal, celebrated in the name of Durga-puja in India. *Dashain* has several connections with Hindu epic stories and myths. It involves an animal sacrifice to the goddess Durga. However, after animal sacrifice, Nepali people feast with their friends, relatives, and families.[110] People receive or give blessings to each other by putting *tika*, a mixture of red pigment and rice, on the forehead. In the past, this festival required the king to bless the people by putting a *tika* on his subjects' forehead, and today, the president fulfills this *dharma* of blessing the citizens.[111] Other religious festivals are dedicated to certain people of the society. The *Teej* festival is chiefly observed by women who keep it for their husbands' longevity. After fasting and taking a holy bath, women spend time together singing and dancing.[112] The third day of the *Tihar* festival is specially dedicated to the relationship between sisters and their brothers.

---

106. Regmi, *Dimensions of Nepali Society*, 134.

107. Vaidya and Bajrachary, *Nepal: People and Culture*, 78–79.

108. Pujari, "Exploring the Effects of the Chariot Festival," 55.

109. Pujari, "Exploring the Effects of the Chariot Festiva," 49. Data shows that 84.1% people participated in the festival with their family and friends for religious participation.

110. Jha, *Hindu Buddhist Festivals of Nepal*, 104.

111. Mocko, *Demoting Vishnu*, 173.

112. Majpuria and Gupta, *Nepal: The Land of Festivals*, 91–92.

While sisters bless their brothers with rainbow color tika and delicious food, brothers give their sisters gifts of money and other things.[113]

Nepali *dharma* is fulfilled by participation in religious functions and rituals related to life events. Such *dharma* of participation provides Nepali people with an understanding of their identity and their specific roles in society. Through such participation and fulfillment of duties, people unite in the family and the community. For the part of their religion, Nepali people practice *dharma* as a way of life without uttering their practices in academic concepts.[114]

Dharma *as Communitarian Consciousness of Nepali People*

Even though everyone participates in *dharma*, it is never limited to a personal matter in Nepali society. Family, caste, and ethnicity define *dharma*, and fulfilling *dharma* is about keeping the tradition and being part of the community. In Nepal, religions are given big names, such as Hinduism and Buddhism; however, they are more about the nexus of indigenous *dharma* of many communities in Nepal. There is no uniformity of practice, but the communities are bound by the *dharma* defined within their context.[115] The *dharma* includes some specific duties for immediate family to the general duties that everyone should observe for their *dharma*.

There are many layers of rituals and celebrations in the Nepali community. Lynn Bennet conducted an anthropological study about the Nepali community to understand the role of high-caste women in society and parsed the community layers.[116] She showed that the parivar, a family, is the first unit in which people must keep their ritual of death and birth for 10 to 13 days as a part of their *dharma*. Then other relatives are obliged to keep the death and birth ritual for at least five days. The relative not so close keeps the rituals for one day.[117] The intensity of *dharma* required in the community differs, but they are united into a single community with this. There are priests, shamans, or lamas (Buddhist priests) in the local community to preside over the *dharma* duty for people and act as the guardian of the particular community's *dharma*.[118] *Dharma* unites

113. Majpuria and Gupta, *Nepal: The Land of Festivals*, 114–15.
114. Kehrberg, *The Cross in the Land of the Khukuri*, 66.
115. Panta, "Religion, Society and State in Nepal," 49.
116. Bennett, *Dangerous Wives, and Sacred Sisters*, 19.
117. Bennett, *Dangerous Wives, and Sacred Sisters*, 21.
118. Sharma and Dixit, "*Dharma* in a Changing Landscape," 11.

The Trinitarian Dharma

small units of families and immediate relatives as a community. Specific festivals and rituals are practiced among their close relative and family members but also as a community. The importance of *dharma* in fulfilling rituals and celebrating festivals falls not only in religious matters but also in making a community.[119]

For example, Rai is a people group that originally resided in the eastern mountains of Nepal. They have a ritual to honor their ancestors, which can be done in their homes. However, a particular aspect of ancestor-related traditions is done collectively as a community presided over by a priest. Nokcho, a village priest, represents the whole community to perform the rituals. The entire village people gather for the community ritual and commemorate their ancestors from whom they inherited their land. As a community, people fulfill their ancestral *dharma* and renew their commitment to the community.[120]

In Nepal, especially in the capital city, Kathmandu, there is a tradition of having a unique community called *Guthi*. They inherit a certain portion of land or fund to maintain temples, and religious ceremonies, and support a religious institution. Such a community's principle goal is to "promote the social welfare of the Nepali people through maintaining religious and cultural traditions and temples, monuments and sites."[121] *Guthis* exists to ensure that the *dharma* is kept well and to provide the community members' welfare. The welfare of the people taken care of by *Guthi* communities is part of religious activity or simply community *dharma*.[122] Because of these *Guthis* the numerous temples, and the festivals are funded and ensure enthusiastic participation. Fulfillment of one's *dharma* by participation in the rituals and festivals is made sure by the activities of *Guthi*. There are many *Guthis* in Nepal to serve the community in different roles and capacities and perform activities related to *dharma*.[123] In other words, *dharma* is not the responsibility of a single individual or a household, but the whole community takes part in the *dharma* as one body.[124]

---

119. Sharma and Dixit, "*Dharma* in a Changing Landscape," 12.

120. Schlemmer, "Following the Ancestors and Managing the Otherness," para 1.

121. Scott, "The Guthi System of Nepal," 4; Ingles, "Religious Beliefs and Rituals in Nepal," 212.

122. Vajracharya, "Role of Guthi in Newar Buddhist Culture," para 1–5.

123. Scott, "The Guthi System of Nepal," 25.

124. Maharjan, "Guthi System: Tracing Indigenous Practices of Heritage Conservation in Kathmandu Valley," ICHCAP, (May 15, 2018). https://www.unesco-ichcap.org/guthi-system-tracing-indigenous-practices-of-heritage-conservation-in-kathmandu-valley/.

Dharma: The Social Foundation

In Nepal, *dharma* plays more than the religious aspect of people's life. Since *dharma* includes festivals, as such, they renew the life of a community. While people are satisfied with their *dharma* involvement, they also get entertained and bonded as a community.[125] Lal Deosa Rai analyzed the *dharma* in Nepal from the ethical and human rights perspective and mentioned that "It is to *dharma* or collective consciousness that the components of the organic whole, namely, the state, the community and all individuals including the monarch, or the highest executive authority owe allegiance."[126]

Dharma leads Nepali society from individuality to the community and makes every individual sacrifice their individuality for the community's good. *Dharma* promotes cooperation and unity in society. In such a harmonious community, Nepali people fulfill their *dharma*.[127] There is always a public dimension in the personal *dharma* of Nepali individuals. Private devotion and religious activities are always accommodating to others. All the general nature of *dharma* activities also includes the individual aspect of personal *dharma* or religiosity. Through public religious events, all individuals achieve fulfillment in their *dharma* as well. Therefore, the Nepali *dharma* community concept cannot be divorced from its association with individual *dharma*.[128]

Dharma: *Social Responsibility of an Individual*

The individual's value is not diminished in Nepali society due to *dharma* and its demand for social involvement. *Dharma*, which is community-oriented, allocates each individual in the community a duty and function to perform. In the community, the goal of an individual life is to fulfill the responsibility of his/her best. Such individual effort has both societal benefits and ensures personal salvation in the world or attainment of *dharma*.[129]

"In Nepal, every household is a member of at least one guthi formed for a specific purpose, like taking care of temples, performing mask dances, playing musical instruments, lighting butter lamps, taking care of stupas or bridges, and many more." This way Nepali people are involved in the ritual activities one way the other.

125. Sharma and Dixit, "*Dharma* in a Changing Landscape," 12.

126. Rai, *Human-Buddhist Tradition*, 52.

127. Rai, *Hindu-Buddhist Tradition*, 56.

128. McKendry-Smith, "Old Gods, New Religions," 122. The study shows that their devotions at home always have space for others to give it a community dimension, at the time congregational religiosity fulfills their very private *dharma* as well.

129. Rai, "Human Rights," 37–46.

The Trinitarian Dharma

Every individual in the community, including kings or political leaders, is expected to perform personal *dharma*, which is for the well-being of the society. A political person has his own political or leadership *dharma*, and he completes his *dharma* of society's development.[130]

The kingship of Nepal, which was abolished after the 2006 political change in Nepal, was also bound by *dharma*, called raj-*dharma* (king's *dharma*). King's *dharma* is evaluated according to the governing of his people.[131] The King's duty of governing is done according to *dharma*, which is for the people's well-being, not the King's enjoyment. Former King Birendra understood his *dharma* as follows,

> The king cannot change this value system (*dharma*). Therefore, he too is governed by this ethical code according to which the King lives and has his being only to protect the people, to dispense justice to them, and to punish the wrongdoers. Indeed, the king embodies the collective identity of the people, and as desired by the people, it is he who grants and amends the constitution.[132]

In a family, everyone has compulsory duties to follow rituals and other obligations. The *Dharma* of the individual is extended to his family responsibilities. In many Hindu families, *dharma* requires a man to marry and produce offspring for familial continuation. The husband of the family must earn a living for the family and ensure his immediate family's well-being. "According to the householder's *dharma* then, one contributes to and participates in [worldly life] and receives his rewards there- whether it is a pleasant sojourn in swarga or a high re-birth.[133] It's not only the head of the family whose individual *dharma* is his familial responsibility, but all family members have allocated vocational duties of *dharma* to identify and follow the appropriate action. By fulfilling their social vocation, everyone fulfills his or her *dharma*.[134]

Newar people group, who mostly live in the Kathmandu valley, are adherents of Hinduism and Buddhism. Some people seek to be monks to achieve their higher *dharma*, apart from worldly life in family and society. Even these monks cannot wholly disregard their duty to the community

---

130. Kattel, "Democracy without Prevalence of *Dharma*," para 10.
131. Nawaraj Chaulagain, "Hindu Kingship," 4.
132. King Birendra, *Newsweek*, 09-10-1973.
133. Bennett, *Dangerous Wives and Sacred Sisters*, 39.
134. Dhand "The *Dharma* of Ethics, the Ethics of *Dharma*," 357.

and family. Society defines one's *dharma*, and an individual keeps it.[135] A Newar individual speaks about his *dharma* accordingly,

> A human being's *dharma* is to care for his family. He has to bring up his children, worship the gods, offer food to the ancestors, and make sure that everything that he has to do is done . . . The highest *dharma* is to care for one's family. This is the *dharma* of human beings.[136]

Glenner and LeVine documented that Buddhist monks and nuns are compelled to work for their families and relatives. A Buddhist monk cannot devote his life to only the monastery's religious matters leaving his widow mother alone at home. While being a monk, he works hard to fulfill his/her duty to his sibling by providing them opportunities and money.[137] Another monk who learned his younger sister was orphaned after his parent's death cannot remain silent on the issue but fulfills his responsibility to his younger sister.[138] These are examples of how even the pursuit of individual *dharma* in a monastery away from society cannot detach from social responsibility. "*Dharma* is not about one's placement on a social scale, and the management of one's relationships on that scale. Rather, it is a simple imperative: *Dharma* is friendliness, which works for the welfare of all."[139] A person's individuality is not diminished in *dharma* by making him or her part of the society, but the person's individuality comes to fulfillment when he/she belongs to a community. The individuality is fulfilled by the participation of *dharma* in the community.[140]

SUMMARY

Hinduism's interaction with various traditional beliefs such as Buddhism and traditional animistic or shamanistic beliefs makes Nepal's present religious context. Therefore, though Nepal is known as a Hindu country, Nepal's religion is different from Hinduism practiced in India. Throughout history, Hinduism was used by political leaders to justify their rules and promote a social system favorable to them. Hindu religious leaders

---

135. Leve, "Subjects, Selves, and the Politics of Personhood," 843.
136. Leve, "Subjects, Selves, and the Politics of Personhood," 843.
137. Gellner and LeVine, "All in the Family: Money Kinship," 158,
138. Glenner and Levine, "All in the Family: Money Kinship," 158.
139. Dhand, "The *Dharma* of Ethics," 367.
140. Dhand, "The *Dharma* of Ethics," 352.

The Trinitarian Dharma

such as priests or Brahmans incited the rulers to enforce the Hindu social system upon those who traditionally did not practice the caste system. As a result, today's Nepali context is born, which has various traditional beliefs still tainted by Hindu elements in society. Today, though Nepal's politics is secular in the constitution, people demand more state involvement and restriction of other religions to promote and preserve their traditional religious system, *dharma*. This is due to *dharma* has become an inseparable part of Nepali life.

Dharma is the foundation, definition, and primary function of the rule of life in Nepali society. First, Nepali people's practical religiosity is that one's religion is defined not by creed or theology but by their *dharma* practices in the community, homes, and personal life. To practice their faith, Nepali people participate in religious festivals and perform rituals related to human life, such as marriage ceremonies and funerals. Secondly, *dharma* is the Nepali people's communitarian consciousness that their *dharma* binds Nepali societies and various castes. *Dharma* gives them a collective identity in society. In the name of Hinduism, *Dharma* also seeks to incorporate all different practices under its wing, giving all Nepalis a national identity of being Nepali. *Dharma* leads Nepali society from individuality to the community and sacrifices individuality for the community's sake. All the individual aspects of *dharma* are ultimately a building block of the community. Lastly, *dharma* is the responsibility of an individual in his family, community, and country. An individual's *dharma* is about fulfilling the dharmic duties as a husband, a wife, a parent, a child, a member of a particular community, a citizen of the country, a king, or a politician. A person's individuality is not diminished, but it is drawn to accomplish his or her association with the community.

Therefore, in the Nepali context, *dharma* points to practical religiosity as the theological method. Any theology in Nepal done outside of their *dharma* practices cannot penetrate Nepali society. Similarly, religion cannot be understood in terms of individuality; instead, it becomes a community force. Nepali theology should note the community aspect of Nepali *dharma*. However, in the present condition, there are several challenges. Nepali *dharma* faces in Nepal, which is made the subject of Nepali contextual theology as well. The following chapter introduces Nepal's social problems related to *dharma* and its relation to Christianity, an outside element of Nepali *dharma*.

3

The Crossroads of Faith

Exploring the Confluence of Christianity and Dharma

DHARMA, SERVING AS THE foundation of the Nepali social system, permeates all aspects of life. It is integral to the examination of social issues such as poverty, gender equality, and social discrimination. One cannot isolate these societal challenges from the influence of *dharma*. Internally, *dharma* is often identified as a root cause of various social problems. Externally, Christianity has been perceived as a challenge to Nepali *dharma*. This chapter delves into the analysis of the current challenges posed to Nepali *dharma*, particularly considering the impact of external factors like Christianity.

SOCIO-POLITICAL PROBLEMS OF NEPAL

Dharma, as a religious system of Nepal, balances various dimensions of Nepali society. It stabilizes the individual lives of people and their identity and function as a community. It also gives a collective identity to be Nepali people. However, as a religious system of Nepal, *dharma* even stumbles against various obstacles in its path. Some point out the social issues as the negativity of Nepali *dharma*. Others call them genuine challenges that Nepali *dharma* needs to tackle. In Nepali *dharma*, the challenges come from the caste system of old Hinduism,[1] a low view of women in the society, and

---

1. Serchan, *Democracy, Pluralism and Change,* 52–53. points out that the Hindu caste system was forced upon even those people who were not originally Hindus. Eventually, the caste system pushed low-caste people to the economically disadvantaged side because they were entitled to be limited to low-ranking jobs.

poverty among the disadvantaged people.² Though these three social issues are discussed independently in this research, they are interrelated, and *dharma* finds itself amid these problems. There is a growing call for a reformation of the Nepali religious system to cope with the challenges.³

Caste System

The caste system is a traditional Hindu way of categorizing people into a hierarchal social ladder. Nepal society has been organized into four Castes: Brahmin, Chhetri, Vaishya, and Sudras. Among them, Brahmin and Chhetri are high class, and Vaishya and Sudras are the lower class. Especially Sudras are called untouchable people of society.⁴ Following are some distinct features of this system: it is a hierarchical system in which one group is on the top, and another is on the bottom, the hereditary basis of membership that a person's caste is inborn, endogamy that people are required to marry within one's caste, and conscious of purity that higher caste people do not have any fellowship with the so-called unclean lower caste people.⁵

This way, we can observe that Nepali society is engaged in a systematic system of discrimination and humiliation of the so-called lower-caste people. Even traditionally, non-Hindu people are also labeled with different castes making them subject to discrimination and humiliation. The statistics show that 29.3% of the population belongs to higher castes (Brahmin and Chhetris), and the rest 70.7% of the population are underprivileged.⁶ A Nepali social anthropologist, Dhor Bahadur Bista, explains the situation by saying,

> In this regard, the past governments of Nepal misled people by creating an unnatural vertical social ladder, framing the legal code accordingly. People with so many different origins and cultural backgrounds cannot possibly be arranged into strict social frameworks. However, the value of the Hindu caste system tends to pervade the entire Nepali situation.⁷

---

2. Dhungana, "Nepali Hindu Women's Thorny Path to Liberation," 39; Birkenholtz, "On Becoming a Woman," 433–64.

3. Majpurias, *Religions in Nepal*, 129.

4. Dilli Ram Dahal, "Social Composition of the Population," 90.

5. Dahal, "Social Composition of the Population." 90.

6. *Statistical Pocket Book Nepal 2010*, 32.

7. Bista, *People of Nepal*, ix.

Some claim that the Hindus brought unity to the country and prevented society from disintegrating. These voices usually come from 'Brahmins and Chhetries,'[8] the most privileged ones in Nepal.[9] In contrast, some other people see such a social system as oppressive to the unprivileged, mostly lower caste people and women.[10] An unfair political system caused the social turmoil which prevails in Nepal. Narendra Prasad Shrestha writes,

> What we find is that the higher classes and castes have the monopoly to get it [opportunities of education, and to advance in society] and lower classes who are on the lower rungs of the social ladder are unable to compete with them because these backward communities have not been made capable due to deprivation and exploitation of equal opportunity or right and education since centuries . . . This allowed the Maoists to grow and spread violence and terrorism.[11]

However, after the re-establishment of a multiparty democratic system in Nepal in 1990, the constitutional position of Nepali minorities was slightly improved. The constitution of 1990 declares that "Nepal is a multi-ethnic, multi-lingual, democratic, independent, indivisible, sovereign, Hindu," constitutional monarchical country where previously Nepali society was always said to be homogeneous.[12] Even so, the constitutional declaration of equality did not guarantee equal treatment in society. While analyzing the relationship between politics and inequality in Nepal's culture, Lawoti and Ghimire report ever-increasing cases of caste-based discrimination. According to them, in 1998, only one case of discrimination was reported; in 2007, the figure reached 61.[13] The eradication of the caste system from Nepal is not likely in the immediate future.

Though people of various ethnicities and languages have always constituted Nepal, the State never published such diversity before the 1950s. The state tried to put all the ethnic groups under the umbrella of a Hindu caste system and presented Nepal as "a homogeneous country in terms

---

8. See the Glossary.

9. Baidhya and Bajracharya, *Nepal: People and Culture*, 26.

10. Serchan, *Democracy, Pluralism and Change*, 51–52. Serchan presents various conflicts in Nepali society that are the result of forcing Hinduism onto the country as a social system.

11. Sharma, *The Road to Democracy and Kingdom of God*, 13.

12. Hutt, "Drafting the Nepal Constitution, 1990," 1035.

13. Lawoti and Guneratne, *Ethnicity, Inequality, and Politics in Nepal*, 44.

The Trinitarian Dharma

of language, religion, and ethnicity."[14] By definition, indigenous people groups are "communities which have . . . [their] . . . own mother tongues and traditional cultures and yet do not fall under the conventional fourfold Verna of Hindu or Hindu hierarchical caste structure."[15] However, the government's social hierarchy system put all indigenous people below Brahmins, Chhetris, and Hindu customs and rituals.[16] Indigenous people make up 31% of the Nepali population, and they remain subject to social and cultural discrimination and oppression.[17]

The Janajati, the indigenous people, and women suffer a similar existence to that of the Dalits, the untouchables. The indigenous people in Nepal are currently struggling to protect their identity, culture, and fundamental rights. Some aspects of the culture of these indigenous people conflict with the Hindu cultures and values. For example, on 26 June 2011, the National Federation of Indigenous Nationalities (NEFIN), an organization working for the rights of indigenous people in Nepal, published a press release citing the case of one 'Tamang'[18] family, belonging to the indigenous people of Nepal, who were accused of eating beef, the cow being a holy animal according to Hindu teaching. Tamang people traditionally eat beef, and they do not consider themselves Hindus.[19] As a result, indigenous people have thought that the Hindu system has suppressed their customs and practices.

Language is another thing that makes the indigenous nationalities of Nepal different from dominant Hindus. Though Nepali is a lingua franca, only 48.6% of the population professes the Nepali language as their mother tongue. It means 51.4% of Nepali people speak other than Nepali as their mother tongue.[20] In Nepal, 70% of the total population is linguistically homogenous, among which 48.6% speak only Nepali, and the rest, 21.4%, do not speak the Nepali language.[21] Nevertheless, the government neglected

---

14. Dahal, "Social Composition of the Population," 84.

15. Dahal, "Social Composition of the Population," 84.

16. Whelpton, *A History of Nepal*, 35. Whelpton names the period between 1743 and 1885 as unification and Sanskritisation, explaining how non-Hindus were forced into the Hindu social system.

17. Dahal, "Social Composition of the Population," 91.

18. An indigenous people group of Nepal who traditionally follow a form of Buddhism. Gautam and Thapa-Magar, *Tribal Ethnography of Nepal Vo. II*, 264–65.

19. Ang Kaji Sherpa, "I was put into Custody for 4 hours" NEFIN, Sunday 26, 2011.

20. Yadava, "Languages," *Population Monograph of Nepal 2003*, 140–41.

21. Yadava, "Languages," 154.

this considerable portion of the population for centuries because the one nation-one language policy overlooked diversity.[22]

Nepali *dharma* has internalized the caste system, and people have adopted it as part of their *dharma*. The higher castes, the Brahmans, Chhetris, and Vaishyas, are afraid of losing their social status if they attempt to disregard the caste system. It is hard for people to be against the community bound by the system of *dharma*.[23] In general, people respecting the caste system are synonymous with following one's *dharma* in society. While many agree that the caste system should be replaced with some liberating systems, *dharma* cannot bring such reform because it seeks to protect the system itself.[24]

Women: The Helpless Sufferers

Since Nepali *dharma* emphasizes rituals and purity laws, certain aspects of such traditions put women at a disadvantage in the family, society, and community. Some of these rituals reflect less trust in women, who are considered weak, vulnerable, and unworthy.[25] Since Nepali *dharma* is Nepal's political system, even those who reject Hinduism are negatively affected.[26] *Dharma* incorporates specific values that favor men over women. As a result, the community gives more importance to sons over daughters. Even among women, widows are deprived of the ritual privileges of other women in society.[27]

Women and children suffer the worst of all in Nepal because they are under religious and social oppression in many stages. It is challenging for Nepali women and children to find a sanctuary. They are equally oppressed and neglected in all castes and people groups. 51% of Nepal's population is female. They suffer various kinds of inequality and oppression in society and their home.[28] The Women's Foundation of Nepal (WFN), an organization that gives voice to women's rights, recorded that 81% of husbands physically abuse their wives, and 21% of men stated that

22. Yadava, "Languages," 143.
23. Bista, *Fatalism and development*, 54–55.
24. Sharma, "Caste, Social Mobility and Sanskritization," 297.
25. Sharma, "Caste, Social Mobility and Sanskritization," 281.
26. Dhungana, "Nepali Hindu Women's Thorny Path," 43.
27. Pandey, "The Symbolic Colour Red," 8.
28. Pantha and Sharma, "Population Size, Growth, and Distribution," 60.

it is acceptable for men to beat their wives.[29] WFN also claims that every 54 minutes, there is a woman raped in Nepal. Many women do not report such crimes because they fear that they will face further discrimination and rejection in society if they reveal such cases.[30]

Women also face a substantial educational disadvantage. National statistics show that 25% of Nepal's girls never enter a primary (elementary) school. 10% of the girls who entered elementary school leave the school before they complete their studies. Almost 35% of Nepali females get no formal education.[31] WFN also records that women in Nepal face other oppression and discrimination, such as being subjected to torture following witchcraft accusations, and bias specific to widows.[32]

Nepal is a society where these outcasts, untouchables, neglected and deprived women and children, and rejected indigenous people groups are struggling to make their way. *Dharma* as a religious system is entangled with all these social problems, with its rituals favoring a specific group of people over the other. Nepali *dharma* makes giving birth to a son almost mandatory to extend family lineage and fulfill their ancestors' *dharma*. Sons are the ones who perform the rituals regarding their dead parents and ancestors. Due to such *dharmic* requirements, sons are given more priority over daughters, from which all the disadvantages against women begin.[33] There is a growing call for the improvising of *dharma* to lift the burden of the women.[34]

Underdevelopment and Poverty

The suffering of the children, women, lower caste, and indigenous people in Nepal is felt on cultural and religious fronts. The whole country is gripped in poverty, growing crime and violence, underdevelopment of

---

29. "Domestic Abuse," *The Women's Foundation of Nepal*, para. 3.

30. "Sexual Abuse," *The Women's Foundation of Nepal*, para. 1–3.

31. Tirtha Bahadur Manandhar and Krishna Prasad Shrestha, "Population Growth and Education Development," 227.

32. "Women's Issues" *Women's Foundation of Nepal*, para. 1–3.

33. Bennett, "Dangerous Wives and Sacred Sisters," 39.

34. Birkenholtz, "On Becoming a Woman," 461. After analyzing a Nepali Hindu scripture which is read my majority of women in Nepal to achieve their personal *dharma*, the author finds it patriarchic and subordinating women and suggest Nepali women to read more progressive writings instead. Pandey, "The Symbolic Colour Red," 8. Calls the women, especially widows to get away with certain oppressive and depriving *dharmic* symbols.

infrastructure, and political instability; thereby, Nepal is one of the world's poorest countries. According to the CIA factbook, Nepal's estimated GDP (per capita) in 2011 was just $1,300, which is 204th among 216 countries in the world.[35] The underdeveloped state of the country has increased the suffering of all parties. A 2004 survey shows that only 37.2% of households had access to electricity, 43.9% of households had piped water, and only 38.7% had a toilet facility in the home.[36] Many Nepali people suffer from a lack of necessities.

The Nepali history study shows that Nepal's present social problems— the caste system, indigenous ethnic groups' rights, issues regarding women and children, poverty, and underdevelopment- came along in history. In the past, the kings and rulers sought to enjoy their power, but they did not consider their subjects' welfare. Nepal's politics always remained unstable, and the rulers had to work hard to protect their position and power; therefore, they paid no heed to the country's development.[37] Nepal was declared a Hindu nation, and the governments and rulers attempted to enforce religious laws and customs as civil law in the country. The whole process of Hinduzisation or Sanskritization happened with the hand of political leaders; the religious leaders had very little influence on the direction of political affairs.[38] Rulers and Brahmans (so-called spiritual leaders in Nepal) alliance existed for their mutual benefit that rulers wanted religious approval of their monopoly while Brahmans wanted political security of their high social status given by Hinduism.

Nepali *dharma* embraces *karma*, and fate, to justify the suffering of these people in society. Though karma means action, general people understand it as their luck or fate in a certain caste or gender, which determines their livelihood in society.[39] *Dharma* rarely states any possibility for anyone to change their future status in the community; most poor and suffering people curse themselves for having such a bad fate. Fatalism comes in the way of the development of Nepali society because *dharma* as a social system is ensnared with such beliefs and practices.[40] Society certainly needs a way

---

35. The Central Intelligence Agency (CIA), "Nepal: Economy," *World Fact Book*, para. 2.
36. Central Bureau of Statistics, "Nepal Living Standards Survey 2003/04."
37. Bista, *Anthropology of Nepal*, 105.
38. Sharma, "Caste, Social Mobility and Sanskritization," 290–97.
39. Bista, *Fatalism and Development*, 77.
40. Khadka, "Spiritual poverty and fatalism a drawback for Nepal," para. 3.

The Trinitarian Dharma

out. In recent times, Nepali *dharma* has been losing its charm, and people are being attracted to other faiths to escape from the injustices and discrimination in the Nepali religious system. Improvising its *dharma* to address social issues and pave the way for justice and equality in society is the way forward of Nepali *Dharma*.[41] The lack of initiative on such reform within Nepali *Dharma* has made it vulnerable to criticism and rejection. These social issues related to *dharma* are where Christianity in Nepal can contribute to society. Through a serious conversation with *dharma* problems, Nepali theology can give an alternative to Nepali society.

NEPALI *DHARMA* ENCOUNTERS CHRISTIANITY

Christianity is not the first foreign religion that Nepali *dharma* had to encounter in its land. Muslim people have entered Nepal as artists and settlers since the 15th century. Some of them were invited to hilly regions in Nepal as trainers of firearms for armies.[42] Muslims lived peacefully with their neighbors following Hinduism, Buddhism, and folk religions.[43] However, since the beginning, Christianity's arrival was not appreciated but seen as the enemy of Nepali *dharma*.[44] No Christian country ever colonized Nepal, nor was it propagated by foreign missionaries. However, the teachings and practices of Christianity are considered to be against Nepali *dharma* and considered foreign *dharma* for Nepali society.[45]

In the 1950s, when the country was opened to the world for the first time in centuries, there were no known Christians in Nepal. With a new political environment in the country, after the collapse of the *Rana* regime and the reestablishment of democracy within the monarchy, many Christians, both foreigners, and Nepali, who received the gospel outside Nepal's borders, began their mission work in the country.

Christianity has been preached in Nepal for at least two centuries. In 1715, Capuchin missionaries resided in Kathmandu and established a church.[46] Eventually, they were barred from the kingdom following the Gurkhas' conquest of the Katmandu Valley in 1768.[47] After that, any conver-

41. Chemjong, "Fake Secularism," para. 1–5.
42. Chemjong, "Fake Secularism," 309.
43. Chemjong, "Fake Secularism," 315.
44. Chemjong, "Fake Secularism," 330.
45. Sherchan, *Democracy, Pluralism and Change*, 59
46. Whelpton, *A History of Nepal*, 37.
47. Perry, *A Biographical History of Church in Nepal*, 10.

sion of Nepali to Christianity happened outside the border. Cindy Perry's research on Nepali Diaspora shows that some Nepali people in India were introduced to Christianity long before Nepal opened its doors to missionaries. Cindy Perry writes, "The almost 100 years of Protestant missionary activity along the borders was excellent preparation for when Nepal finally opened her doors . . . Slowly, one by one, Nepali men and women began to respond to the message."[48] The Nepali, who responded to the missionaries' message and converted to Christianity at the border, later carried the same message into Nepal when the door was open in 1950.[49]

The environment was not missionary friendly in Nepal due to restrictions on the missionaries and Christians that they did not have permission to promote their religion or convert any Nepali to Christianity. Despite such limitations, Christianity flourished. Nepal allowed mission organizations such as United Missions to Nepal (UMN) and International Nepal Fellowship (INF) to help develop the country. However, they strictly prohibited them from involving in religious matters.[50] Yet, the missionaries' presence was a witness for Christ, and slowly people came under their influence. Despite the restrictions, statistics show that Christianity grew from 0% to 0.3% in 50 years.[51] The Nepali believers, who received the gospel through the missionaries at the borders, took charge of planting Churches.[52]

Nepal's church flourished and grew to encompass a half-million members in less than 50 years. One of the leading Nepali magazines, *Nepalitimes*, suggested that there are almost one million church members in Nepal.[53] Government records show that only 0.4% of Nepali are Christians. This is due to the complicated procedure of officially changing religions on government records. People do not inform officials about the change of their religion.[54] Though the exact number of Christians is difficult to determine, the government record itself certainly shows that Nepal's Christian population is growing. *Christianity Today*'s report in 2000 hinted that there are

48. Perry, *A Biographical History of Church in Nepal*, 57.

49. Perry, *Nepali Around the World*, 358; Karthak, "Gyani Shah," 59–61, an example of how a Nepali woman met missionaries on the Nepal-India border, was converted and later planted a church among the poorest of the Nepali community.

50. Lindel, *Nepal and the Gospel of God*, 130–31. Sharma, "A History of the Pentecostal Movement in Nepal," 299.

51. See Figure 1.

52. Perry, *A Biographical History of the Church in Nepal*, 83.

53. "Rising Christian Population" *Nepalitimes*, para. 1–4.

54. Dilli Ram Dahal, "Social Composition of Population," 104.

The Trinitarian Dharma

400,000 Christians. In 2004 the same publication reported the number had increased to 500,000, and then 700,000 in 2006. John Barclay mentions that there were over 2,799 churches in Nepal in 2007. He further estimates the total number of Christians to be 800,000 by 2009.[55] The *Presbyterian Herald*, which frequently covers Nepal's missionary activity, gives the estimated number of around one million believers.[56] Therefore, it is considered that Nepal's population is far greater than shown in government statistics, and the church in Nepal is growing at a rapid pace.

It is worth noting that the growth did not happen because there were no hindrances against the growth of Christianity. Even after introducing so-called democracy, Nepali Christians never enjoyed real freedom because the country always remained the official Hindu Kingdom and religious liberties were strictly limited. In his analysis of the process of making and content of Nepal's 1990 constitution, Michael Hutt points out some discrepancies in religious freedom and quotes the lines from the constitution that "Every person may profess his own religion as handed down from ancient times and may practice it having regard to tradition. Provided no person shall be entitled to convert another person from one religion to another."[57] Hutt further writes, "Under this article, many people had received prison sentences for allegedly converting Nepali citizens to Christianity."[58]

There have been all sorts of attempts to hinder the growth of Christianity in Nepal. In response to a journalist's claim that even as an official Hindu country, all religions were treated equally in Nepal, Ramesh Khatri, a prominent leader and scholar of the Nepali Christian community, summarized the evidence as follows:

> From 1962 many Nepali Christian leaders found themselves in prison for no other reason than their faith in Jesus Christ. One in Okhaldunga succumbed to police torture and is the first known Nepali Christian martyr. When Nepal became democratic in 1990, two British MPs, David Alton and David Atkinson pleaded with KP Bhattarai's interim government for the release of 60

---

55. Stephen, "Briefs: The World," para. 1–2; Stephen "Terror on Top of the World," para 3; Akkara "New Life for Nepal," para. 1–2.

56. Barclay, "The Church in Nepal: Analysis of Its Gestation and Growth," 189. Finlay, "Text Message: Impression of Nepal," 13.

57. Hutt, "Drafting Nepal's Constitution 1990," 1029.

58. Hutt, "Drafting Nepal's Constitution 1990," 1029.

The Crossroads of Faith

Christians behind bars. One elderly pastor in Dharan has been in and out of jail 14 times.[59]

In 1983, Nichonor *Tamang*, a leader in the Nepali Church, arrested for teaching and preaching, was given a notice of seven days to leave the country.[60] Though freedom of religion was mentioned in Nepal's constitution, Christians suffered persecution when they engaged in evangelism. When the ban on political parties was lifted in 1990, Christians' suffering did not end. The churches and Christian organizations are not allowed to be registered, and there are no registered churches or Christian organizations in Nepal.[61]

Although the state does not systematically persecute Christians, it has always remained challenging for Christians to live in Nepal. Despite the imposed restrictions, the government did not dispatch a team to find and prosecute Christians; it mainly acted on the reported cases of Christian activities. Khatry outlines the situation saying, "Although the present democratic government of Nepal is not officially anti-Christian, . . . [The] suspicion of Christians and missionaries, first shown in 1760 by the founder-king of modern Nepal, continues."[62] The challenge that Christians face in Nepal is not only political; there are also social challenges. In Nepal, Christians are looked at differently, as if they are outsiders. In an interview with a national weekly magazine, the *Nepali Times*, a Christian woman reflected on her experience thus: "Non-Christian [Nepali People] perceived me as less of a Nepali at best and more of a traitor at worst . . ."[63] The whole Christian community feels as if they are outsiders. Even the leaders of the Nepali Christian community characterize their experience as that of an outcast. Tirtha Thapa of the Nepal Christian Fellowship once said, "I hope that when people see that Christians are respected by the leaders of the country, the general attitude toward us will slowly change." Loknath Manaen from the Bible Society of Nepal said, "We need to . . . show that we as Christians are part of Nepali society."[64] These voices echo the overall feeling of rejection felt by Nepali Christians.

59. Khatry, "Unsecular," para. 1.
60. Tamang, "Church in Nepal," 151.
61. Khatry, "Church and Mission Relationship in Nepal—Forty Years Ahead," 302.
62. Khatry, "Church and Mission Relationship," 302.
63. "Being a Christian in Nepal is both a great privilege and a positive challenge," *Nepali Times*, no 533 (December 24–30, 2010), para. 1–10.
64. "Christmas in Nepal," *Christian Century*, 106.

The Trinitarian Dharma

The Church in Nepali Society: Thriving but Challenged

Despite the difficulties in Nepal, which hinder the non-Hindu religion's flourishing, Christianity has multiplied in Nepal. The Christian population grew by 1400 times that it developed from 3,891 Christians in 1981 to 10,1976 in 2001. Dilli Ram Dahal, in his comparative analysis of national statistics between 1981 and 2001, concluded that

> The Christian population, who were not even reported in the 1952/54 census, numbered only 458 in the 1961 census and reached 101,976 in the 2001 census. Between the 1991–2001 censuses, the number of follower of Christianity has increased more than 226 percent. Conversion of religion is not an easy task in Nepal. One could be jailed for converting to Christianity and more certainly for proselytizing. But the fact is that Christian populations are increasing dramatically in Nepal, and not only Hindus (particularly the low caste Hindus) but also Buddhist populations (such as *Tamang*) are converting themselves to Christianity over the years.[65]

There are a few features that have helped the Nepali church to grow despite an unfavorable environment. For example, both the foreign missionary leaders and the Nepali church agree that the Nepali church's achievement results from the fact that the church and missions are independent. As a result, the church has been led by Nepali leaders from the beginning of its establishment. It has never been a church controlled by non-Nepali.[66] While evaluating the relationship between the church and foreign mission groups in Nepal, Ramesh Khatry states, "the Nepali Church was independent and self-reliant right from the beginning." Khatry says that the Nepali church's strength is that "it grew up being self-supporting, self-governing, and self-propagating."[67]

---

65. Dahal, "Social Composition of Nepal," 105.
66. Burgoyne and Lindell, "Nepal," 453.
67. Khatry, "Church and Mission Relationship in Nepal- Forty Years Ahead," 302.

Figure 1—Distribution of Population by Religion
in Nepal, 1951-2021 Censuses[68]

	1951	1961	1971	1981	1991	2001	2021
Hinduism	88.87	87.69	89.39	89.50	86.51	80.62	81.2
Buddhism	8.59	9.25	7.50	5.32	7.78	10.74	8.2
Islam	2.54	2.98	3.04	2.66	3.53	4.20	5.2
Kirat	-	-	-	-	1.72	3.60	3.2
Christianity[c]	-	0.0048	0.02	0.03	0.17	0.45	1.8
Other	-	0.0752	0.05	2.49	0.29	0.39	0.4
Total	100	100	100	100	100	100	100

Mission organizations and Nepali churches have worked hard to translate the gospel into the local people's language. This led to the second important factor behind church growth in Nepal, the publication of the Bible, and other literature in the Nepali language.[69] The work was pioneered by William Carey and his team in 1821, who translated the New Testament into Nepali. As the work was completed in an older language style, the Bible was not circulated among Nepali communities.[70] However, with the Bible Society of India and Ceylon's help, the Nepali leadership produced a fresh one. In April 1894, Ganga Prasad Pradhan received the responsibility to translate the Bible into the Nepali language. In 1902, they completed the New Testament translation, and in 1914 published the first whole Bible in Nepali.[71] Various missionaries lent a hand in improving the situation. A commentary written in the Nepali language by Thomas Hale, a medical missionary for more than 25 years, can be taken as an example.[72]

---

68. figures are given in percentage of the total population of the census year. *Kirat* religion was never included in the census before 1991. It was part of Hinduism by the state. There was no known Christian population at the time of the census. 2021 data is derived from a Preliminary report published by Nepal Census Bureau in https://censusnepal.cbs.gov.np/results/cast-ethnicity; accessed: February 8, 2024.

69. Perry, *A Biographical History*, 85.

70. Khatry, "William Carey- The First Publisher of Nepali," 42.

71. Perry, *A Biographical History of Church in Nepal,* 85, 119.

72. Hale, "My Pilgrimage in Mission," 37.

The Trinitarian Dharma

The next factor that led to the church's growth is often pointed out to be its indigenous, Nepali style of worship. The Nepali managed the church in a Nepali way, which was more suitable for its people. Khatry elaborates on the contextualized form of worship in Nepal, saying, "[Nepali Christians] have developed their style of worship and their own hymns; they have developed their own wedding customs; castism has no place in the church, and there are intermarriages between groups and castes; they have had difficulties with funerals . . . and the church wants to introduce cremation."[73]

Other features demonstrate a distinct Nepali flavor in worship, which, it is thought, has contributed to the growth of the church. This includes the "predominant use of indigenous songs and tunes, meeting on Saturdays (Sunday not being a public holiday in Nepal), gender-segregated seating on the floor."[74] These characteristics certainly prevent a newcomer in the church from experiencing a cultural shock. Instead, they can quickly adapt to this new cultural group.

If the Nepali church cannot retain or further develop the characteristics mentioned above, it will undoubtedly lose momentum, and growth will come to an end. There is an increasing concern among the leaders inside and outside Nepal that the church is becoming more dependent on outsiders or the missionaries who financially help the church activities, and their voices are louder in the church's internal affairs. The financial assistance for an individual church came through denominational or organizational relationships, which led the particular local church to isolate itself from the national church bodies.[75] Ramesh Khatry calls for the relationship between the church and missionary organizations to be adequately handled so as not to diminish the church's independence.[76]

Though the church is growing in numbers and has grown from statistically zero to a million members in just over fifty years, it is still a minority in a Hindu-dominated society. The Nepali church wants to be heard in society, and it wants to be recognized officially as a *bona fide* Nepali community. Christians have not received the rights and freedom that others enjoy in this so-called democratic society. Compass Direct News, an online news portal covering church persecution worldwide, posted the news in Nepal in April 2011. The news is about the legal battle that involved Nepali Christian's

---

73. Khatry, "Church and Mission Relationship in Nepal," 303.
74. Barclay, "A Description and Analysis of the Growth of the Church in Nepal," 2006.
75. Thapa and Knoble, "Western-National Church Partnerships, 484.
76. Khatry, "Church and Mission Relationship in Nepal," 342.

demand for a burial ground and their concern about religious freedom in the future, given that a new constitution was being drafted.[77] Since 2006, the interim constitution declared that Nepal is a secular state, Christians have been fiercely targeted by the public, as if Christians are the ones who drafted the constitution.[78] The majority of Hindu people thought that constitutional changes harmed Nepali *dharma* and way of life and blamed Christianity for its negative impacts.[79] The church needs to respond to the accusations and appropriately present itself to the general public.

An Encounter of Nepali Dharma and Christianity

In larger Nepali society, there is displeasure about the spread of Christianity in Nepal. Many accuse Christianity that propagates cultural imperialism by making Nepali Christians renounce their culture, rituals, festivals, and indigenous identities. As a result, Nepali Christian converts are stripped of their identity of being Nepali people.[80] This calls for the abandonment of the Western elements of Nepali Christianity and the adaptation to a more characteristically Nepali expression of faith so that the Nepali church will be at home in Nepal. Some have concerns about the contextualization of the Christian message, while others call for contextualizing its practices.[81] After their conversion, when Christians refuse to take part in the traditional rituals and religiosity, they are accused of abandoning their *dharma* and disrespecting their family and community.[82] Such a Christian attitude certainly creates conflict within the family and the community. Christians are often excommunicated from the family and deprived of their right to ancestral property and land.[83] Christianity directly comes to an odd with Nepali *dharma*.

---

77. Compass Direct News, "Nepal Christians Begin Legal Battle for Burial Ground," para. 1–4; "Nepal Plans New Criminal Code Forbidding Evangelism" para. 1.

78. "Secular Strife," *Nepali Times*, para 1. The article blames that secularism was made in the country because of the pressure from NGOs funded by Christian, Islamic, and Buddhist countries and asks the government a reason for making the country lose its identity as a Hindu state.

79. Jha, "Secularism in a diverse state," *Nepalitimes*, para. 5. Jha points out that many Nepali people interpret the secular state means cow slaughter, which is against their *dharma*.

80. Basnet, "Bankrupt Faith and Cultural Imperialism," 1–3.

81. Bergh, "Contextualization of the Gospel in the Church of Nepal," 33.

82. Kehrberg, *The Cross and the Land of the Khukuri*, 117.

83. Gibson, *Suffering and Hope*, 154–55.

The Trinitarian Dharma

There have been some suggestions for the Nepali church from those who have researched Christianity in Nepal. Ian Gibson, who observed the struggle of converting Nepali people to Christianity brought in Bhaktapur city, a city adjacent to the capital city of Kathmandu, argues that ethical superiority among Nepali Christians is required to win over the disgruntled family members and neighbors in the community.[84] Similarly, Kehrberg, whose research is mainly concentrated on Nepali Christians' dual identity, one being Christian and the other being Nepali, suggests Nepali Christians find a way to participate in community life while being faithful to their belief.[85] Similarly, Ole Kirchheiner conducted his study on the change of way of living of Nepali Christians after and before conversion and saw the need to negotiate socio-religious boundaries by Nepali Christians.[86] Sung Im Shin, a Korean scholar, studying Nepali culture from a Christian perspective, has pointed out that Hindu festivals such as *Dashain* can be the subject of critical contextualization for missions among Nepali Hindus.[87] Cindy Perry sees the contextualization question as a renewed opportunity to witness Christ and replace the current identity of Christianity as a Western religion in the eyes of the Nepali.[88] It is a theological task to demonstrate that Christians belong to Nepali society and are not driven by outsiders. Nepali Christianity cannot but relate to the *dharma* of the community.

SUMMARY

This chapter has mainly argued that in the Nepali social context, the concept of *dharma* plays a central role, and the community and individual lives of people, and therefore becomes the social platform upon which Nepali Christianity can build its contextual theology. Though Nepal is known as a Hindu-majority country, it was not always like that. Hinduism in Nepal is different from that of India because it has retained its ancient form and is syncretized with Nepal's indigenous people's Buddhist practices and folk religions. Throughout the centuries Hindu values have overridden other religious traditions. As a result, a unique religious system

---

84. Gibson, *Suffering and Hope*, 165.

85. Kehrberg, *The Cross and the Land of the Khukuri*, 120.

86. Kirchheiner, Culture and Christianity Negotiated in Hindu Society: A Case Study of a Church in Central and Western Nepal, iii.

87. Shin, "A Mission Strategy through the Contextualization of Dashain Festival in Nepal," 200–202.

88. Perry, "Bhai-Tika and Tij Braka," 18.

became prevalent in Nepal, where *dharma* as a religion of Nepali people stands for its social values, practices, and culture.

Dharma is the system with which all religions, social, and family practices are defined and directed. This chapter has pointed out three critical aspects of *dharma*. First, though we may see certain strains of the philosophy behind *dharma*, it is not concerned with doctrine but mostly a practical-oriented religious aspect of Nepali people. In other words, to participate in social life as defined by *dharma* is the religion of Nepal. Second, *Dharma* is the community consciousness of Nepali people. *Dharma* is not so much the personal righteousness of an individual. Even individual *dharma* is tied to family, the community, and the country. *Dharma* unifies individuals into a community as one body. Lastly, *Dharma* is the social responsibility of every Nepali people. The individual's value is not diminished by *dharma*; it is rather redefined by his/her responsibility toward his/her society. For instance, an individual husband's *dharma* is to provide for the family's needs while the personal *dharma* of a wife is to take care of the house. Individual *dharma* is not separated from the community and social responsibility.

This chapter also shows how *dharma* is entangled with social problems such as the caste system of Hinduism, the suffering and plight of women in society, and poverty. These social problems exist in society because, historically, they are incorporated into *dharma*. Many Nepalis consider that not respecting such a system is going against *dharma*. Such a state shows that *dharma* needs to be redefined so that it can solve such social issues.

Christianity arrives at the land known as a Hindu country and is run by the social system of *dharma*. Individual Christian converts are considered betrayers of the *dharma* and against the social norm. They are called outsiders. Nepali Christianity needs to find a way to be part of society. It requires a theology that can help Nepali Christians retain their identity of being Nepali and make their presence in the community, especially for the suffering people. Nepali Christianity has no other choice than to utilize *dharma* in the process of making their contextual theology. By dealing with the concept of *dharma*, Nepali Christians will be able to construct a way to be part of Nepali society and, at the same time, bring a meaningful impact regarding the social problems that *dharma* is not able to overcome by itself.

4

Apostles' Creed to Social Trinity

Navigating the Trinitarian Journey

WHEN CHRISTIANITY WAS COMPLETING its final lap around the world in the twentieth century, Nepal was one of its final destinations to be conquered.[1] In neighboring countries like India, China, Myanmar, Bangladesh, and Pakistan, Christianity has transformed "into a local or indigenous religion, with their ecclesiastical structures, liturgy, and prayers, spirituality, theology, art and architecture, music and song and dance" but in Nepal, it is yet to show its true Nepali colors.[2] Ever since Nepali Christianity struggled to adjust to Nepali culture, the progress on the theological front has been slow and invisible.[3] Since this research explores how Nepali Christianity can be contextualized, it focuses on the concept of the Trinity, the core of Christian theology, as a tool for dialogue with Nepali *dharma*.[4] The assumption

---

1. Kim, "A Missiological Assessment of the State and Christianity in Nepal," 213.

2. Phan, *Christianities in Asia*, v, 4. C. Phan explains various forms of Christian religions in Asia, including Nepal's neighboring countries: India, Bangladesh, Pakistan, and China but does not discuss Nepal, illustrates the lack of recognition of development of Nepali Christianity.

3. Kirchheiner, Culture, and Christianity Negotiated in Hindu Society, 301–3. The ethnographic study shows that Nepali Christianity is struggling to negotiate the cultural gap by differentiating Nepali cultural elements into *Sanskriti* and *Sanskar* negotiable and non-negotiable items.

4. Phan, "Systematic Issues in Trinitarian Theology," 13. Phan stresses that "the trinitarian mystery is unquestionably enthroned at the heart of Christian theology."

Apostles' Creed to Social Trinity

is that the Trinity has taken various forms in various contexts; it can be contextualized in a Nepali way to serve the Nepali context.[5]

This chapter, 'The Trinitarian Journey,' examines the development of the trinitarian doctrine throughout the centuries. The goal is to analyze the social interpretation of Trinity in the works of Jürgen Moltmann, Leonardo Boff, John Zizioulas, Catherine M. LaCugna and argue that the social understanding of Trinity can be taken as a suitable conversation partner to Nepali *dharma*, which stands for practical religiosity, community consciousness and social responsibility of an individual in the society.

THE FOUNDATION OF TRINITY: THE APOSTOLIC WRITINGS AND EARLY CHURCH

The doctrine of the Trinity[6] came forth when the doxologies found in the apostle's writing clashed with Greek philosophy demanding further explanation.[7] The early development of the doctrine resulted from various ecumenical councils, in which the Church Fathers attempted to sort out heresies concerning three divine persons, their relationship with each other, and the hierarchy between them. The creed confessed by protestant churches throughout the world today was finalized in the Council of Chalcedon and documented in the Nicene Creed.[8] Throughout the centuries, the doctrine has gone through various stages of dogmatization and theorization. Though the term Trinity is not in the Bible, and it is purely a product of the church's history, we can trace the trinitarian origin in the biblical narratives where the metaphoric naming of the Father and Son and their association with the Holy Spirit began.[9] The trinitarian doctrine was formulated when the early church approached the Bible with particular questions raised by their socio-political context. Afterward, the Trinity is used as a tool to read the biblical text.[10]

---

5. Kärkkänen, *The Trinity: Global Perspective*, xxii. Kärkkänen mentions various contextual attempts at doing theology in Trinity. Some of the examples are as follows: Jong Young Lee's East Asian Trinity in Taoist YinYang principle; Raimon Panikkar's cosmotheandric vision of Trinity; Leonardo Boff and Justo L. Gonzales' Hispanic-Latino Liberation perspective on Trinity; others.

6. Tertullian, "Against Praxeas," *Early Christian Writings*, para 2.

7. Marmion, Declan, and Nieuwenhove, *An Introduction to the Trinity*, 6.

8. Bettenson and Maunder, editors, "Nicene Creed," 27–29.

9. Wainwright, "Like a Finger Pointing to the Moon," 33–34.

10. Wainwright, "Like a Finger Pointing to the Moon," 35.

The Trinitarian Dharma

Monotheism of the Old Testament continued in the New Testament, but soon it took a variant form due to the divine attributes associated with Jesus of Nazareth. Though early believers were still rejecting any other gentile gods, they shifted towards adopting Jesus in their monotheistic fold.[11] Before his resurrection, the disciples did not clearly understand who Jesus was. However, the Easter experience added a new dimension to His identity. After His resurrection, His birth, work, teaching, and crucifixion were confirmed to be divine. Gospel writers identified Jesus to be God. Mark named him the Son of God while Matthew and Luke gave their account of the miraculous birth of Jesus, which originated from the Holy Spirit. Similarly, in his logos Christology, John spoke of the pre-existence of Jesus, who came from God.[12]

The majority of the Biblical text put forth the idea of a binitarian God, explicitly focusing on the Son and the Father's self-distinction and unbroken unity.[13] Yet, the relationship between the Spirit and the Father and between the Spirit and the Son is implicitly found. The biblical account emphasizes the interrelation between the Father, Son, and the Holy Spirit; however, their interrelation is not clarified. The Bible showed the trinitarian consciousness of an interrelated Triad of the Father, the Son, and the Holy Spirit, which became a foundation for later generations' trinitarian discussion.[14]

The second-century Christianity inherited the ambiguity about their monotheistic conviction and the existence of the person of Jesus Christ and the Holy Spirit's activity in the Church as recorded in the Biblical texts.[15] For the next three hundred years, the Church struggled between modalism, which disagrees with the distinction of the Father, the Son, and the Holy Spirit, and Tritheism, the existence of three independent Gods. They also equally faced the challenges of Gnosticism,[16] Monarchianism,[17]

---

11. Hurtado, "Observation on the 'Monotheism' affirmed in the New Testament," 53.

12. Dünzl, *Brief History of the Doctrine of the Trinity*, 4–6.

13. Bucur, "Is Binitarian Monotheism a First Step toward Trinitarian Theology?," 32. Binitarian is an early attempt to formulate the doctrine of God which is monotheistic and comprises the Father and the Son.

14. Kärkkäinen, *The Trinity: Global Perspectives*, 15.

15. Kelly, *Early Christian Doctrines*, 87.

16. Perkins, "Gnostics," 466. Gnosticism attacked the Church of reading the biblical text literally and worshiping the God of *Judaism*; They also rejected the idea of Jesus' death and resurrection.

17. Lyman, "Monarchianism," 764–65.

and Arianism.¹⁸ Tertullian (c.160–220) is credited to be the first person to use terms such as Trinity, persons, or substance in a theological discussion. He fought back the teaching, which cannot "reconcile the sovereignty of Father with the participation of the Son and the Holy Spirit in the Lordship of the Father."¹⁹

The trinitarian doctrine was the outcome of the early church's responses to various teachings that emphasized only one aspect of the triadic relationship over the other. For example, Arius thought that attributing divinity to other than the Father diminished the Father's dignity and did not acknowledge the Son's co-eternity with the Father.²⁰ Unlike Arius, Docetists viewed the Son as co-equal with the Father but could not reconcile the divinity with the suffering and death of Jesus Christ; therefore, they declared Christ's human body was a phantasm.²¹ Gnostics went further and said the incarnation of Jesus to be unreal and said Jesus to be unborn and without form.²² Praxeans and Sabellianism, also known as modalism, tried to reconcile the Son and Holy Spirit within a single person of God. Many saw these views differed from what is recorded in the apostolic writings and declared such teachings as heretics and attempted to correct them.²³ Trinitarian theology eventually took its form in the councils where Church leaders debated various instructions on the intra-divine relationship.

Tertullian was at the forefront of dealing with the controversies and published scores of writings against Gnostic and Monarchianist teachings.²⁴ Tertullian first rejected the Gnostics' premise, who believed that God could not be born, or he would remain God with his idea of God's freedom.²⁵ He sought to re-establish the biblical notion of historical birth, death on the cross, and resurrection of Jesus to counter the Gnostic's idea that the bodily incarnation of Jesus is a phantom. His response underlined the unity and continuity of salvation as the God of the Old Testament.²⁶

---

18. Arius, "The Letter of Arius to Eusebius, Bishop of Nicomedia, C. 321," 43; Williams, "Arianism," 107–8.
19. Baker, *Introduction to the Early History of Christian Doctrine*, 138–39.
20. Stead, "Arius in Modern Research," 23.
21. Bettenson and Maunder, editors., *Documents of the Christian Church*, 38.
22. Bettenson & Maunder, *Documents of the Christian Church*, 39.
23. Bethune-Baker, *Introduction to the Early History of Christian Doctrine*, 7
24. Sider, "Tertullian," 1108.
25. Tertullian, *On the Flesh of Christ*, para 1–2.
26. Tertullian, *On the Flesh of Christ*, para 1–2.; Ashwin-Siejkowski, *The Apostles'*

The Trinitarian Dharma

Like Tertullian, Hippolytus of Rome (c. 170–235) also resorted to the mystery of God while refuting the idea that incarnation and divinity are irreconcilable.[27] Both Tertullian and Hypollytus concluded that the Father, Son, and the Holy Spirit are of the same divine substance distributed in all three but not separate divine persons.[28]

However, the issue was about the possibility of three persons in one Godhead, but Arius's position to Eusebius was about the hierarchy within the Trinity. He could not profess that the Father and the Son are equal in authority. Arius highlighted the unique condition of the Son being begotten, which separates him from the Father.[29] Arianism met with strong opposition in the Council of Nicaea (325), where Athanasius of Alexandria condemned it with his affirmation that the Son's essence is the same as that of the Father and, therefore, is fully divine.[30] The Council of Nicaea condemned Arius for being a heretic for diminishing the divinity of Jesus and concluded with the affirmation of trinitarian doctrine and divinity of the Son and the Holy Spirit.[31] The Nicaean creed outcome is that the Trinity was confirmed and established as the correct understanding of Christian God and made available for further development as a doctrine.

Coupling with *dharma*, this early development of trinitarian theology promises a great deal of interaction and cooperation. The early development did not separate trinitarian theology from the believers' religious experience, which suits the practical religiosity of Nepali *dharma*. However, these trinitarian ideas are more focused on the intra-trinitarian relationship; therefore, the early church's theology did not fully articulate the trinitarian relationship to human living.

THE GROUNDWORK OF TRINITARIAN THEOLOGY: THE CAPPADOCIAN FATHERS AND ST. AUGUSTINE

Differences existed even among those who accepted the trinitarian statement of the Nicaean Creed. The pre-Nicaean trinitarian discussion did not

---

Creed, 22; Tertullian, "The Incarnation of the Logos," 34.

27. Hypollytus, "Against Beron and Helix," para. 1.

28. Ashwin-Siejkowski, *The Apostles' Creed*, 31–32; Kelly, *Early Christian Doctrines*, 113.

29. Arius, "The Letter of Arius of Eusebius, Bishop of Nicomedia," 42.

30. Phan, "Development of Trinitarian Doctrine," 7.

31. Wlgt, "Council of Nicaea; Nicene Creed," 27. Bettenson and Maunder, *Documents of the Christian Church*, 44.

involve the issues of the Holy Spirit like that of the Son. The implication of the trinitarian doctrine to Christian life was not established yet, and it was left for the coming generations to explore.[32] The post-Nicaean development of the Trinity took two separate paths, Christianity in the east and Christianity in the west. Though the whole group's strict characterization into one or the other approach, generally, their theology falls into "the essentialist approach," for the western church, the Latin Christianity, and "the personalist approach" for the eastern church the Greek-Orthodox Christianity.[33]

Trinity of the East: The Divine Perichoresis

In the late fourth century, the three leading scholars from the Cappadocia, Basil of Caesarea, his brother Gregory of Nyssa, and Gregory of Nazianzus, contributed to solidifying the decision of the Council of Nicaea and further developed the trinitarian doctrine.[34] Up to the Nicaean creed, the discussion focused only on the Father and Son relationship. These Cappadocian Fathers incorporated the equality of the Holy Spirit in the trinitarian relationship.[35]

Basil of Caesarea (c. 330–379), also known as the great, confronted the views against the Nicaean Creed, the Neo-Arianism, which refused the same status of the Son as the Father, and Sabellianism, which denied the distinction between the two.[36] He was one of the pioneers to argue for the Holy Spirit's divinity and stand against the idea that the Holy Spirit is God's creation.[37] Basil's argument against neo-Arianism was that the concept of a greater and lesser God leads to pagan polytheism. Belief in monotheism demands faith in God's same substance in both the Son and the Father.[38] In Basil's epistemology, God is incomprehensible, and therefore a mystery. Just as God's unbegottenness is one aspect of the divine essence, the Son's begottenness is another aspect of the incomprehensible divine substance. Therefore, it is unreasonable to attribute them to the hierarchy.[39] In the perfect substance of God, there is no limited semiperfect substance of the

---

32. Kärkkäinen, *The Trinity*, 44.
33. Phan, "Systematic Issues in Trinitarian Theology," 15.
34. Marmion and Nieuwenhove, *An Introduction to The Trinity*, 69.
35. Bernard, *History of Christian Doctrine*, 133.
36. Smith, *St. Basil the Great*, 85.
37. Smith, *St. Basil the Great*, 85.
38. Smith, *St. Basil the Great*, 86.
39. Marmion and Nieuwenhove, *An Introduction to the Trinity*, 71.

The Trinitarian Dharma

Son.[40] Basil stood against Sabellianism, saying that believing in three persons does not necessarily lead to tritheism rather than Godhead's unity.[41] Basil's argument for the Holy Spirit's divinity came from his convictions that the scriptural references speak of the Spirit's association and relation with the Father and the Son to bring out salvation, and there is scriptural evidence of the work and the dignity of the Spirit.[42]

Gregory of Nazianzus (c. 335–395) joined with Basil to argue for the Trinity, and he argued that the Trinity is not an extension to the monotheism of Judaism; instead, it is the gradual self-revelation of God the Father in his work of creation, the Son in the redemption, and the Holy Spirit in the sanctification. The Son and the Holy Spirit were not explicit in the Old Testament, but the Trinity is revealed for the church.[43] Godhead is mysterious, "one in distinction and distinct in connectedness," and is not fully comprehensible.[44] Therefore, Gregory resorted to the divine economy to address trinitarian theology because, for him, the Trinity is neither about metaphysics nor a mathematical equation to prove. Instead, the Trinity is the representation of the divine economy in its most profound and fullest meaning.[45] Gregory tried to dilute the misunderstanding caused by the terms *ousia* and *hypostasis*, saying they are not different as understood by many.[46] However, he articulated the Trinity as a relationship between the three persons but not in abstract terms. The Spirit's proceeding and Son's begottenness are not temporally conditioned. It means the Trinity is the eternal relationship between the three. In the trinitarian relationship, an individual believer enters into the trinitarian life.[47]

Gregory of Nyssa (c.329–389) elaborated Holy Spirit's divinity as initiated by Basil and the relational nature of the Trinity as explained by Gregory of Nazianzus. He mainly spoke for the unity of the Trinity because many

---

40. Smith, *St. Basil the Great*, 89.

41. Kelly, *Early Christian Doctrines*, 264.

42. Kelly, *Early Christian Doctrines*, 261. Basil of Caesarea, "Basil of Caesarea on the Work of the Holy Spirit," 163–64.

43. Gregory of Nazianzus, "Gregory of Nazianzus on the Gradual Revelation of The Trinity," 163–64.

44. Gregory of Nazianzus, *On God and Christ*, 36, 45.

45. Beeley, *Gregory of Nazianzus on the Trinity and the Knowledge of God*, 195.

46. Gregory of Nazianzus, *On God and Christ*, 70.

47. Beeley, *Gregory of Nazianzus on the Trinity*, 197.

objections regarding three *hypostases* were raised.[48] However, the dissection of unity is not dominated by God's substance or essence but rather by God's economy as it did with Gregory of Nazianzus and Basil. "Godhead" does not signify a specific nature but an operation."[49] Rather than opting for non-relational analogies, the younger Gregory made the work of the salvation the argument to show the trinitarian inter-relationship.[50]

We can understand the Cappadocian fathers' articulation of God's mystery in the distinction between *ousia* and *hypostasis*, which can be comprehended through the divine economy involving all three Divine persons.[51] Here a believer finds access to the trinitarian life. Trinity is about the mysterious divine unity that opens out into three persons who always interrelate into unity in their divine economy. From early on, the Trinity is where God and the world come together so that human beings participate in the divine life. Cappadocian father has been an inspiration for the recent development of social attributes of trinitarian God in theologians like Jürgen Moltmann and others.[52]

Trinity of the West: A Path to Abstraction

While from Eastern Christianity, there were three main advocators of the Trinity according to the Nicaean Creed and its further developments, among the Latin theologians, St. Augustine of Hippo (c. 354–430) stood highest in the post-Nicaean scene. Augustine's exposition of the Trinity remained influential for centuries to come. Even at the turn of the second millennium, people trace Augustine's writings to draw the trinitarian road map.[53] Like the Cappadocian Fathers, Augustine's theology on the Trinity developed as a reaction to the ani-Nicaean teachings attacking the trinitarian belief affirmed in the creed. Unlike earlier writers, Augustine, rather than attempting to prove it, sought to expose the meaning of faith

---

48. Marmion and Nieuwenhove, *An Introduction to the Trinity*, 77.
49. Gregory of Nyssa, "Gregory of Nyssa on Human Analogies of the Trinity," 161.
50. Nyssa, "On Human Analogies," 162.
51. Anatolios, "Discourse on Trinity," 447.
52. Moltmann, *History and the Triune God*, 73. Moltmann uses Basil's idea to argue for the Spirit's involvement in the Father's work.
53. Joseph, *An Indian Trinitarian Theology of Missio Dei*, 129.Ployd, *Augustine, the Trinity, and the Church*, 4. Ployd argues that Augustine's trinitarian theology is not only abstract but like that of Cappadocian Fathers, is about knowing God through participation.

The Trinitarian Dharma

in a trinitarian God.[54] Augustine's theological exploration was his effort to know God, i.e., to participate in trinitarian life. He was not limited to reflecting on God's economy but also on the psychology and triads of the human mind to elaborate on the Trinity.[55]

Augustine spoke against neo-Arianism's argument of inequality between the Son, the begotten, and the Father, the unbegotten. Augustine's view was from the relationship perspective that one is the Father and the other is the Son, but for their existence, both are of the same substance, and there was no hierarchy in the Trinity.[56] Augustine maintained a difference between who God is in His relationship with human beings and with himself.[57] The immanent relationship within the Trinity is also meaningful to a human being. By extending the Holy Spirit to human beings, we become part of the trinitarian relationship. With the Holy Spirit's presence, the fruit of love and joy, the relationship between the Trinity and the creation is made real and meaningful.[58]

Augustine moved his argument from the relational trinitarian image toward the impersonal argument of the human mind beyond any realm of the divine economy. In such views, Augustine spoke of the faith in a trinitarian God being carried out in mind, which reflected God's image. In other words, faith is limited to knowing God rather than living a life concerning the trinitarian God.[59] With such arguments, Augustine maintained the relationship between the trinitarian God and the creation. However, the argument is no longer about the economy expressed in the incarnation and the Holy Spirit's procession rather abstract speculations. Here, Augustine moved away from the community concept to a more individualized relationship with the trinitarian God because the analogy of the mind represents an individual rather than a community.[60]

Augustine's trinitarian theology was intended to be significant in the Christian life, and he certainly did not intend to make it irrelevant to Christian living. There are undoubtedly many implications for Christian

---

54. Kelly, *Early Christian Doctrines*, 271–72.
55. Marmion and Nieuwenhove, *An Introduction to the Trinity*, 85.
56. Anatolios, "Discourse on Trinity," 44. St. Augustine, *On the Trinity*, chapter 8.
57. St. Augustine, *On the Trinity*, Book 5.11.12 & Book 5.12.13.
58. St. Augustine, *On the Trinity*, Book 6.10.11.
59. St. Augustine *On the Trinity*, Book 14.8.11. & Book 14.12.15.
60. Kärkkäinen, *The Trinity*, 50. Kärkkäinen speaks of Augustine's failure to capture the trinitarian image as a community to human community.

life in Augustine's trinitarian theology. Nevertheless, the Christian life is not a subject that makes trinitarian theology like that of the Cappadocian Fathers. Since there is a movement of Augustine's trinitarian thought from a divine economy to the physiological analysis, we can conclude that Western trinitarian theology that took its roots in Augustine became abstract and irrelevant to Christian life and the human community.[61] Though it would be unfair to characterize Augustine's theology as abstract speculation, he has become the source and inspiration for the abstract Trinity of theologians such as Thomas Aquinas.[62]

The Cappadocian Fathers and St. Augustine both provided a groundwork for theology for their contemporaries and the theologians of the immediately following centuries and the centuries and millenniums to come. The twenty-first-century theologians who speak of the Trinity in terms of social relationships or God's being trace their concept to the groundwork laid by the Cappadocian Fathers and St. Augustine. The extent of the nature of the discussion may vary in today's discussion; however, the theme is already laid out by these great theologians.[63] trinitarian theology is relevant for Christian living, though socio-political implications for various social contexts are not theological. However, the *dharma* and trinitarian theology of St. Augustine and the Cappadocian fathers can initiate a dialogue on the subject of practical religiosity. More importantly, the Cappadocian fathers' divine community concept provides a theological agenda for making theology in a *dharma* context.

THE DOGMATIZATION OF TRINITY: MADE INAPPLICABLE FOR CHRISTIAN LIVING

After the Cappadocian Fathers and St. Augustine's groundwork, the development of the theology of the Trinity took a philosophical and abstract path. The Christian influence shifted toward the West from where Catholicism and the other protestant denominations appeared, and the impact of the Latin theologians such as Anselm of Canterbury and Thomas Aquinas has become excessive.[64] From St. Augustine to the modern-day, trinitarian theology took its path via scholasticism's intellectuality, the authority of the traditions and scripture during/after the reformation,

---

61. Barnes, "Latin Trinitarian Theology," 79.
62. Khaled, Anatolios, "Discourse on the Trinity," 451.
63. Marmion and Nieuwenhove, *An Introduction to the Trinity*, 94.
64. Allison, *Historical Theology: An Introduction to Christian Doctrine*, 210ff.

and skepticism of the 19th-century enlightenment.[65] In the course, the doctrine of the Trinity adopted St. Augustine; yet, it ignored the social implications that he laid out in his early Trinitarian theology. As a result, trinitarian theology was made indifferent to Christian living.[66]

Rationalization of God in Medieval Scholasticism

During the Medieval Age, the Trinity was one of the central subjects of Christian theology; however, it was subjected to extreme rationalization. The rational arguments and utilization of metaphysics rather than the Biblical revelations made the trinitarian theology more abstract and disconnected from salvation history and the real Christian life.[67] Such rationalization of the Trinity was reflected in Anselm of Canterbury, Richard of Victor, and Thomas Aquinas.

Anselm based his inquiry on the mystery of the Trinity in Augustine's works that use psychological analysis leaving out the argument on the Trinity from the perspective of the incarnation and the procession. Anselm repeated St. Augustine's statement that "the mind itself is the image and mirror of the supreme being."[68] Rather than exploring the content of the belief to bring out an understanding of God, Anselm's inheritance of the Augustinian concept was an attempt to explain the Christian concept of God and other aspects of Christian belief.[69] Anselm did not struggle with the belief in the Trinity because he accepted the creed. He attempted to make such a three-in-one more reasonable.[70] Therefore, he used abstract human reasoning to argue for the Trinity so that belief in the Trinity is suitable for the human mind because, for him, truth should be reasonable enough to believe. Anselm's arguments inferred that even the things from the scripture should be made rational to accept them.[71]

Richard of St. Victor, another Medieval theologian known for their theology of the Trinity, used the analogies of love familiar to present-day trinitarian theology such as Jürgen Moltmann. However, Richard of St.

---

65. Marmion and Nieuwenhove, *An Introduction to the Trinity*, 96–97.
66. Sanders, "Entangled in the Trinity," 175.
67. Friedman, *Medieval Trinitarian Thought from Aquinas to Ockham*, 135–36.
68. Anselm, *Monologion*, 401.
69. Evans, "Anselm's Life, Works and Immediate Influence," 12.
70. Williams, "God who Sows the Seed and Give the Growth," 612.
71. Adams, "Anselm on Faith and Reason," 45. Anselm, *On the Procession of the Holy Spirit*, 401.

Victor's Trinity as the loving community was more like Anselm's rational argument than the present-day exposition of the dynamic of the Trinity's interpersonal relationship as expressed in the divine economy.[72] In Richard's analogy, love is an ontological argument and is only limited to the divine persons rather than a divine-human relationship.[73] Richard maintained the distinction between the sacred love relationship with the creation and ontological divine love.[74] God's trinitarian love is part of the supreme good. His love argument is so abstract that Love is supreme, and therefore God is not deprived of supreme, which demands the loving member of the Trinity.[75]

Thomas Aquinas is the eminent Medieval theologian who built on the Augustinian foundation.[76] He used Augustine's treatise "On the Trinity" as a measuring stick to confirm the acceptability of trinitarian theology.[77] Aquinas used natural reasons to explain the trinitarian doctrine.[78] In his 'Treatise on the Most Holy Trinity,' though he states that the Trinity is revealed in the scripture, Aquinas moved to defend rather a philosophical concept of God, who cannot be divided, and he did not see it necessary to base the arguments about Trinity on the God's economy of salvation.[79] Thomas Aquinas remained in the psychological category when he discussed the Son's processions and the Holy Spirit as God's intellect and will.[80] Though Thomas Aquinas used the concept of "love" to discuss the second procession of God, the Holy Spirit, he separates himself from making the Trinity the Divine community of Love. Like with Richard of Victor, Aquinas' Love analogy and discussion of Love did not have any social implications.[81]

Trinitarian theology of Anselm of Canterbury, Richard of St. Victor, and Thomas Aquinas illustrated the severe rationalization. They sought to

72. McGrath, "Richard of St. Victor on Love Within the Trinity," 178. Marmion and Nieuwenhove, *An Introduction to the Trinity*, 98.

73. Richard of Victor, *On the Trinity*, Book 3. II., 117.

74. Richard of Victor, *On the Trinity*, 116.

75. Richard of Victor, *On the Trinity*, Book 3. IV, 119.

76. KärKkäinen, *The Trinity: Global Perspectives*, 50.

77. Aquinas, "Theology, Faith and Reason. On Boethius On the Trinity, 1–2 (1257)," Part 2-6, Aquinas' appreciation of Augustine's idea of the Trinity is illustrated by his countless references to Augustine's writing when he made his arguments.

78. Aquinas, "Theology, Faith and Reason . . ." Part 2-6, Article 4, ebook.

79. Aquinas, *Summa Theologica*, 339.

80. Aquinas, *Summa Theologica*, 335.

81. Aquinas, *Summa Theologica*, 342.

The Trinitarian Dharma

accommodate Christian faith in the Hellenistic philosophical understanding of God. Therefore, theology became a more philosophically appropriated understanding of God, completely ignoring trinitarian revelation in the economy of creation, incarnation, and the Holy Spirit's involvement in the Church.[82] Trinitarian theology addressed the rational scholastic mind rather than the believers' life. This makes scholastic trinitarian theology and *dharma* too far for a productive dialogue. As the foundation of the Nepali religion, *Dharma* stands opposite to the rational character of medieval trinitarianism. These theological developments have detached the link between people's lives. They can give very little to the questions of *dharma* regarding community consciousness.

Scriptural Turnabout of Trinity during the Reformation

Reformation marked the separation between Catholics and Protestantism and a shift of power from the church institution to the scripture. The Reformation principle of Sola Scriptura was useful in reformulating the church's traditional teachings, such as salvation by faith alone, and it also provided an opportunity for the redefinition of specific theological topics.[83] The Reformation doctrine of the Trinity did not indicate such departure from the Medieval articulation; instead gave it continuity while providing its legitimacy through the scripture.[84]

Martin Luther, the chief instigator of the Reformation, who belongs to the Augustinian camp, initiated various traditional theological topics and made his mark on the theology of the Trinity. Though Martin Luther departed from the scholastic and medieval enrichment of human reason for the discussion of faith, he affirmed such effort when they talked about the mystery of the Trinity. While Martin Luther initiated the possibility of a radically different trinitarian theology than the Medieval ones with his sola scriptura principle, his position on the Trinity remained more like

---

82. Understanding of God such as, "God = that than which a greater cannot be thought," originated from Philosophy and is connected to the Christian faith. Such tendencies made theology abstract and foreign to what is been spoken in the Bible. Charles J. Kelly, "Classical Theism and the Doctrine of the Trinity," *Religious Studies* 30.1 (1994) 67.

83. Chun, "The Trinity in the Protestant Reformation," 129.

84. Marmion and Nieuwenhove, *An Introduction to the Trinity*, 130.

Medieval theology. He argued that the trinitarian doctrine belonged to the matter of reasoning rather than faith.[85]

Luther did not see a need to justify the doctrine of the Trinity; instead, he took it as the faith statement and explained it with biblical reference.[86] Therefore, he did not seek to develop a new trinitarian theology but used what had been done to understand the Bible. Luther's most significant contribution to trinitarian theology was that he gave biblical language to the scholastic philosophical doctrine.[87] Martin Luther infused the language of the divine economy into the Medieval trinitarian thought that the knowledge of God sprang from the salvation work on the Cross.[88]

John Calvin, who is mostly known for dogmatizing reformation outcomes, utilized the sola scriptura principle to produce in-depth theology in every subject. Unlike medieval scholars, Calvin did not prove the Trinity or give a new theology on the Trinity; instead accepted the Trinitarian creed and used it to develop other doctrines. The trinitarian doctrine was affirmed by the scripture.[89] However, John Calvin built his theology on the trinitarian principles of the Church Fathers, and he also accepted some extra-biblical philosophical arguments of scholasticism.[90] Calvin steered his theology between the distinction of economic and immanent Trinity and justified a relationship between the Christian life and the Trinity. Therefore, the Trinity is not just a philosophical inquiry but an interpretation of scripture. The prayer itself is a trinitarian action involving the Father, Son, and the Holy Spirit."[91]

Though Calvin did not demonstrate his opposition to the Medieval abstract theology, he showed his distaste for it.[92] Calvin was not fond of using non-biblical terms in trinitarian theology, however, but out of

---

85. Luther, *Disputation against Scholastic Theology,* 73rd page,

86. Luther, *Creed,* 273.

87. Chun, "The Trinity in the Protestant Reformation," 130. Chun points out the retention of the Medieval doctrine of the Trinity in Martin Luther's theology pointing out similarities discussed in Augustine's writing and others.

88. Luther, *Heidelberg Disputation,* 102.

89. Merkle, *Defending the Trinity in the Reformed Palatinate,* 15. Calvin used Gen. 1:26 to point out the trinitarian work and also hinted that the plural form of the word Elohim may point to the Trinity to be revealed in the New Testament.

90. Chun, "The Trinity in the Protestant Reformation" 137.

91. Krohn, "The Triune God who Speaks," 54–56.

92. Calvin, *Institutes of Christian Religions,* Book 1. 2. 4, 243,

necessity, he agreed to use terms such as hypostasis, persons, and Trinity.[93] Calvin maintained the distinction between God's immanence and the economy. For him, God's economy speaks of the Trinity's threeness while the unity is separated from the economy.[94] Calvin completely ignored the begottenness of the Son and the Holy Spirit when talking of their unity.[95] Calvin disagreed with Augustine that the human mind was the Trinity's image after the fall of Adam.[96] However, for Calvin, God's image is in the human soul, mind, and heart. He spoke of human as an individual term, not a community, and God, as the Trinity also loses the implication for community as expressed by the Cappadocian Fathers.[97]

The Reformation theologians Luther and Calvin both marked the return to the Scripture and God's economy to discuss the Trinity. They did not promote the philosophical speculation about God and made the Trinity important to believers' lives, showing some relevance to *dharma*. However, they retained the abstract, individual aspect of God and human relations. The emphasis was on an individual's relationship with God rather than as a community. As the community of God, the Trinity is relevant not only for individual humans but also for human society and is left to be discovered by the coming generation of theologians. Nepali *dharma*, being a community consciousness of people, needs more than practicality for individual life.

Nullification of Trinity: During/after the Enlightenment

Reformation's return to scripturally based theology did not last long when it was overtaken by the wave of rationalization during the Enlightenment period. However, this upholding of human reason was different from the Medieval one in that this time, the reason nullified the revelation.[98] The age that witnessed social advancement saw that theology was possible with reason alone. Christianity can be justified by reason, and the

93. Calvin, *Institutes*, Vol. 1 Book 1.13.5.

94. Lee, "The Relationship between the Ontological Trinity and the Economic Trinity: 95.

95. Calvin, *Institutes*, Vol. 1. Book 1.13.25.

96. Calvin, *Institutes*, 2. 4.

97. Calvin, *Institutes*, 2. 3.

98. Grenz and Olson, *20th Century Theology: God and the World in a Transitional Age*, 21. Grenz and Olson say that "Reason and nature opened the way for the third principle of the Enlightenment mindset—'autonomy.' As noted earlier, in this epoch autonomous humans dethroned external authority as the arbiter of truth and action." This way humans did not need the revelation.

Apostles' Creed to Social Trinity

revelation was not necessary to develop a theology.[99] This age gave birth to a theology solely dependent on reason or completely separated from the matter of faith. Both types of theology had significant implications for the doctrine of the Trinity.

John Locke (1632–1704) is the prime example of the one who believed that Christian faith could be justified by reason or to believe anything claimed in theology. It should be justifiable by reason.[100] Just like with any theological topic, John Locke sought to make the Trinity persuasive.[101] While Locke understood that the doctrine of the Trinity is difficult to comprehend, he thought through scripture, and one can come to the certainty of the teaching.[102] Matthew Tindal (1657–1733) was ready to forego the revelation related to faith if it contradicted the reason.[103] However, Emmanuel Kant (1724–1804), though he associated morality with reason, saw morality as the goal of any religion.[104] Kant evaluated and upheld the religion based on its moral implacability. Kant favored Christianity mainly because he thought it had moral associations.[105] However, he disregarded the aspect of the Trinity, which, for him, has no moral value. For Kant, the trinitarian doctrine has "no practical relevance at all."[106] Kant's stance against the Trinity was that it lacked practical value and that its metaphysical nature is the opposite of real human life. In Trinity, there is no human participation.[107]

When it was a trend to nullify the Trinity that it was not rational to believe three in one concept, Georg Wilhelm Friedrich Hegel (1770–1831) gave a philosophical reinterpretation.[108] Hegel's philosophy was different from Medieval metaphysics. For Hegel, reality is active and developing, and such understanding stands against the classical idea, such as God is unchangeable. Hegel put God behind the process of reality. Hegel devised a law of dialectic, "the triad of thesis–antithesis–synthesis," to explain the

---

99. McGrath, *Historical Theology*, 186.
100. Marmion and Nieuwenhove, *An Introduction to the Trinity*, 142.
101. Locke, *Reasonableness of Christianity: as Delivered in the Scriptures*, 159.
102. Locke, *A Second Vindication of the Reasonableness of Christianity*, 99.
103. Marmion and Nieuwenhove, *An Introduction to the Trinity*, 142.
104. Grenz and Olson, *20th Century Theology*, 29.
105. Kant, *The Philosophical Theory of Religion*,
106. Kant, *The Conflict of Faculties*, 65.
107. Kant, *The Conflict of Faculties*, 67.
108. Marmion and Nieuwenhove, *An Introduction to the Trinity*, 148.

The Trinitarian Dharma

dynamics of reality.[109] In Hegel's dialectical philosophy, God is eternal, as the Father, which is the thesis. God enters the world through the Son's incarnation, which stands as the antithesis of the dialectic. Lastly, in the Holy Spirit's realm, God reunites the world with himself, which is the synthesis.[110] Unlike Kant, for Hegel, the Trinity has moral implications, he says, "True liberation is to be found in Christianity, in the Trinity."[111] God as the spirit, if not understood as Trinity, is an empty word, and Trinity is the key to making theology relevant[112] At the time of scientific advancement and optimism of human reasoning which abandoned anything deemed irrational, Hegel attempted to show the worth of trinitarian doctrine with his inventive metaphysics.

Schleiermacher, a Romanticist theologian, argued not emphasizing reason but human feeling and imagination to reconstruct Christian theology.[113] He constructed theology based on experience, thereby rejecting both revelation and reason. For him, the essence of religion lies not in the proof of God or the supernaturally revealed doctrine but in human life.[114] Though many doctrines were made relevant to Christian living during the Reformation, Schleiermacher thought that the doctrine of the Trinity remained untouched in its scholastic form.[115] Regarding Trinity, he emphasizes God's unity and that all three persons share the same essence of God. However, for him, the essence of God is less abstract than with other theologians. Love and wisdom are two attributes of God that constitute the essence of God.[116] Though Schleiermacher brought human experience into the realm of theological discussion, his focus on the unity of the Threeness of God missed the dynamism of the Trinity as the divine community relevant to

---

109. Grenz and Olson, *20th Century Theology*, 33–35. In Hegel's dialectic, "First a thesis arises. This immediately generates its antithesis. The two are then merged in their synthesis."

110. Marmion and Nieuwenhove, *An Introduction to the Trinity*, 150. Hegel, *Lectures on the Philosophy of Religion* Vol. I *Introduction and Concept of Religion*, 126.

111. Hegel, *Lectures on the Philosophy of Religion* Vol. II *Determinate Religion*, 156.

112. Helmer, "Christian Trinitarian Thinking after the Reformation," 162.

113. Grenz and Olson, *20th Century Theology*, 43.

114. Olson, *The Journey of Modern Theology*, 135–36.

115. Schleiermacher, *The Christian Faith in Outline*, 63. Schleiermacher, *The Christian Faith*, 114.

116. Schleiermacher, *The Christian Faith in Outline*, 732.

the human community. Schleiermacher's divine and human relationship derived from the experience is individualistic.[117]

Though rejected many traditional understandings of trinitarian theology, the theology of this age of scientific advancement raised several questions that no future theology could avoid. Trinitarian theology, which was treated as an abstract theology, demanded its practical and moral implications. They also pointed out the possibility of understanding God differently from classical metaphysics. This theology also brought the human experience into the theological realm. Though such theological developments departed from many classical renderings, they stuck with the individualistic approach when they talked about morality and experience, which is a much-desired subject in dialogue with Nepali *dharma*.

THE RECHARACTERIZATION OF THE TRINITY AND ITS SOCIAL IMPLICATION

At the turn of the last century, the world experienced two world wars, which reflected negatively towards the optimistic human reason suggested by the Enlightenment era. Theology, particularly about the Trinity, was forced to make profound reflections based on the social turmoil.[118] From the twentieth century onward, trinitarian theology took its social form and the various human experiences have become a theological subject. Trinitarian theology ceased to become the neutral talk of God. Rather, it is transformed into a theological address to society's problems.[119]

Trinity Made the Center of Christian Theology: Barth and Rahner

Two of the most prominent theologians, Karl Barth and Karl Rahner, made Trinity the center of the theological enterprise. While Barth made it the measuring rod for all of his theology, Karl Rahner opened the possibility of making trinitarian life relevant to Christian living. The influences of Karl Barth and Karl Rahner are evident in the works of later twentieth-century theologians.[120]

---

117. Schleiermacher, *The Christian Faith in Outline*, 747.
118. Olson, *Journey of Modern Theology*, 296.
119. Ford and Muers, editors, *Modern Theologians*, 429–30.
120. Kärkkäinen, *The Trinity: Global Perspectives*, 76.

The Trinitarian Dharma

Karl Barth stood against the Nazi government of Germany and developed a theological system that is the purely trinitarian revelation of God. Karl Barth saw that liberal theology, which was keen to make theology acceptable to human reason and culture, failed to stand against the Nazi ideology. Consequently, he sought to rescue theology from human reason and philosophy and put it under the category of God's self-revelation.[121] For Barth, the revelation of God is the only way to know God.[122] Karl Barth's trinitarian theology springs out of his revelatory foundation. Trinity is what God revealed about himself, and revelation is the Trinity. He made Trinity the main subject of God, not just an interpretation. By putting the Trinity at the forefront of theology, Barth countered Kant and Schleiermacher's dismissal of the Trinity on the grounds of irrelevancy toward morality.[123]

By this, Karl Barth rejected all sources of theology other than God's revelation. Karl Barth spoke of the transcendence of God in the language of revelation. Though he said God's revelation in the language of the economy of revelation, God is still transcendent from the human side. God makes Himself revealed and significant to them. In human history, God surrendered Himself to human contemplation, human experience, human thought, and human speech.[124] However, Barth placed God's revelation so high that it has no space for human experience in trinitarian theology. God's economy of the incarnation and the Holy Spirit's involvement in the world. Trinity is the communion of a threefold God enacted through Jesus and mediated through the Holy Spirit. The trinitarian God that Barth spoke of is transcendental.[125] Barth emphasized God's unity and spoke three modes instead of the persons to avoid personality that suggested the difference from unity.[126] Through the concept of revelation, Barth sought to bring God to the human sphere.

When Karl Barth developed his theology of reconciliation, he explained God's essence as the Love that makes the trinitarian unity extend to the creation in the work of creation, redemption, and reconciliation.[127] Barth finally made the trinitarian essence, love the basis for the God-human

---

121. Grenz and Olson, *20th Century Theology*, 68–69.
122. Barth, *Church Dogmatics* Vol. 1 *The Doctrine of the Word of God*, 295.
123. Barth, *Church Dogmatics* Vol 1.1, 312.
124. Barth, *Church Dogmatics* Vol 1.1, 315.
125. Barth, *Church Dogmatics* Vol 1.1, 321–22.
126. Grenz and Olson, *20th Century Theology*, 73.
127. Barth, *Church Dogmatics* Vol. 4 *the Doctrine of Reconciliation*, 43.

Apostles' Creed to Social Trinity

relationship and relationship between humans. Barth opened the divine life for humans, saying that the essence of God, which is love flows toward us. The trinitarian relationship is imparted to the human relationship by transferring love, which is a trinitarian action.[128] Karl Barth's theology did not involve history in his theological enterprise, and he failed to make an explicit claim that the Trinity is a community of God bound in love. However, his theology envisioned a trinitarian community based on the trinitarian essence, love, and later theologians developed it.[129]

Like Barth, Rahner is known for his contribution to trinitarian theology, and his theology came as a reaction to the negligence of the trinitarian relevance for Christian life. Rahner attempted to rescue Trinity from being an abstract theology. He made God's self-revelation in salvation history the departure point for his trinitarian theology.[130] Unlike Barth, who saw the possibility of Revelation only in God, Rahner's self-communication happens in human history.[131] For him, it is impossible to understand Trinity outside of the economy of salvation. His famous statement on the subject is "The economic Trinity is the immanent Trinity, and the immanent Trinity is the economic Trinity."[132] Rahner did not entertain the idea of treating each member of the Trinity in general because, in the economy of salvation, at least Logos God is a man and is particular of Him. He took the hypostatic union as the place where God can have his proper relation to the world and the Son and other divine persons also enter into the hypostatic union.[133] God self-communicates himself to his creatures as Father, Word, and the Spirit. This self-communication of God is limited to his communication to the world in salvation history and the inner-self communication of God's inner life. Rahner thought that if we distinguish God's self-communication with the world from his inner self-communication, God's relation to the world becomes indifferent.[134] For Rahner, God's self-communication in the economy is the only way to

---

128. Barth, *Church Dogmatics* 4.2, 778.
129. Ibid., 779; Kärkkäinen, *The Trinity: Global Perspectives*, 72.
130. Kärkkäinen, *The Trinity: Global Perspectives*, 77.
131. Marmion and Nieuwenhove, *An Introduction to the Trinity*, 168.
132. Rahner, *The Trinity*, 22.
133. Rahner, *The Trinity*, 23, 25, 35.
134. Rahner, *The Trinity*, 37–38.

The Trinitarian Dharma

know the immanence of God. By doing this, he rejected all the speculation and separation of God's economy from His inner being.[135]

Though Rahner grounded the Trinity in God's self-revelation, in his discussion on God's unity, he resorts to the concept of essence, not found in the economic Trinity. Like Karl Barth, Rahner emphasized God's Oneness over the Threeness that the one nature is expressed in modes of being of the Son and the Holy Spirit.[136] Rahner declined to use the term person because three-person can be misunderstood as three consciousnesses and three centers of activities can lead to the heretic teaching of three-fold God. Therefore, Rahner calls the church to reconsider the use of the term three persons. Rahner's use of history as the point to discuss God's self-communication becomes distant and transcendent because he directed it to God's distant future.[137] For Rahner, God's self-communications have two modes, truth, and love, toward history, but he does not make this history important to the trinitarian life. Regarding the two ways, Rahner said, "This self-communication, insofar as it occurs as truth, happens in history; and that insofar as it happens as love, it opens this history in transcendence towards the absolute future."[138]

Both Barth and Rahner's contribution to trinitarian theology is that they made the economy of salvation the starting point of theology. Barth made trinitarian theology his foundation to develop other theologies. Though both theologians connected human history to the understanding of transcendence, they maintained the separation of God's transcendence from human history. For both, the Oneness of God is the trinitarian inner life. Trinity, as a unity of communion of a three-person aspect, is non-existent in both theologians. With their theologies, both Barth and Rahner were able to make trinitarian theology the center of theological discourse tossed aside during the Enlightenment. However, they did not develop it as a theology relevant to Christian living, which was the challenge posed by Emmanuel Kant.[139] Nepal needs a theology suitable for Christian living because social issues are the main subject of Nepali contextual theology.

---

135. Rahner, *Foundations of Christian Faith*, 136.
136. Coffey, "Trinity," 104.
137. Rahner, *The Trinity*, 57.
138. Rahner, *The Trinity*, 98.
139. Marmion and Nieuwenhove, *An Introduction to the Trinity*, 195.

Trinity as a Divine Community

Though the developments of trinitarian theology during the early twentieth century put the Trinity at the center of the theological enterprise, it still concentrated on God's oneness, reaching toward the creation from above. It restricted the relational aspect of the trinitarian God and failed to make it essential not just for the cognitive part of human faith but also for society.[140] However, their approach, discussion of the Trinity in God's economy rather than philosophical speculation, paved the way for the next generation of theologians to develop a trinitarian theology that speaks relational nature and provides insight into Christian living. Such developments happened among the theologians of various camps such as Eastern Orthodox churches, mainline protestant scholars, Catholics, and theologians from different contexts and people groups.[141]

The solution to the failure of making trinitarian theology relevant to the Christian community was introduced by the theologians of the other isle, the Orthodox church. Dumitru Staniloae, the most significant Orthodox theologian, brought the trinitarian doctrine to create his ecclesiology based on the living communion of trinitarian persons.[142] For Staniloae, the weaknesses of Western Christianity lie in their failure to make Trinity the Church's experience. While Catholic church leadership diminished the Holy Spirit's involvement in the Church, Protestants failed to acknowledge the importance of community by emphasizing the individual divine-human relationship.[143] In Staniloae's work, Trinity is similar to Barth and Rahner in that it is the revelation in God's economy. He argued that God is revealed to us in His economy.[144] However, unlike both Barth and Rahner, Staniloae did not limit the Trinity to understanding God; rather, he made the Trinity the goal of Christian living. Trinity represents the unity of the love of God. Therefore, such a trinitarian community is reflected in the community of

---

140. Richard Swinburne, "The social theory of the Trinity," 419–37. In this article Swinburne shows his preference of the Social Trinity over the ones speak Unitary one and argues that such social aspects have been found in the western thought.

141. Theologians like Zizioulas, Moltmann, Pannenberg, and LaCugna developed their theology from the proposal of Karl Rahner and Karl Barth. Some as their criticism against them others as further development of their theology. Kärkkäinen, *The Trinity: Global Perspectives,* 87.

142. Louth, "Review Essay: The Orthodox Dogmatic Theology of Dumitru Staniloae," 253. Williams, "Eastern Orthodox Theology," 584.

143. Roberson, "Dumitru Staniloae on Christian Unity," 107–11.

144. Staniloae, *Theology and the Church,* 75.

The Trinitarian Dharma

believers.[145] Here, not only is a woman/man understood as God's image, but the Christian community reflects the triune community of God, from where our love for one another originates.[146]

John Zizioulas is another Eastern Orthodox theologian who expanded on Dumitru Staniloae's trinitarian theology.[147] Zizioulas develops a concept of being in a community as ontology. He departs from the long-standing tradition established since the time of St. Augustine regarding a human individual as the trinitarian image. The image of God is no other than the way of being in a relationship with others.[148] However, Zizioulas does not dismiss each person's individuality in the collectivity; instead, he believes that the community generates individuality to its fullest. Within the Trinity, the emphasizing triune communion does not threaten the unity of God because "the love of God bridges the gulf of otherness."[149] "The expression 'God is love' signifies that God subsists as Trinity, that is as a person and not as substance. Love is not an emanation or 'property of the substance of God . . . Love, as God's mode of existence hypostasizes God, constitutes His being."[150]

This trinitarian Characteristic is equally meaningful for the understanding of the human community as well. Zizioulas's theology counters Kantian criticism against the Trinity's practicality for Christian life and claims that there is no other model for communion between God and humans than God as trinitarian.[151] Trinity is relevant for Christian living when trinitarian life opens for participation in human history. The world is united with the Trinity, and none of the trinitarian members lose their particularity in such communion. However, in the trinitarian life, Zizioulas still holds the idea of hierarchy in the Trinity because "the Father out of love . . . begets the Son and brings forth the Spirit."[152] If the communion of Trinity is not based on equality, can it advocate a society of equality?

---

145. Staniloae, *Theology and the Church*, 78.

146. Staniloae, *Orthodox Dogmatic theology*, 245.

147. Kärkkäinen, *The Trinity: Global Perspectives*, 90.

148. Zizioulas, *Being as Communion: Studies in Personhood and the Church*, 15.

149. Zizioulas, *Communion and Otherness: Further Studies in Personhood and the Church*, 24.

150. Zizioulas, *Communion and Otherness*, 46.

151. Zizioulas, *Communion and Otherness*, 4.

152. Zizioulas, *Being as Communion*, 41.

Jürgen Moltmann received and utilized Eastern Orthodox theologians' attempt to express the Trinity as the community relevant to Christian living.[153] Moltmann becomes radical in rejecting the classical transcendental understanding of God. For him, the Trinity is historical (including the suffering) and is for the transformation of history.[154] Moltmann adopts Barth and Rahner's line that the Trinity is founded on the self-communicatory revelation of God. Moltmann becomes more specific in that the Trinity is expressed in God's work on the cross. "The formal principle of knowledge of the cross is the doctrine of the Trinity."[155] The historical experience that Jesus suffered on the Cross is the trinitarian experience.[156] Moltmann finds the experience of suffering common in both God and humans by which we can understand the triune God.[157] Jürgen Moltmann speaks for integrating the human experience of the Trinity with God's experience of history.[158]

Moltmann's argument is in line with Karl Rahner, who spoke of God's self-communication, i.e., revelation, as God's inner self-communication. For Moltmann, God's revelation contains God's suffering and love. God's inner suffering of love is not a weakness or limitation of God that Moltmann speaks of, as some have speculated; instead, it is God's freedom and love.[159] Like the Orthodox theologians Zizioulas and Staniloae, Moltmann opted for the three persons over Barth and Rahner's modes of being. Rather than resorting to divine oneness to speak of three-person unity, Moltmann speaks of the unity of three distinct persons, the Trinity. For now, and here, Moltmann only iterates of the Trinity as God's social unity bound in love. The transcendental unity of God is pushed for eschatological consummation.[160] Moltmann's theology is not against God's unity; instead, he refuses to equate God's Unity to homogeneity. Moltmann believes in God's unity while maintaining the distinctiveness of the Son and the Holy Spirit. God's unity and community are not abstract; instead, it's where people

---

153. Munteanu, "Dumitru Staniloae's Influence on Jürgen Moltmann's Trinitarian and Ecological Theology," 24.

154. Grenz and Olson, *20th Century Theology*, 180.

155. Moltmann, *The Crucified God*, 241.

156. Moltmann, *The Crucified God*, 243.

157. Moltmann, *The Trinity and the Kingdom*, 4.

158. Moltmann, *The Trinity and the Kingdom*, 5.

159. Moltmann, *The Trinity and the Kingdom*, 34. Grenz and Olson, *20th Century Theology*, 186. Grenz and Olson have their reservation against Moltmann's approach that he is making God too dependent and conditioned with the history.

160. Moltmann, *The Trinity and the Kingdom*, 149.

experience freedom and receive their calling for reconciliation towards such a relationship in history.[161] Moltmann's trinitarian theology shows God in terms of faithfulness, compassion, and love rather than abstract concepts such as immutability and impassibility.[162]

From the Catholic side of the aisle, Catherine M. LaCugna advocated for the trinitarian theology relevant to Christian living. LaCugna's trinitarian theology incorporates various developments of Zizioulas, Barth, Rahner, and Moltmann.[163] For her, the Trinity is the cornerstone of theology, and she sought to recover the practical aspect of this theology lost in its development.[164] She aims to resolve the gap between revelation and the transcendence of trinitarian God in the contemporary theological field.[165] She sees the problems with the metaphysics of the dogmatic theology, which made the Trinity abstract. Like theologians Barth, Rahner, Moltmann, and Zizioulas, LaCugna starts theology afresh by going into the salvific history of Jesus, the Holy Spirit, and the Trinity. However, her focus is on the *oikonomia* concept to argue for the Trinity's social aspect grounded in God's revelation in the salvation history.[166]

LaCugna traces the social relevance of God in St. Augustine's work. However, her position on Trinity differs from that of Jürgen Moltmann. Though she sees the practical relevance of the Trinity, she sees that actual human history has no relevance to the trinitarian life itself.[167] However, in her stance on the transcendent Trinity, she stands with God's economic attributes over metaphysics. God is free from the bondage of history means he is open to love and relate to his creature rather than autonomy and self-sufficiency.[168] Though LaCugna adopts Rahner's principle that "the economic Trinity is the immanent Trinity and vice versa," she parts from him and uses the term person rather than Rahner's modes of being. LaCugna argues that only God's personhood makes the relationship

---

161. Moltmann, *History and the Triune God*, 25.

162. Marmion and Nieuwenhove, *An Introduction to the Trinity*, 176.

163. Kärkkäinen, *Trinity: The Global Perspective*, 178–19. Grenz, *The Social God and the Relational Self*, 53.

164. LaCugna, *God for Us: The Trinity and Christian Life*, 1.

165. Groppe, "Catherine Mowry LaCugna's Contribution to Trinitarian Theology," 730–31.

166. LaCugna, *God for Us*, 28–29.

167. LaCugna, *God for Us*, 86.

168. LaCugna, *God for Us*, 169.

possible between God and us.[169] LaCugna advocates for plurality in her approach to the Trinity and emphasizes that "no single method or formula can adequately communicate the mystery of God."[170]

The theologians of social trinitarianism brought the Trinity to the center of theological enterprise and argued for its relevancy for the community and people's practical lives. Subjects of Nepali *dharma* such as practical religiosity and community consciousness can be discussed with social trinitarianism. Social trinitarianism approaches society in a holistic manner, which resonates with Nepali *dharma*. The social Trinity, in its theological basis on God's economy of salvation and participation in history, welcomes human experience into the theological process. Therefore, the social Trinity is well suited to have a dialogue with *dharma*.

SUMMARY

This chapter explored the development of trinitarian theology, finding its major traits and developments. Trinitarian theology has always revolved around the Oneness and Threeness concept. Theologians resorted to philosophy to argue the reasonableness of the Trinity, and it was made abstract and irrelevant for practical life. When the trinitarian concept was under attack for its irrelevancy for Christian living and unreasonableness, newer developments emerged. The significant development of trinitarian theology happened during the 20th century when the Trinity was understood in community concept and considered relevant for Christian living.

The development of the Trinity since the latter half of the century, commonly known as the social Trinity, can be the base for a contextual theology of Nepal. Human society plays a vital role in the social Trinity, and at the same time, the social Trinity makes the Christian community involved in the trinitarian role in their context. In the social Trinity, the Nepali context, which is elaborated on in the next chapter, finds space for its meaning and mission. Since the social Trinity opens itself for humanity, many human society dimensions become part of the social Trinity. The social Trinity is a promising platform upon which Nepali Theology can take its shape. The following chapter implores the social Trinity's multiple dynamics and dimensions by discussing its proponents and opponents in the process.

---

169. LaCugna, *God for Us*, 305.
170. Groppe, "Catherine Mowry LaCugna's Contribution," 763.

5

Building Bridges

The Social Trinity as the Cornerstone of Constructive Theology

THE TRINITY DOCTRINE IS brought to the center of theological enterprise by theologians like Jürgen Moltmann, John Zizioulas, Catherine M. LaCugna, and Leonardo Boff, whose theologies are commonly referred to as the social Trinity. They established the Trinity as the central Christian doctrine, which is "relevant to the life of individual Christians, to the life of the Church and beyond."[1] Other theologians such as Wolfhart Pannenberg, Collin Gunton, Mirsalov Volf, Stanley J. Grenz, and many others also advocate teachings on God that can be categorized as social trinitarianism. At present, the trinitarian doctrine in its social form has increased its roots in various directions such as contextual theologies like liberation and feminist theologies, ecclesiology, theology of religions, and even eco-theology.[2] Even the theologians, who avoid being associated with Moltmann's line of thinking, make

---

1. See the previous chapter for the development of the doctrine of the Trinity and the arrival of the Social Trinity in particular. Kilby, "Perichoresis and Projection: Problems with Social Doctrines of the Trinity," 432.

2. Platter, "The Trinity, Social Justice, and the Missio Dei," 1. Bacon, "Thinking the Trinity as Resource for Feminist Theology Today," 442. Argues that thinking of God as a Trinity works as the theological resource for feminism. Moe, "From a Trinitarian Theology of Religion to a Trinitarian Theology of Religions," 293. For Moe, the social Trinity provides a hermeneutical approach to embracing the religious other. Boff, *The Cry of the Earth, Cry of the Poor*, 156. Boff says, "Trinity helps us to delve deeper into understanding our common home, planet Earth, the universe, and its future."

Building Bridges

theology relevant for Christian living and mission and develop their version of a relational and community-oriented Trinity.³ However, such social development of the trinitarian theology was not universally welcomed, and many theologians, especially those who would like to be called evangelical theologians, were cautious in such an approach.⁴

Though many theologians, who advocate the social or relational concept of the Trinity, point the root of their theology to the Church Fathers' trinitarianism, the term "social Trinity" is new. It denotes the Trinity's relational and community concept proposed by theologians like Jürgen Moltmann, John D. Ziziouals, Catherine LaCugna, Leonardo Boff, and others.⁵ The Social Trinity collectively speaks of relational trinitarianism, which has implications for the church's social life and beyond because it was developed to make the Trinity relevant to people's lives, the church, and society.⁶ The Greek term, *perichoresis*, is the foundation of divine diversity, egalitarian unity of Godhead, and the central concept of the social Trinity.⁷ Such distinctive characteristics are claimed to be founded in the history of God's economy as recorded in the biblical narratives where interaction between divine persons occurs. The Trinity's historical orientation is not confined to the past but is made relevant for current and future history, demonstrating ecclesial, social, and political significance.⁸ This study of social trinitarianism concentrates on two concepts, the *perichoresis* and the historical orientation of God.

---

3. Plantinga Jr. "Gregory of Nyssa and the Social Analogy of the Trinity," 352. Analyzing the Cappadocian Father's argument, Plantinga argues for the trinity as the unity of God, but he refuses to name it a society like that of human beings. Though he seeks to be different, inherently he is standing for the Trinity as the relational unity of God that the social Trinity speaks of.

4. The following articles are some examples of criticism of the social Trinity. Norman, "Problems for the 'Social Trinity'-Counting God," 3–13.; Kilby, "Perichoresis and Projection: Problems with Social Doctrines of the Trinity," 432–45; Hasker, "Objections to Social Trinitarianism," 421–39.

5. Kinnison, "The Social Trinity and the Southwest: Toward a Local Theology in the Borderlands," 1.

6. Kilby, "Perichoresis and Projection," 432.

7. Kinnison, "The Social Trinity and the Southwest," 4.

8. Holmes, "Three Versus One? Some Problems of Social Trinitarianism," 78.

The Trinitarian Dharma

PERICHORESIS: UNITY OF THE THREE DIVINE DIVERSITY

Social trinitarianism shuns the traditional model of understanding the Trinity, which begins with God's oneness and seeks to accommodate the three persons in one divine substance. Their new approach speaks of the Trinity, a community of three persons, and confirms their unity.[9] The social trinitarianism's contempt of the former is that such an approach is based on the metaphysical concept that "God is supreme substance," and such an idea is understood by pointing out the world's finitude. As a result, God is separated from the world and made abstract and irrelevant to the Christian life.[10] However, the new approach is also accused of promoting tritheism in the name of the Trinity as a society of three individual Gods.[11] Social trinitarianism adopts the ancient Greek concept of *perichoresis* to explain three divine persons' relationality.[12]

Perichoresis is used by Greek fathers to express the communion between the two natures of Jesus Christ and the trinitarian persons. Perichoresis speaks of intimate fellowship that one makes room for the other. Christ's divinity and humanity make room for each other.[13] Similarly, perichoresis stands for Trinity to express the intimate communion of the three divine persons. In Christology, perichoresis represents the inseparable unity of two distinguishable human and divine aspects of Jesus, but it speaks of the divine oneness of three distinct divine persons in the Trinity.[14] Such use of perichoresis in Christology and Trinity has been the subject of debate.[15] The perichoresis constitutes "the society of the three divine persons," commonly known as social trinitarianism.[16]

The mutuality and equality of three persons form the basic thesis of social trinitarianism, and the misconception of tritheism is raised against

---

9. Moltmann, *The Trinity and the Kingdom*, 149. The choice between the "Oneness of God" and "Threeness of God" as the departure for trinitarian doctrine is a choice between philosophy and biblical narratives respectively.

10. Holmes, "Three Versus One?, 10–14.

11. Norman, "Problems for the 'Social Trinity,'" 5–6.

12. Kilby, "Perichoresis and Projection," 435.

13. .Lawler, "*Perichoresis*: New Theological Wine in an Old Theological Wineskin," 49–50.

14. Lawler, "Perichoresis," 53.

15. Crisp, *Divinity and Humanity*, 1–32. Crips argues that *perichoresis* is not suitable to make argument for incarnation where two kinds of attributes should be interacted, however it is plausible to speak of relationship of persons in the Trinity.

16. Moltmann, *Trinity and the Kingdom*, 198.

such an approach.[17] While advocates of social trinitarianism use the term person to highlight the inter-connectedness, mutuality, and eternal co-existence of the Trinity, others observe it as being too individualistic and three independent divine.[18] Jürgen Moltmann and Leonardo Boff extensively utilize perichoresis to argue against tritheism and advocate the social aspect of trinitarian divine life and its relevance to human society. Both Moltmann and Boff argue that the perichoretic person is not about independent individualism; rather, it is about the eternal bond of three persons. The characteristic of each person is not their separateness but an unbreakable relationship.[19] Boff adds, "By the joining of the three persons in creating (perichoresis), everything comes interwoven with relationship, interdependencies, and webs of intercommunion."[20]

Social trinitarianism attempts to tackle not only God's unity but also the relevancy of trinitarian doctrine to practical life. Therefore, while making a case for the unity of three persons in perichoresis, Moltmann emphasizes that each trinitarian person's distinctiveness is not diminished in such unity. As a result, the relationship they advocate is not just superficial but real and dynamic. Moltmann states: "The doctrine of the perichoresis links together in a brilliant way the threeness and the unity, without reducing the threeness to the unity or dissolving the unity in the threeness. The unity of the triunity lies in the eternal perichoresis of the trinitarian persons. Interpreted *perichoretically*, the trinitarian persons form their own unity by themselves in the circulation of the divine life."[21] In social trinitarianism, the Trinity is not merely a mathematical equation or a sound philosophical argument. Rather, it is where believers experience the communion of God and with God. It does not entertain the separation between God and the world. Instead, it seeks to advocate for their relationship. Therefore, perichoresis comes to the social trinitarian stage to argue for the unity of three divine persons and create a perichoretic link between God and the creation. Boff says, "In Christian trinitarian language, perichoresis captures the relationship of mutual presence and

---

17. Kärkkäinen, *Trinity: Global Perspectives*, 290. Shows his doubt on Boff's social trinitarian theology's ability to unite the three divine persons in one.
18. Heidi Russell, *The Source of all Love: Catholicity and the Trinity*.
19. Boff, *Trinity and Society*, 5–6; Moltmann, *Trinity and Kingdom*, 175.
20. Leonardo Boff, *The Cry of the Earth, Cry of the poor*, 166.
21. Moltmann, *Trinity and Kingdom*, 175.

The Trinitarian Dharma

interpenetration between God and the universe or between the three divine persons among themselves and with all creation."[22]

Two main aspects of trinitarian life, mutuality, and egalitarianism, are emphasized to establish the Trinity as a model for human society. Therefore, social trinitarianism, rather than just accepting God's inner being as a mystery, uses the perichoresis to advocate mutuality and egalitarianism. In this way, the Trinity can be a model for an inclusive and loving human society.[23] Among social trinitarianism advocates, Catherine M. LaCugna refuges to discuss God's inner being even in relational terms. However, she strongly advocates the Trinity as the most practical theology.[24] LaCugna speaks Trinity in terms of God's relationship with us, rather than God's inner relationship.

> The central theme of all trinitarian theology is relationship; God's relationship with us and our relationship with one another. The doctrine of the Trinity is not an abstract conceptual paradox about God's inner life or a mathematical puzzle of the 'one and three.' The doctrine of the Trinity is in fact the most practical of all doctrines . . . it helps us articulate . . . how personal conversion is relation to social transformation; what constitutes the 'right relationship,' within the Christian community and in society at large . . .[25]

While LaCugna is strong on Trinity's social implication, refusing to elaborate on the trinitarian inner relationship loses her claims' core. The doctrine of the Trinity helps us articulate our right relationship within and outside of the Christian community.[26] Thereby, elaboration of the perichoretic aspect of the trinitarian inner life by Moltmann and Boff can supplement LaCugna's emphasis on the applicability of the Trinity to the human community.[27]

---

22. Boff, *Cry of the Earth*, 24.
23. Kinnison, "The Social Trinity and the South West," 5–8.
24. LaCugna, "The Practical Trinity," *Christian Century*, 679.
25. LaCugna, "Practical Trinity," 679.
26. Kärkkäinen, *The Trinity: Global Perspective*, 191.

27. LaCugna, *God For us*, 265–78, 305. Though not critical of the idea that perichoresis takes place with God, and is model for human community (belonged to Moltman and Boff), LaCugna focuses on her idea that "God for us is who God is as God," to assert that God is personal. She refuses to distinguish between if it is plural of singular but speaks person is relational. Such idea is incomplete, if Trinity is not viewed as a relational communion.

TRINITY: THE EGALITARIAN DIVINE RELATIONSHIP

John Ziziuolas speaks of the Trinity in terms of the ontology of relation; however, he does not bring the concept of perichoresis to define trinitarian unity. Zizioulas differentiates himself from those who advocate immanent trinitarianism but advocates hierarchical trinitarianism while making Trinity the church's image. He says, "The Father as 'cause' is God, or the God in an ultimate sense, 'not because he holds the divine essence and transmits it' . . . but because he is the ultimate ontological principle of divine personhood."[28] Though Zizioulas speaks of the hierarchy of personhood, not as a divine essence, such a monarchial understanding makes the trinitarian community less egalitarian.[29] Zizioulas's Trinity, according to the ontology of communion, differs from the classical trinitarianism that the personhood of the Father, not His substance is the source of the Son and the Holy Spirit.[30] Miroslav Volf argues against the Monarchianism of Zizioulas and defines the trinitarian relationship as follows.

> Moreover, within a community of perfect love between persons who share all the divine attributes, a notion of hierarchy and subordination is inconceivable. Within relations between the divine persons, the Father is for that reason, not the one over against the others, nor "the First," but rather the one among the others. The structure of trinitarian relations is characterized neither by a pyramidal dominance of the one (so Ratzinger) nor by a hierarchical bipolarity between the one and the many (so Zizioulas), but rather by a polycentric and symmetrical reciprocity of the many.[31]

Similarly, Pannenberg voices the trinitarian subordination that trinitarian communion is not a one-way proceeding from the father and the other two being just recipients. Rather they are in mutual co-operations who cannot exist without the other in their eternal being.

> The Son is not subordinate to the Father in the sense of ontological inferiority, but he subjects himself to the Father. In this regard, he is himself in eternity the locus of the monarchy of the Father. Herein he is one with the Father by the Holy Spirit. The monarchy

---

28. Zizioulas, *Being as Communion*, 130.
29. Gunton, *Father, Son and Holy Spirit*, 73–74.
30. Zizioulas, *Communion and Otherness*, 30.
31. Volf, *After our Likeness*, 217.

of the Father is not the presupposition but the result of the common operation of the three persons.[32]

Collin Gunton puts perichoresis as the solution to diffuse the confusion from God's economy, where subordination is in play. He rejects the option of immanent trinitarianism that One God's involvement in the world in mutual action of the Three is not possible. In perichoresis, the unity in diversity and mutual equality in functional subordination is established.[33] Shielding against all kinds of subordinationism, Gunton says though the Son and the Spirit are in the economy, "they (the Son and the Spirit) are not subordinate, for, without his Son and Spirit, God would not be God."[34] In the perichoretic relationship, God's hierarchization does not exist because only mutuality and equality exist in trinitarian life.[35] Moltmann says, "Each person receives the fullness of eternal life from the other."[36]

THE OPENNESS OF GOD: HISTORICAL TRINITY

One of the social Trinity's distinctive features is that a trinitarian relationship is not limited to the divine inner being, but the inner being relates and opens toward the world. Social trinitarianism finds its deepest root in God's involvement in society, as revealed in the scriptures. It seeks to be a practical doctrine relevant to present history.[37] Social trinitarian relation to the world and history is twofold: first, it finds root in God's involvement in history, and second, it opens toward the present history and seeks to make a meaningful presence in it. This relationship with history is not separate from the divine inner relationship characterized by perichoresis. Here what Karl Rahner said, "the immanent Trinity is the economic Trinity, and the economic Trinity is the immanent Trinity," come to life.[38]

Moltmann comes to the forefront to promote the historical orientation of Trinity.[39] He argues that the trinitarian heavenly image reflects

32. Pannenberg, *Systematic Theology*, Vol. 1, 324.
33. Gunton, *The One, the Three and the Many*, 164.
34. Gunton, *Father, Son and the Spirit*, 73.
35. Boff, *Trinity and Society*, 146.
36. Moltmann, *Trinity and the Kingdom*, 174.
37. Brink, "Social Trinitarianism," 336. Among four characteristics of social trinitarianism that Brink points out two are "historical re-orientation," and "practical relevance."
38. . Boff, *Trinity and Society*, 114. Boff quotes Rahner's famous quote to show how Rahner's vision comes to reality in Social Trinity.
39. Moltmann, *Trinity and Kingdom*, 19. Moltmann calls his trinitarian theology "a

Building Bridges

God's participation in history and grounds God's eternal natural love in the historical event of the cross.[40] By showing the connection between the world and God in history, Moltmann emphasizes different divine characteristics than the abstract philosophical attributes that God involved in the historical event of the cross, cannot be immovable, impassible, and beyond history.[41] With Trinity, Moltmann connects 'the biblical history' with 'the here and now history' of the Spirit and God's 'eschatological history.' The historical orientation of the Trinity binds the biblical revelation of God with the present history of the Spirit's work, which anticipates the eschatological history of the Kingdom of God. In such an eschatological orientation, we can perceive the trinitarian relationship of differences and unity.[42] "In the presence of God in history, we find a perichoresis of the times: his future in his present, and his presence in his future."[43] Moltmann's historical Trinity not only participates in the world's history but also creates space for history in the Trinity. Believers' fellowship is not only with God but also with God. Moltmann says, "Through his mercy, Jesus opens up to others God's relationship with himself and takes men and women into his relationship with God."[44]

Such historical orientation of the Trinity has implications for the believer's life in history. Trinitarian unity calls for Christian unity, and the freedom of God anticipates the freedom of believers from all bondage. Trinitarian openness toward history calls for the Church's participation in the world and solidarity with the suffering, hungry, and oppressed.[45] Trinity enters into a reciprocal relationship with history. As Moltmann underlines:

> Christ in us makes us the anticipation of redeemed humanity and the overture to the new creation of all things. We in Christ brings us into the space of movement of God's coming kingdom . . . We in the Spirit: here we are person, and the Spirit is our living space. The Spirit in us: there the Spirit is person, and we are its living space and its dwelling . . . All things in God: here God is the living space of his world the space which receives everything and takes

---

historical doctrine of God."

40. Moltmann, *Trinity and Kingdom*, 26, 32.
41. Moltmann, *Trinity and Kingdom*, 45.
42. Moltmann, *Trinity and Kingdom*, 65, 212.
43. Moltmann, *Sun of Righteousness, Arise!*, 165.
44. Moltmann, *History and the Triune God*, 34.
45. Moltmann, *Trinity and the Kingdom*, 47, 202. Moltmann, *History and the Triune God*, 41–43.

up everything. Then all created beings find in God their 'broad place where there is no more cramping.' God in all things: there God finds his space for living and dwelling in his new creation: and God will dwell with them, and all created beings will participate in the indwelling livingness of God.[46]

Like Moltmann, Boff expresses the historical orientation of the Trinity, saying, "The God-Trinity, which had been present in human history, now through the Son and the Holy Spirit, sent by the Father, took on human history as its own and dwelt among us as in its dwelling place."[47] Both Moltmann and Boff understand the Trinity from the viewpoint of God's participation in the history and significance of the Trinity. While Moltmann elaborates on God's inner relationship from a historical perspective, Boff focuses on the relationship between the trinitarian community and the Trinity. Boff says, "Father, Son, and Holy Spirit have always been present in the history of men and women, communicating their love, taking human endeavors into the divine communion of the Three Persons."[48] Historical orientation rescues trinitarian theology from being only abstract rational discourse. As Boff contends: "Therefore, in order to know the Father, we must see how the Son acts. His actions and words give us access to the Father. This is not an abstract and metaphysical approach; rather, in it, the Father is revealed through history, by way of a revealing gesture through the course of his Son's life among his sons and daughters."[49] Though it is not as expounded as in Moltmann's theology, Boff sees the relationship between God and history in the eschatological perspective that it is on the movement toward eschatology where "God will be all in all."[50] God's involvement in history and making history part of the trinitarian life, the history, and the world get its trinitarian character. Boff states, "By the joining of the three persons in creating everything comes interwoven with relationships, interdependencies, and webs of intercommunion. The cosmos is shown to be an interplay of relationship because it is created in the likeness and image of the God-Trinity."[51] The Holy Spirit is active in making world history part of trinitarian history. "The Spirit acts universally in

---

46. Moltmann, *Sun of Righteousness*, 166–68.
47. Boff, *Trinity and Society*, 10.
48. Boff, *Trinity and Society*, 26.
49. Boff, *Trinity and Society*, 32.
50. Boff, *Trinity and Society*, 53.
51. Boff, *Cry of the Earth, Cry of the Poor*, 166–67.

all men and women, not in just one of them, as the Son does in Jesus . . . The Spirit is present in multiplicity and diversity, creating communion."[52] A believer anticipates God's eschatological kingdom, which is inaugurated in present history, and participates in it.[53]

Zizioulas envisions the trinitarian connection with the world in the work of the Son and the Spirit, and the church is the product of the divine economy.[54] Such trinitarian history is related to the church's understanding of communion, which is the image of the Triune communion of God.[55] Zizioulas places the church in between the world's history and the eschatological history that the church's eschatological nature is to be incarnated in the world.[56] Zizioulas takes the Eucharist as the defining aspect of the church, which links the church to the apostolic church and the history of Christ. The presence of the Spirit in the Eucharist gives the church an eschatological course.[57] Church receives communion from Christ and the Holy Spirit's presence in the Eucharist.[58] Thereby, for him, the Eucharist is more than a sacrament. He argues: "[The Eucharist] is the eschatologization of the historical word the voice of the historical Christ, the voice of the Holy Scripture which comes to us, no longer simply as "doctrine" through history but as life and being through the eschata. It is not a sacrament completing the word, but rather the word becoming flesh, the risen Body of the Logos."[59] In the Eucharist, God converses with us and enters into trinitarian communion, and the whole creation finds a place in the Trinity through the church.[60] Zizioulas speaks more about the church's relational and communal nature than the church's mission in the world. However, he understands that it is the church's responsibility to bring the creation into the trinitarian life.[61]

Following Zizioulas' notion of the personhood of the Monarchical Father, Catherine M. LaCugna refuses to elaborate on the trinitarian

52. Boff, *Trinity and Society*, 208.
53. Boff, *Jesus Christ Liberator*, 286–87.
54. Zizioulas, *Being as Communion*, 19
55. Rikheim, "Johannes Zizioulas," 438.
56. Zizioulas, *Being as Communion*, 20.
57. Zizioulas, *Being as Communion*, 22.
58. Zizioulas, *Being as Communion*, 22–23.
59. Zizioulas, *Being as Communion*, 22–23.
60. Zizioulas, *Being as Communion*, 7
61. Zizioulas, *Communion and Otherness*, 43.

The Trinitarian Dharma

inner being but insists on making the Trinity relevant to the Christian life. She speaks of the intimate connection of the Trinity with history.[62] She says, "The doctrine of the Trinity is the shared life between God and creature."[63] Trinity is the place where God and his loved ones as one. LaCugna disjoins *theologia*, the mystery of God, from *oikonomia*, the salvation history, and focuses on the *oikonomia* to advocate the practical aspect of the Trinity for Christian living.[64] Trinitarian theology provides God's relational nature; therefore, our communitarian life in Christ and the Spirit is the starting point of any reflection on the Trinity.[65] Trinity stands for a connection of human life into the heart, life, and identity of God where "hierarchy nor inequality, neither division nor competition," exist but only love and diversity.[66]

The Triune God's historical work extends itself to the world so that the world can take part in the trinitarian life. As the community, the church resulted from trinitarian work in history becomes a hub to communicate trinitarian salvation and love to the world.[67] The communitarian image of trinitarian God becomes the vocation of the people, especially the church in the world. "God's intention is for those who are in Christ to participate in his destiny and thereby replicate his glorious image."[68]

THE ASSESSMENT OF SOCIAL TRINITARIANISM

While appreciating the social trinitarianism's attempt to ground the Trinity in the history of salvation, Kärkkäinen questions the threeness of God as the problem in Boff, LaCugna, and Moltmann.[69] While LaCugna is intentionally quiet on the issue of God's inner being, Moltmann and Boff repeatedly emphasize the perichoretic unity of God. We should note that social

---

62. LaCugna, "The Baptismal Formula, Feminist Objections, and Trinitarian Theology," 245. LaCugna says, "Trinitarian theology is not concerned with providing an abstract metaphysics of God's "inner life" but with elaborating the essentially personal and relational nature of God." LaCugna not only avoids the metaphysical explanation of God but also refuses to speak God's relational life as we find in the theologies of Jurgen Moltmann, Leonardo Boff and John Zizoulas whom she agrees.

63. LaCugna, *God for us*, 377–78.

64. LaCugna, "The Practical Trinity," 682.

65. LaCugna, "The Baptismal Formula," 245.

66. LaCugna, "The Baptismal Formula," 246–49.

67. Irvin, "The Trinity and Socio-Political Ethics," 401.

68. Grenz, *The Social God and The Relational Self*, 225.

69. Kärkkäinen, *The Trinity: Global Perspectives*, 121, 192 and 290.

trinitarianism seeks to establish a genuine relationship between three divine persons, not just three modes of being of the same impersonal substance. Kärkkäinen's complaint of tritheism in Moltmann, Boff, and LaCugna is an attempt to force them to use the metaphysical language to define the Trinity, which they intentionally seek to avoid.[70] As Collin Gunton says, in defense of relational Trinity "a perichoresis which dissolves particulars is no longer perichoresis, being rather an unrelational homogeneity."[71] Unless spoken in the language of perichoretic unity, such unrelational homogeneity leads to unrelational abstract trinitarianism.

William Huskar resorts to the metaphysical explanation of the Trinity that the relational nature of the Trinity fails to do justice to the Godhead who is ultimately a single concrete being. He believes that the only way to justify the ultimate Oneness of God is to psychological analysis where men can have multiple streams of experience.[72] Like Hasker, Ralph Norman also objects to social trinitarianism, which, according to him, ultimately leads to tritheism.[73] *Perichoresis* is the unity of divine persons and does not speak of the unity of divine nature. Similarly, Normal points out the social trinitarianism's refusal to admit that three persons are of a single divine substance.[74] These arguments are purely metaphysical and insist on the singular substance of God shared by all persons.[75] While standing the philosophical soundness, these arguments fail to reflect on the scriptural references that speak of the Father, Son, and the Holy Spirit as simultaneously independent persons. Even to make a metaphysical case for the multiple divine substances, Richard Swinburne states that God is love, and love does not exist without sharing. This explains that multiple divine individuals are possible when metaphysical attributes are understood alongside ethical attributes. The existence of multiple divinities is not possible if their substance does not differentiate them.[76] Swinburne makes a logical argument that multiple divine substances are necessary if we even try to argue any kind of trinitarianism. "If 'the Father' is the name of a person who is not the same person as the Son or the Spirit, then it

70. Moltmann, *Trinity and Kingdom*, 175; Boff, *Cry of the Earth*, 152.
71. Gunton, *The One, the Three and the Many*, 186.
72. Hasker, "Objection to Social Trinitarianism," 421.
73. Norman, "Problems for the Social Trinity," 5.
74. Donnell, "Trinity as Divine Community," 21
75. Hasker, *Metaphysics and the Tri-personal God*, 257–58.
76. Swinburne, "Trinity," 20–24.

The Trinitarian Dharma

cannot also be the name of a God (or a substance) who is the same God (or substance) as the Son and the Spirit. And if we deny that 'the Father' etc. do have clear uses, we deny any clear content to the doctrine of the Trinity at all."[77] However, Swinburne's argument is even more plausible when he says that the life of Jesus in salvation history cannot be different from life before incarnation.[78] This argument also answers those who stand against social trinitarianism, saying that unless the Son, fully participates in the divinity of God, cannot be a savior.[79] Swinburne argues that unless the Son was the Son from eternity could not identify with our suffering to redeem us. A metaphysical argument about the Trinity would always be incomplete if not brought before the revelation of the salvation history, which stands more with social trinitarianism.

Kilby argues against the use of perichoresis to construct the relational Trinity and make it relevant to the Christian life. He makes an argument from the opposite direction that social trinitarianism is a projection of current social value to construct the Trinity and reflect it to the world as a social norm. For him, Moltmann and others bring the understanding of human relationships to understand God. *Perichoresis* is only an excuse to show three divine persons' unity, which is three individual projections. Kelly accuses Moltmann and Boff of using the modern individualistic concept of person to argue against divine essence's homogeneity as claimed in classical trinitarianism.[80] For them, the distinction of each divine head is as important as their unity.

> The concept of person must therefore in itself contain the concept of unitedness or at-oneness, just as, conversely, the concept of God's at-oneness must in itself contain the concept of the three Persons. This means that the concept of God's unity cannot in the trinitarian sense be fitted into the homogeneity of the one divine

---

77. Swrinburne, "Trinity," 33.

78. Swinburne, "A Posteriori Arguments for the Trinity," 13–27. Swinburne argues, "There is a good a priori argument for the doctrine of the Trinity, from the need for any divine being to have another divine being to love sufficiently to provide for him a third divine being whom to love and by whom to be loved. But most people who have believed the doctrine of the Trinity have believed it on the basis of the teaching of Jesus as interpreted by the church. The only reason for believing this teaching would be if Jesus led the kind of life which a priori we would expect an incarnate God to live in order to identify with our suffering, make atonement for our sins, and to reveal truth to us; culminated by a miracle which God alone could do and which would also authenticate the teaching."

79. Metzler, "The Trinity in Contemporary Theology," 2.

80. Kilby, "Perichoresis and projection," 441.

substance, or into the identity of the absolute subject either, and least of all into one of the three Persons of the Trinity. It must be perceived in the perichoresis of the divine Persons.[81]

For Boff, *perichoresis* is the solution for the concept that "God as the absolute subject actualized in three distinct modes or three distinct modes of subsistence." Such a view cannot do justice to the revelation of salvation history, where three distinct subjects are interrelated.[82] Kelly seems to be suspicious of social trinitarianism's claim of the practical relevance of trinitarian doctrine. He questions, "Does the Trinity need to be relevant? What kind of relevance does it need to have?" As he claims, it should be limited to the confession of faith. This paper puts Kilby's objection aside by quoting Catherine M. LaCugna:

> The doctrine of the Trinity is not an abstract conceptual paradox about God's inner life or a mathematical puzzle of the 'one and three.' The doctrine of the Trinity is in fact the most practical of all doctrines. Among all other things, it helps us to articulate our understanding of the gospel's demands; how personal conversion is related to social transformation; what constitutes 'right relationship' within the Christian community and in society at large; how best to praise and worship God; and what it means to confess faith in and be baptized into the life of the God of Jesus Christ.[83]

Perichoresis stands for unity as a trinitarian community that divine Threeness and oneness are not distinct and envisions no hierarchy and domination in the divine fellowship.[84] In this way, perichoresis shows not the similarity of the trinitarian community and the human society but communicates that the trinitarian God relates to the world and history.[85]

SUMMARY

In social trinitarianism, perichoresis is the foundation of divine diversity and unity. In other words, with the *perichoresis* concept, the oneness of God does not contradict the threeness of God. *Perichoresis* does not stand

---

81. Moltmann, *Trinity and the Kingdom*, 150.
82. Boff, *Trinity and Society*, 137.
83. LaCugna, "The Practical Trinity." 678.
84. McDougall, *Pilgrimage of Love*, 97–99.
85. Gunton, *Father, Son and Holy Spirit*, 23.

The Trinitarian Dharma

for intra-divine relations alone, but it also advocates God's connection to the world.[86]

Social trinitarianism, in its perichoretic theme, is suitable to make a relationship with the context. Though the perichoretic argument for God's unity is always questioned in the theology of the West, in Africa, and Asia, it is home to the community concept of the divine in their traditional belief system. Plurality and singularity are not opposite categories, but they co-exist together. Perichoresis speaks for mutuality and egalitarianism of trinitarian life, which can be considered the model for human society. Social trinitarianism advocates for mutuality and equality in human society as well. *Perichoresis* stands against the hierarchy and unjust concentration of power on certain individuals or institutions.[87] Contextual theologies can model their theology after the perichoresis of the social Trinity to speak against the social issues of inequality and injustice.

Third, another distinctive feature of the social Trinity is the historical openness of God. God is accessible and welcoming at the same time. Trinity becomes part of history, and history becomes part of the Trinity.[88] For contextual theology, its context is part of God's trinitarian history. Historical issues of a given context come under the trinitarian scope. God takes part in their historical activities.

---

86. McDougall, *Pilgrimage of Love*, 97, 107.
87. LaCugna, *God for Us*, 276–78.
88. Jurgen Moltmann, *Sun of Righteousness*, 156–57.

6

In Action

*Unveiling the Social Trinity
in Contextual Engagement*

SINCE CHRISTIANITY EXTENDED ITS border toward the global south, reflecting on the contextual issues has become a new Christian theological task. Though Christianity did not remain a Western religion but has a global presence, the Western academic world is reluctant to acknowledge the need for contextual theology. It considers the contextual reflection of the Christian faith as being inferior to the Western counterpart.[1] Jung Young Lee, who attempted to produce his work, *Trinity in Asian Perspective*, expressed that Third World theologies are considered "subsidiaries to the Western perspective," instead, he intends to "complement" the Western theology with his work.[2] Contextual theology is not an option; rather, it is a theological imperative, and it has no other choice than to take "present human experience" into account to construct a contextual theology.[3]

Constructing a contextual theology is a challenging task because the context comes with different beliefs and social issues. The social Trinity, which holds plurality and diversity in its life, can be a resource for dealing with diverse contextual challenges.[4] The openness of the social Trinity toward history is best suited to make contextual issues theological subjects. While

---

1. Parrat, *An Introduction to Third World Theologies*, 1.
2. Lee, *Trinity in Asian Perspective*, 12.
3. Bevans, *Models of Contextual Theology* 3–4.
4. Marmion and Nieuwenhove, *Introduction to Trinity*, 225.

The Trinitarian Dharma

trinitarian theology enables God's presence as transcendent and immanent in history, it also opens a path of articulating God's relation to the different contexts in different forms and theologies.[5] This section explores the roles that the social Trinity has played or can play in theologies concentrating on contextual issues such as liberation and contextual theologies.

LIBERATING ACTION OF SOCIAL TRINITY

The main distinctive characteristic of liberation theology is that it is rooted in the experience of everyday life in poverty. Such experience relates to the interpretation of the scripture, resulting in discovering new hope in God's purposes amid oppression and deprivation.[6] Trinity plays the central role in bringing human experience into theological enterprise, and it becomes the agenda of liberation theology. "Because the Trinity is not only a mystery; it is "agenda," at once home and destiny: we come from it, we live in it, we are going to it."[7] Liberation theologies such as Latin American liberation theologies and Feminist theologies developed with the Western trinitarian concept than those from the non-Western world, such as Minjung and Dalit theologies. In contrast to the individualism of European and North American societies, societies in Latin America, Africa, and Asia value community and societal relationships.[8] Therefore social trinitarianism has become/can become the understanding of Biblical God in liberation theologies.

Latin American Liberation Theology

In Latin American liberation theology, the Trinity speaks of God's involvement in the history of humankind through the incarnation of the Son, and the presence of the Holy Spirit is in the present history of suffering people.[9] God is love which is not just for speculation but for imitation, as Justo L. Gonzales writes:

---

5. Peter Scott, *Theology, Ideology and Liberation*, 214.
6. Rowland, "Introduction: The Liberation Theology," 1–2.
7. Casaldaliga and Vigil, *The Spirituality of Liberation*, 70.
8. Kärkkäinen, *The Trinity: Global Perspective*, 272.
9. Gonzales, *Manana: Christian Theology from a Hispanic Perspective*, 112–13. Gonzales particularly criticizes the immanent trinity (essential Trinity in his own term) but accepts economic (social) trinity. Immanent trinity takes God as a puzzle to be solved than an example to imitate.

In Action

> This love of God, however, is not only something we receive, or something we must praise. It is also something we must imitate, for if God is love, life without love is life without God; and if this is a sharing love, such as we see in the Trinity, then life without sharing is life without God; and if this sharing is such that in God the three persons are equal in power, then life without such power-sharing is life without God.[10]

Understanding God apart from experience in the community is not possible. Trinitarian God is intertwined in the people's history and has a place for it. According to Gonzales, Trinity means "God's very being is for-otherness," and the trinitarian work of the Son opens a path for the church to take part in God's love. Such trinitarian work makes us truly human beings for others in society.[11] Similarly, Gustavo Gutierrez says that "to be saved is to reach the fullness of love; it is to enter into the circle of charity which unites the three Persons of the Trinity."[12] Trinity becomes the category for believers to participate in God's work in history. In Latin American liberation theology Trinity is God's communion, which seeks to create the human community according to God's love and desires to use the church for the purpose. As Gutierrez writes:

> The basis for fellowship is full communion with the persons of the Trinity. The bond which unites God and humanity is celebrated—that is, effectively recalled and proclaimed—in the Eucharist. Without a real commitment against exploitation and alienation and for a society of solidarity and justice, the Eucharistic celebration is an empty action, lacking any genuine endorsement by those who participate in it.[13]

Boff is the most recognized Latin American theologian using the social Trinity for the liberation theology cause. Boff presents trinitarian communion as a critic of and inspiration for human society. He brings Trinity to point out its distinction with both capitalism and socialism.[14] He speaks of capitalism as follows,

10. Gonzales, *Manana*, 115.
11. Gonzales, *Manana*, 155.
12. Gutierrez, *A Theology of Liberation: History, Politics, and Salvation*, 144.
13. Gutierrez, *A Theology of Liberation*, 150.
14. Kärkkäinen, *Trinity*, 287. Kärkkäinen criticizes Boff's intention to be critical of both socialism and capitalism saying, "too naïve" and principles drawn from Trinity are too general to be critical of socialism and capitalism. However, personally, I disagree with Kärkkäinen that his criticism is against the whole idea that social trinity stands for, ie.

The Trinitarian Dharma

> Liberal-capitalist society... means the dictatorship of the property-owning classes with their individualistic and business interests always shored up by mechanism of state control... So, by their practice and theory, capitalist regimes contradict the challenges and invitations of trinitarian communion. They are not a vehicle for people in general and Christians in particular to experience the Trinity in history.[15]

For Boff, Trinity stands critically against the so-called socialism, which speaks of everything collectively and disregards personal differences.[16]

In Latin American Liberation theology, the social context is the place for trinitarian action. It is transformed into "the image and likeness of the communion of the divine persons," and it envisions the church's place in the trinitarian communion and action in the transformation process.[17] Latin American Liberation theology can present a model for Nepali contextual theology where it needs to call the church for solidarity with the low caste people, discriminated women, and poor people of the society. Social trinitarianism can be a tool for critique and inspiration. Trinitarian openness and fellowship of love compel the Nepali church to address contextual social issues.

Black Theology

While the southern neighbors, the Latin American theologians, worked out a full-fledged trinitarian theology to advocate God's justice and solidarity for the freedom of the suffering in their context, Black theology of independence, in particular, spoke of the same mainly focusing on God's involvement in the history without a fully detailed trinitarian theology.[18] Black theology does not dip into the mystery of God. Instead, they take their experience of suffering to understand God; thereby, some theologians tend to take it for granted regarding the divine nature.[19] Without

---

Social relevance of divine life. Boff's criticism of capitalism and socialism makes us think about society in God's point of view and prevents us from putting too much trust in the existing social political system. Though we cannot be optimistic of such proposal would bring any change, however, it can be a good motivation of Christian communities to be involved in the society.

15. Boff, *Trinity and Society*, 149–50.
16. Boff, *Trinity and Society*, 151.
17. L. Boff and C. Boff, *Introducing Liberation Theology*, 51–52.
18. Díaz, "Black Latin American and US Hispanic Perspective," 260–61.
19. Walker, Jr., "Theological Resources for a Black Neoclassical Social Ethics," 36–37.

being critical about the language of God, but being focused on the liberating work of Jesus Christ, Major J. Jones accepts the Barthian view of the Trinity as the three modes of God rather than three persons. Jones seeks to understand God in Christ, who is the redeemer of the soul and Black people's historical suffering.[20]

However, James Cone broadens the liberating act of God in Christ and in Yahweh, views that the Barthian model of God conflicts with what Black Theology stands for because Barth's monotheistic modalism offers no room for black liberation.[21] Cone finds God's involvement in human history in the Biblical narratives and argues that any authentic theology sides with the poor and suffering because both Yahweh and Jesus Christ worked for the liberation of the suffering people.[22] Cone finds Jürgen Moltmann's theology of hope applicable to black liberation theology because Moltmann's theology of hope speaks of the eschatological future and calls for participation in the present struggle for liberation from suffering.[23] Though we cannot find the concept of trinitarian communion of God fully developed in James Cone's work, he speaks of the church as the community called by God to participate in his mission to liberate the suffering people. For him, "Participating in the historical liberation of God is the defining characteristic of the Church," and further argues that the "church is that community that participates in Christ liberating work in history . . . ."[24] I argue that for James Cone's Black liberation theology, the social Trinity provides an appropriate view of the mystery of divine life, which calls the black communities into the divine life to participate in the liberation of Black people. After all, for Cone, "there can be no Christian theology that is not social and political."[25]

Nepali contextual theology can develop a potential partnership with social trinitarianism to convey the message that God in Christ is the deliverer of the people from their injustices like Black liberation theology. Dalits and women in Nepali society find a theological language in social trinitarianism to express God's plan and desire to be involved in their history. The message of hope associated with the trinitarian eschatology can call the Nepali church to participate in God's liberation and justice in society.

20. Jones, *The Color of God: The Concept of God in Afro-American*, 82–84.
21. Cone, *A Black Theology of Liberation*, 115.
22. Cone, "Biblical Revelation and Social Existence," 166, 173.
23. Cone, *A Black Theology*, 245.
24. Cone, *A Black Theology*, 229–30.
25. Cone, "Biblical Revelation," 174.

The Trinitarian Dharma

Feminist Theologies

Feminist theology is committed to the justice of women and their liberation. This theology focuses on women's historical struggle from males' dominance in the economy, and social and religious spheres and seeks to dismantle the structures that caused women's suffering.[26] While some feminist theologians do not regard Trinity as a necessary topic for them, others view it as a symbol of patriarchal male dominance. However, some feminist theologians value social trinitarianism's relationality and use relational expressions such as mother, friend, and lover to bring the relational dynamics to their theological enterprise.[27]

Elizabeth A. Johnson observes that the language of the Trinity is misused throughout the century by the theologian separating it from God's work of salvation. She argues that "if the Trinity is not grounded in the experience of salvation, the triune symbol will remain in the dust, defeated."[28] Most discussions concentrated on one God vs. three Gods that ignored God's mission in history. Johnson shows her suspicion of the traditional argument on the Trinity that legitimizes the way men rule society, family, and women.

> The doctrine of the Trinity emerged within a patriarchal and imperialist culture ... This political reality melded with the name of God the Father to produce the view that divine authority rules over the world in the same way that men rightly rule the household and the state ... This had disastrous consequences for the symbol of God, which took on the contours of a self-sufficient masculine Father-God. It also had pernicious effects on Christian self-understanding, both politically and in the family, and especially on women.[29]

Johnson uses images like Sophia-Jesus, Sophia-Spirit, and Mother God to transform classical theism into a holistic view of God. Such an addition of the mother image reveals the relatedness of God and the world.[30] However, such interchange of words from "Father to Mother" or use of the "Sophia-God" image is not limited to conceptual as some suggest.[31]

26. Grey, "Feminist Theology," 113.
27. Soskice, "Trinity and Feminism," 139.
28. Johnson, *Quest for the Living God*, 211.
29. Johnson, *Quest for the Living God*, 208.
30. Johnson, *She Who is: The Mystery of God in Feminist Theological*, 231.
31. DiNoia, "Knowing and Naming the Triune God," 187. DiNoia argues against

Johnson seeks to establish the Trinity in relational terms. She says, "The threefold, interwoven aspects of the encounter with the one holy mystery point to Sophia-God, who is not a monolithic block but a living mystery of relation, to herself and us."[32] To dismantle such, Johnson resorts to the economic Trinity that speaks of God according to His divine acts in human history through 'incarnate Word and renewing Spirit.'[33] Johnson appreciates Jürgen Moltmann and Leonardo Boff's social trinitarianism and sees its acceptability from the feminist perspective.[34] She coins the inclusive term Sophia-God's holy mystery for Trinity, which is a "self-communicating mystery of relation, an unimaginable, open communion in herself that opens out freely to include even what is not herself."[35] This way the idea of social trinitarianism comes into full action in Elizabeth A. Johnson's feminist liberation theology.

Similarly, Anne E. Carr questions the maleness of God in traditional theology and Christian life and thinks that giving more feminine symbols has to do with the "reorientation of Christian imagination from idolatrous implications of exclusively masculine God-language."[36] While Carr understands God from women's relational experience, she wants a new image that can be relevant for the present history and express the message of life, death, and resurrection of Jesus. However, she does not settle with terms like a mother, sister, or friend.[37] Rather than suggesting/giving feminist names to God, Carr opts for a reinterpretation of the symbols used and finds other symbols in the Bible that are inclusive and redemptive. She proposes that Feminist theologians use contemporary reformulation of God's concepts to bring women's experience in the quest for a fuller

---

revision of traditional trinitarian language because it does not achieve the objective of feminist theology. DiNoia states that the tradition language of God the Father, Son and Holy Spirit stand for the love and revision of such subvert and obstruct the loving initiative. However, the revision suggested by Elizabeth A. Johnson is not limited to name and terminology, but it seeks to establish a way to make it more relatable for the women who have been suffering under the male domination. Using the term Mother God interchangeably with Father God opens easy and relatable access to God what DiNoia is speaking of.

32. Johnson, *She Who is,* 211.
33. Johnson, *Quest for Living God,* 210.
34. Johnson, *She Who Is,* 220.
35. Johnson, *She Who Is,* 233.
36. Carr, "Anne Carr on Feminism and the Maleness of God," 213.
37. Carr, *Transforming Grace,* 147.

The Trinitarian Dharma

understanding of God. God's feminine image should include the liberating, relational, eschatological, and mystical nature of God, and she argues that the Trinity is such an image.[38] Anne E. Carr states,

> [The] symbol of God as Trinity provides women with an image and concept of God that entails qualities that make God truly worthy of imitation, worthy of the call to radical discipleship that is inherent in Jesus' message. The Trinity includes all the suggestions of suffering and finally triumphant relationality when interpreted biblically and not simply metaphysically or abstractly: death and resurrection, relationship in God, and so also in the human community of grace.[39]

When Carr leads the feminist theology as the transforming grace that springs out of the women's experience and the Christian message, she calls for the church's renewal. The image of the Trinity includes the notion of liberation, relational eschatology, and mystical God.[40] Social trinitarianism can be the Nepali church's theological language for a fellowship based on equality and mutual and relational for Nepali women. Inclusive and redemptive trinitarian theology can be a voice for women subjected to discrimination and abuse in the traditional *dharma*.

Minjung Theology

Minjung theology is a "Korean contextual theology of suffering people" that was the Christian response to Korean people's social and political struggle in the 70s and 80s.[41] It comes as a criticism of society from the perspective of the poor. Minjung is the subject of Korean history who has *han*, the feeling rose out of the unjust experiences of people.[42] Minjung theology is a Korean liberation theology that attempts to resolve the *han* of Minjung (people).[43] Minjung theology differs from Latin American liberation, Feminist, and Black theologies because it uses non-western methods to do theology and does not follow Western categories such as Trinity, Christology, ecclesiology,

---

38. Carr, *Transforming Grace*, 148–56.
39. Carr, *Transforming Grace*, 156.
40. Carr, *Transforming Grace*, 214.
41. Chung, "Introduction: Asian Contextual Theology of Minjung and Beyond," 1.
42. An, "Minjung Theology," 199–204.
43. Kim, "Minjung Theology in Contemporary Korea," 415.

and other doctrines.⁴⁴ From the social Trinity perspective, one can see originating theology from the event of Jesus and making people's experiences as theological subjects for dialogue and cooperation.

Ahn Byung Mu, the pioneer of Minjung theology, said that he does not do his theology with metaphysics but with Jesus's life and teachings. The context of Jesus's life and the people around him are also equally crucial for Minjung theology because it uses the stories to tell their theologies rather than explaining concepts.⁴⁵ Ahn Byung-Mu makes a connection between the event of Jesus to the event of the *minjung*, as he says, "Jesus is present in the suffering of the minjung.⁴⁶ Minjung theology derives its understanding of God from the life of Jesus Christ. Ahn Byung-Mu makes his confession saying, "I experience the God event in the Jesus event. For me, therefore, the Jesus event is the sole reference."⁴⁷ It is significant to note that Ahn dislikes Barthian's understanding of God, who is detached from human reality.⁴⁸ Though the phrase "preferential option for the poor" is not found in Minjung theology, it expresses the same sentiment when it says God unconditionally stands with the Minjung.⁴⁹ Minjung theology rejects the doctrine of the Trinity and its ontological discourse about God but concentrates on God's involvement in history and people being part of God. Ahn Byung-Mu argues,

> I do not deal with the doctrine of the Trinity. . . . It is preferable to see in Christ both the Holy Spirit and God. If we view Christ and the Holy Spirit as events, rather than falling for an ontological view of them as persons, then they are different expressions of various aspects of what the minjung do. Minjung as such is not anything great when considered individually or collectively. What is remarkable is the event of self-transcendence. I believe we can refer to this as missio Dei, the continuation of the Jesus movement, and the presence of the Holy Spirit.⁵⁰

Though we cannot trace the trinitarian concept of a community of God in Minjung theology, we certainly see Minjung as Jesus' community,

---

44. An, "Minjung Theology," 205.
45. Ahn, "Jesus and Ochlos in the Context of His Galilean Ministry," 34–35.
46. Ahn, *Stories of Minjung Theology*, 63.
47. Ahn, *Stories of Minjung Theology*, 116.
48. Ahn, *Stories of Minjung Theology*, 104.
49. Ahn, *Stories of Minjung Theology*, 114.
50. Ahn, *Stories of Minjung Theology*, 122.

The Trinitarian Dharma

free from all hierarchy and discrimination which is expecting the eschatological fulfillment in the second coming of Jesus. In Minjung theology, the church's mission is to participate in the Minjung cause, which is God's mission.[51] Though Minjung theology does not speak the language of social trinitarianism, I argue that it does not stand against it. Minjung theology stands against Western metaphysical theology, which is abstract and unrelated to people. In its emphasis on God's involvement in history, Social trinitarianism agrees with Minjung theology. Social trinitarianism and Minjung theology both strive to make God relevant for a community of people. If we put both together, social trinitarianism can help Minjung theology be more understandable in a non-Korean setting. Minjung theology provides the way it can be part of minjung liberation.

Though Korea's Minjung concept is substantially different from the Nepali *dharma*, theology needs to ovoid Western philosophical ontology and be practically oriented in both contexts. Social trinitarianism itself rejects the metaphysical language of God and makes trinitarian understanding relevant to people's lives. Therefore, while the trinitarian divine community can stand for Minjung as Jesus' community, it can also stand for a *dharma* community in the Nepali context.

Dalit Theology

Dalit[52] theology is the liberation theology that emerged due to the discrimination against Dalits in Indian society, which also exists within India's Christian churches.[53] Dalit theology is a reaction to classical Indian theology, which failed to establish a relationship between God and people's suffering. Classical Indian theology did not serve the purpose of liberation and humanization but legitimized the unjust social order.[54] Like Minjung Theology, Dalit theology too refuses to be developed after the categories of Western theology. Therefore, the explicit notions of the Trinity and such are absent in it. However, Dalit's theology takes God's involvement in history through the Son as the reference for theological construction.

---

51. Ahn, *Stories of Minjung Theology*, 127–32.
52. The untouchable people according to the caste system of India.
53. RajKumar, *Dalit Theology and Dalit Liberation*, 21.
54. Hebden, *Dalit Theology and Christian Anarchism*, 34–36. Hebden states, Thus, the Missionary God emerged as a literate God, a God of the powerful who tended to the poor out his mercy and with consideration of their ignorance.

It recognizes divine solidarity with the oppressed Dalits in the act of the Cross.[55] Dalit theologians avoided making trinitarian formulations because such trinitarian theology would lead to the philosophizing of their theology and distract from the real liberation cause.[56]

God in Dalit theology is open to history and active in their history. In the process, Dalits find God in their midst, and their relationship with God becomes their new identity. John Jeyaharan from the Tamilnadu Theological Seminary writes in his reflection on the Lord's Prayer, "'Our Father', gives courage to Dalits. They boldly say that God is our Father as a protest against non-Dalits who are suppressing their identity. They have pride in claiming God as "Our Father," who is above all human fathers."[57] Dalit theologians emphasize God's continual involvement in history. Dalit liberation is God's continual act in history that "the Holy Spirit defends the poor and makes them present in history . . . . But the Spirit defends them and enables them to assert their presence and demand their share in shaping human destiny."[58] Dalit theology envisions an inclusive community where marginalized people become part of God's mission, the process of liberation.[59] Though Dalit theology does not explicitly claim social trinitarianism, Dalit theology can be the appropriate theological subject of social trinitarianism. In vision and methods, Dalit theology is very social trinitarian in nature.

CONTEXTUALIZED COLOR OF SOCIAL TRINITY

Christianity broadened its territory from its traditional cultural context to the world, and it encountered various cultures and religions.[60] Christian theologians have no other choice than to address the existence of multiple religions and have made their perspectives and attitudes toward them in the name of inclusivism, exclusivism, and pluralism.[61] Overemphasis on certain convictions by Christians did not allow a meaningful dialogue with other religions. Some Christians emphasize the exclusivity of Jesus Christ

55. Devasahayam, ed., *Frontiers of Dalit Theology*, 58–59.
56. Hebden, *Dalit Theology*, 116.
57. Jeyaharan, "A Dalit Reading of Lord's Prayer," 359.
58. Arockiadoss, "The Spirit of New Creation an Exploration into Dalit pneumatology," 443.
59. Larbeer, "Dalit Identiy—A Theological Reflection," 391.
60. Jerkins, *The Next Christendom*, 72.
61. Moe, "A Trinitarian Theology of Religions," 234.

The Trinitarian Dharma

as God's unique incarnation and the Bible as the only authority regarding God. They do not show a positive attitude toward dialogue with other religions.[62] Christians with such emphasis tend to dismiss other faiths as wrong and heretic, closing any possibility of dialogue and relationship. Social trinitarianism, which speaks of the plurality and diversity inherent in the divine life, became a new resource to deal with the challenges and problems caused by religious diversity.[63]

Other theologians tend to depart from Christian particularities and speak of God in more general terms. John Hick, who is known for the pluralistic philosophy of religion, opts for a non-trinitarian approach to establish the relationship between Christianity and the world religions. He argues that Jesus, as the incarnation of the trinitarian God, is a myth, and he seeks to bring Mohammad, Moses, Guru Nanak, and Kabir on the same bench with Jesus.[64] Hick's position is being so open to world religions that it becomes unacceptable to anyone because he speaks God apart from the particulars of manifestations in history. His pluralistic concept is not identified with any beliefs and is detached from all religious traditions.[65]

Paul Knitter, another theologian, seeking to argue from a pluralistic point of view, does not seek to equalize all religions philosophically. Instead, Knitter adopts a correlational approach to liberation.[66] Unlike Hick, Knitter does not dismiss the doctrine of the Trinity instead accepts the relational nature of God that trinitarian doctrine teaches Christianity. He argues that putting faith in the Trinity is to speak of a divine relationship to the creation.[67] Knitter brings a relational understanding of the Trinity to dialogue with other religions. For example, he argues that *sunyata*, the Buddhist concept of reality, corresponds with the Trinity. In light of the insight gained from Buddhism, he reinterprets Trinity that "God is the field—the dynamic energy field of Interbeing—within which, we live and move and have our being' (Acts 17:28). Or, from the divine perspective, there is 'one God above all things, through all things, and in all things' (Eph. 4:6)."[68]

---

62. McDermott and Netland, *A Trinitarian Theology of Religions*, 39.
63. Marmion and Nieuwenhove, *An Introduction to the Trinity*, 225.
64. Hick, *The Metaphor of God Incarnate*, 53, 111.
65. Marmion and Nieuwenhove, *An Introduction to the Trinity*, 228.
66. Marmion and Nieuwenhove, *An Introduction to the Trinity*, 229.
67. Knitter, *Without Buddha*, 32/246.
68. Knitter, *Without Buddha*, 33/246.

Even those who emphasize the particularity of Jesus in their faith consider the Trinity a model for the theology of religions.[69] Gavin D'Costa, an advocate of the trinitarian model for a dialogical theology of religions, rejects the pluralist approach but seeks a constructive dialogue that results in Christians learning about other religions while reflecting on their conviction in the process.[70] The characteristics of the Trinity, such as the plurality of persons in a single Godhead and external relation of Triune God, help Christian theology to recognize and design their relationship with the world religions.[71] The following subsections will exemplify the role that the social Trinity has played or can play in developing a relationship with world religions.

Trinity in Hindu-Buddhist Context in India

Trinity has been the topic of discussion ever since Christianity met Hinduism in India. Missionaries who brought Christianity to India were surprised to discover that Hinduism had a triune divine concept before their arrival.[72] However, those early observers did not approach Hindu leaders, considering them as their equal dialogue partners. Instead, they viewed them as heathens who happened to know some mystery of the Trinity. In the nineteenth century, more constructive studies on the Trinity from Indian perspectives emerged.[73]

Among various branches of philosophy within Hinduism, the philosophy of *Advaita* (non-duality) appealed to Christian theologians to draw relevance to trinitarian theology. *Advaita* challenged Christianity to build a relation between truth and life to overcome the gulf between God's transcendence and the reality of life. Theologians drew parallels between

---

69. Moe, "A Trinitarian Theology of Religions," 235; McDermott and Netland, *A Trinitarian Theology of Religions*, 47; Chung, *Constructing Irregular Theology*, 83. While being critical of a pluralist vision on Trinity, Chung seeks to engage Trinity with a Yin-Yang perspective.

70. D'Costa, "The Pluralist Paradigm in The Christian Theology of Religions," 223. While D'Costa is seems to be very against the idea of Trinity in Moltmann's theology, saying it compromises makes God dependent on History, in his argument of Pannikkar's theology he seeks for a relational Trinity over metaphysical one. D'Costa, *Christianity and World Religions*, 14 and 203.

71. Moe, "A Trinitarian Theology of Religions," 235.

72. Clooney, "Trinity and Hinduism," 309–10.

73. Clooney, "Trinity and Hinduism," 313, 317.

The Trinitarian Dharma

Christian concepts such as *perichoresis* and *Advaita*.[74] In Vedanta, Brahman, the Absolute, is *Saccidannanda* meaning "the Absolute as *Sati* (being), *Cit* (consciousness/ intelligence), and *Ananda* (bliss)." Though the Brahman, the absolute is thought to be without and yet able to be attributeless is described in a threefold way, which is considered parallel to Christian trinitarian doctrine.[75] Keshub Chunder Sen, the founder of the Church of New Dispensation, correlated the Trinity with *saccidananda* a combined word for *sat* (Truth), *chit* (good), and *Ananda* (bliss).[76] Brahmabandhab Upadhyay, a student of Sen, further developed the *saccidananda* concept of Trinity and defined it as the following.

> I adore the *Sat* (Being), *Cit* (Intelligence) and *Ananda* (Bliss), the highest goal . . . the Father, Begetter, the Highest Lord, unbegotten, the rootless principle of the tree of existence . . . the increate, infinite Logos or Word, supremely great, the Image of the Father, one whose form is intelligence, the giver of the highest freedom, the one who proceeds from the union of *Sat* and *Cit*, the blessed Spirit (breath), intense bliss.[77]

Though Upadhyay upholds God's homoousian classical catholic teaching in the Trinity, he disagrees that God is unknowable and unapproachable. For him, *Ananda*, or the Spirit in the traditional language, represents God's relational and personal nature. Creation is out of the flow of Spirit.[78] With *saccidananda*, Upadhyay maintains God as revealed in the Bible while bringing new insights of *advita*, to reformulate the doctrine in Indian philosophy. One thing we should note is that, for Upadhyay, the three persons of Trinity, though defined in the seemingly nonpersonal terminologies, always maintain their distinction in the godhead.[79]

Swami Abhishiktananda, a French monk who immersed himself in Hindu philosophy, is known as a pioneer of the inculturation of spirituality.[80] Abhisiktananda adopted Hindu philosophy for Christian theology, and he reconciled *Advaita* and Christianity. Trinity understood in

---

74. Collins, *Christian Inculturation in India*, 86.
75. Bob Robinson, *Christian Meeting Hindus:*, 302.
76. Clooney, "Trinity and Hinduism," 317.
77. Upadhyaya, *The Writings of Brahmabandhab Upadhyay*, 66.
78. Joseph, *An Indian Trinitarian Theology of Missio Dei*, 121.
79. Upadhyaya, *The Writings of Brahmabandhab Upadhyay*, 142.
80. "The Life of Swami Abhishiktananda," para 4.

light of *Advaita* reveals that being is essentially a koinonia of love.[81] Like Upadhyay, He also utilized the *Sat-Chit-Ananda* concept to relate to the Father-Son-Holy Spirit of the Trinity.

> [T]hat Being, *sat*, opens itself at its very source to give birth eternally to the Son, and in him to countless creatures, each of which in its own way will forever manifest and celebrate the infinite love and mercy of God; that being is essentially "being-with," communion, *koinonia*, the free gift of the self and the mutual communication of love; that self-awareness, *cit*, only comes to be when there is mutual giving and receiving, for the I only awakes to itself in a Thou; that the supreme and ultimate felicity, *ānanda*, is fullness and perfect fulfillment, only because it is the fruit of love, for being is love.[82]

Though Hindu philosophy is metaphysical in characteristics like Hellenistic philosophy upon which Western Christian theology was developed, both Upadhyay and Abhishiktananda have expounded the distinction of their theology from Vedanta to show God as *saccidananda* is a relational Triune God.[83] Mainly, Abhishiktananda reflects what we find in social trinitarianism that in the unity of God, the particularity of Persons is not reduced. As he says, "Difference in identity is the proper subsistence of the inner being of the Trinity. Not difference, nor identity exclusively, but difference in identity, best describes (conceptually) the way in which the Persons are united together and are distinct in their particular functions in the Divine Self-Awareness."[84]

Raimundo Panikkar, born in a multi-religious, Catholic, and Hindu family, brings his multiple backgrounds and utilizes them in his theological exploration. He is one of the first theologians who related the Trinity to other religions.[85] For Panikkar, the Trinity is not limited to Christianity, but it is common to other religions such as Buddhism, Hinduism, and Abrahamic religions. He argues that the spirituality of the word in Abrahamic faiths, the Nirvana experience of Buddhism, and the "Hindu

---

81. Oldmeadow, *A Christian Pilgrimage in India*, 141.

82. Swami Abhishiktananda, *Saccidananda*, 176, quoted in Oldmeadow, *A Christian Pilgrimage in India*, 141.

83. Joseph, *An Indian Trinitarian Theology*, 183.

84. Wayne. "Abhishiktananda's Contemplative Theology," quoted in Oldmeadow, *A Christian Pilgrimage in India*, 143.

85. Kärkkäinen, *The Trinity*, 336–37.

The Trinitarian Dharma

advaitic experience of the non-duality of self and the Absolute," all are related to the Trinity.[86]

Similar to Abhishiktananda, Panikkar brings *Advaita* to renounce dualism and reformulate the Trinity. He writes, "*Advaita* also tries to avoid dualism. It does not renounce making sense of things but recognizes that reality is not split asunder into two irreconcilable fields of good and evil, Being and Non-being, subject, and object, rational and irrational, spiritual and material, or the like."[87] Panikkar defines reality with *Advaita* and Trinity that it is neither One nor Many because it is non-dual *Advaita* and trinitarian.[88] For Panikkar, the Trinity is the category to understand reality, and the reality is trinitarian. What Panikkar calls the radical Trinity, that immanent Trinity is limited because it limits God's presence in creation. Here for Panikkar, the *advaitic* intuition comes to rescue the immanent Trinity by making the Trinity experience in history while rescuing God from the historical trap with its non-linear understanding of history and time.[89]

Without even speaking in the language of social trinitarianism, Panikkar advocates the trinitarian doctrine that social trinitarianism is seeking to achieve. Panikkar rejects the idea of the Trinity as three modes of being of a single substance of God and, at the same time, three substances in oneness. For him, the idea of a divine essence is replaced with a relationship. He says, "Ultimate reality is neither One (Being, or anything real) with three modes nor Three (substances, beings) within a single abstract oneness—*neti*. The Trinity is a pure relationship, and here lies the great challenge and the profound transformation. If the Divine were a substance, we would have three Gods; if the Divine is the infinite relationship, this relationship also enters all creatures and Man in a special way."[90] Many theologians can always be suspicious of Panikkar's trinitarian vision, which he models to a pluralistic form. Jesus is the living manifestation of the divine, and confessing Jesus as one's living manifestation of God does not lead to rejecting other manifestations of the divine in other religious traditions. Panikkar does not argue that all manifestations of God, Krishna, Buddha, Jesus, and many others in world religions are the same, but he claims that they importantly function as the mediator

---

86. Hall, "Radicalizing the Trinity," 52.
87. Panikkar, *The Rhythm of Being*, 223.
88. Panikkar, *The Rhythm of Being*, 227.
89. Panikkar, *The Rhythm of Being*, 262.
90. Panikkar, *The Rhythm of Being*, 225.

between divine and human beings.⁹¹ Kärkkäinen argues that Panikkar holds on to Traditional Christian trinitarian ideas and constructs pluralistic trinitarianism, divorcing it from salvation history.⁹² However, I claim that even if one sticks to the trinitarianism derived from salvation history, he/she doesn't need to create a wall that prevents any interreligious dialogue. This research notes that Panikkar attempts to provide a common language, making the interreligious dialogue possible.⁹³ If our only intention is to keep the difference, our mandate to love others is superficial. Along with Panikkar, I argue that interfaith dialogue is the trinitarian praxis of loving our neighbors. Panikkar writes, "God is the unique locus where my selfhood and my neighbor coincide, consequently the one place that enables me to love him as he loves his own self without any attempt at molding him."⁹⁴

Another major criticism against these attempts at the Sanskritization (Hindu inculturation) of Christian theology by Upadhyay, Abhishiktananda, and Panikkar is Hindu (Sanskrit) philosophical ideas in theology undermine the liberation voices of the Dalits and indigenous people. For them, the root of their suffering is caused by the caste system rooted in Hindu traditions.⁹⁵ The trinitarian relationality can be imported into this Indian indigenized theology to critique elite Hindus' hegemony and empower the Dalits and indigenous people.⁹⁶ My conclusion is that social trinitarianism is in play even in the indigenization of Christianity in India. Further utilization of trinitarian social concepts strengthens the mission of indigenization as well as liberation.

Trinity Encounters Neo-Confucianism in East Asia

In East Asia, Confucianism is the cultural milieu in which Christian theology has no other option but to engage.⁹⁷ Though East Asians profess various religious affiliations, it is argued that they do not cease to be Confucians. Therefore, "Doing East Asian theology necessarily involves the

---

91. Panikkar, *The Rhythm of Being*, 364.
92. Kärkkäinen, *The Trinity*, 343.
93. Panikkar, *The Interreligious Dialogue*, 46.
94. Panikkar, *The Interreligious Dialogue*, 49.
95. Kuruvila, "The Incarnation and the Cross," 220–23.
96. Joseph, *An Indian Trinitarian Theology*, 190.
97. A. C. C. Lee, "Contextual Theology in Asia," 519–20.

The Trinitarian Dharma

study of Confucianism as a theological task."[98] Jung Young Lee is the pioneer of theology from the perspective of Confucianism, who was joined by Hyeup Young Kim and others.

Jung Young Lee developed the theology of change as an alternative to Western theology based on a static and substantial ontology of Greek philosophy.[99] Like what Panikkar attempted with *Advaita,* Lee brought the *yin-yang* concept to overcome Western theology's dualism. Lee writes, "The *yin-yang* is not only a symbol of complementary dualism but also of non-dualism. The coexistence of dualism and non-dualism in yin-yang symbolic thinking provides a hermeneutic advantage in interpreting the trinitarian symbol of the divine nature."[100] In Jung Young Lee's theology, *yin-yang* serves as a symbol for the Trinity and a concept to understand various trinitarian dynamics and relationships. For example, the dual nature of the Son is understood in the *yin-yang* concept "divinity and humanity, resurrection and death, pain and love, or lordship and servanthood." At the same time, Lee symbolizes the Spirit as *yin* as the feminine member and the Father as the *yang,* as the masculine member.[101] Just like, Panikkar used the trinitarian concept to understand the universal reality as well as other religious systems, Jung Young Lee uses the *yin-yang* concept not only to formulate trinitarian theology but also as a key to understanding the reality of all religious and social aspects of life as well as the cosmos. He writes, "The *yin-yang* symbolic thinking is not simply representative of East Asian thought but also is a key to understanding distinctive characteristics of an East Asian approach to reality."[102] *Yin and yang* stand for opposite but united, a relative, relational, and complementary characteristic that is both/and way of thinking and manifestation of change.[103]

> Since *yin* and *yang* are relational symbols, yin cannot exist without yang or yang without yin. Moreover, yin and yang are related to each other because they include each other. This inclusiveness can be simply symbolized by the proposition 'in'. . . . The Father and the Son are one in their inness, but also at the same time, they

---

98. Kim, *A Theology of Dao,* 59.

99. Chung, "The Asian Pursuit of Trinitarian Theology in a Multireligious Context," 148. Lee, *The Trinity in Asian Perspective,* 62.

100. J. Y. Lee, *The Trinity in Asian Perspective,* 18.

101. J. Y. Lee, *The Trinity in Asian Perspective,* 19.

102. J. Y. Lee, *The Trinity in Asian Perspective,* 22.

103. J. Y. Lee, *The Trinity in Asian Perspective,* 22–32, 53.

are three because 'in' represents the Spirit, the inner connecting principle which cannot exist by itself. In the inclusive relationship, two relational symbols such as *yin* and *yang* are trinitarian because of 'in,' which not only unites them but also completes them.[104]

Lee brings the yin-yang relationship to revise Rahner's rule because Rahner's formula does not retain the difference between the economic and immanent Trinity. Instead, he says, "The immanent Trinity is *in* the economic Trinity, and the economic Trinity is *in* the immanent Trinity. This rule will help us retain their distinctiveness as well as their unity."[105] Lee makes Jesus the key to understanding the Trinity that He is in between the Father and the Spirit as a connecting principle. *Yin-yang* explains death and resurrection, and redemption is the act of change.[106] As the earth's mother, the Spirit is the immanence of the Trinity that opens the world, and the Father as the masculine figure is the creative and moral principle of all. All these make up a trinitarian family where hierarchy and coequality coexist between three persons.[107] Lee states, "the trinitarian structure is fundamental to the human community and is the primordial unit of life. The divine Trinity can then serve as the archetype of the human family and the basic unit of all things in the world."[108] Though his theology is more like an alternative to Western metaphysics, Jung Young Lee concludes that the Trinity is the building block of life and society. For him, Trinity is even more relevant for a pluralistic society where the difference is part of a relationship while retaining their identity.[109] Though Lee seeks to formulate trinitarian theology in Confucian terms after the yin-yang concept, his theology resonates with what social Trinitarians stand for. The social relevance of Trinity, and Trinity as a union of divine community when each person does not cease to exist.[110] Though Lee refuses to use the term persons in Trinity, his articulation is not a non-personal abstract concept. As he writes, "In the trinitarian principle, the distinction among the three is essential. The father is the father because he is different from the Son

---

104. J. Y. Lee, *The Trinity in Asian Perspective*, 58.
105. J. Y. Lee, *The Trinity in Asian Perspective*, 68.
106. J. Y. Lee, *The Trinity in Asian Perspective*, 77–90; Wessels, *Images of Jesus*, 156.
107. J. Y. Lee, *The Trinity in Asian Perspective*, 123, 158.
108. J. Y. Lee, *The Trinity in Asian Perspective*, 150.
109. J. Y. Lee, *The Trinity in Asian Perspective*, 200–201.
110. Kärkkäinen, *Trinity*, 321. Kärkkäinen observes that yin-yang thinking comes close to Zizioulas' idea of communion as the primary manner of existence over substance.

and the Spirit. The Son is the son because he is different from the Father and the Spirit. Moreover, the Spirit is different from the others, because she is neither the Son nor the Father. When their differences are denied, they lose their identity as a member of the Trinity."[111]

Heup Young Kim follows Jung Young Lee's line and uses the Daoist philosophy for constructing theology. Kim affirms that Lee's *yang* in *yin* and *yin* in *yang* concept is in line with Leonardo Boff's affirmation of perichoresis, while it also promotes the ontology of relationship spoken by Zizioulas.[112] Paul S. Chung, who is cautious of reformulating the Trinity in Daoism like Lee, argues that Dao serves as God's trinitarian self-communication to history.[113]

The Communitarian Reformulation of Trinity in Africa

Theology in Africa cannot but consider the African religious context to which Christianity has come into tension. African inculturation theology employs the common intellectual crystallizing point for all the African people.[114] African trinitarian reflections utilize social analogies such as community concepts, and various African cultural features provide the ground for Christian interpretation of the Trinity in the African context.[115] Among African theologians who have attempted to formulate trinitarian theology in African terms are A. O. Obgonnaya and Charles Nyamiti.

Ogbonnaya is a Methodist theologian from Nigeria who has given an African interpretation of the Trinity from the communal nature of African life. He draws inspiration from Tertullian's theology in which even monarchy is perceived as communal and that monarchy belongs to all members of the Trinity, not only the Father.[116] For Ogbonnaya, the traditional African understanding of community involves human beings, ancestors, and spirits across time and space. Such a relationship among the members of the community is permanent and inescapable in Africa. Thereby, he constructs the doctrine of God after the concept of community because personal interconnection within the community is the African

---

111. J. Y. Lee, *The Trinity in Asian Perspective*, 201.
112. Kim, *A Theology of Dao*, 71.
113. Chung, *Constructing Irregular Theology*, 84, 98.
114. Owino Kombo, *The Doctrine of God in African Christian Thought*, 7.
115. Kärkkäinen, *Trinity*, 356–57.
116. Kärkkäinen, "Trinity, Triune God," 912.

key to understanding God.[117] In the African context, the community is more than a gathering of people, rather it is an ontological relatedness bound in the past and the future. Historical events and future anticipations are commonly shared.[118] Ogbonnaya shuns the terms monotheism and polytheism and crafts a category as "divine as a community," emphasizing God's relationality and ontological equality.[119] In his own words:

> The concept of the One is present in African religions but so also is the concept of the many . . . The concept of the Divine as a community actually does more justice to African conceptions of God. For this, we need another term, a word like communotheism, a community of gods. Community in the African sense will reflect better the affirmation of both the one and the Many than the categories of monotheism and polytheism. The noun communotheism communicates the idea that Divinity is communal.[120]

Ogbonnaya argues that Tertullian's theology reflects the African concept of "divine as community one," emphasizing ontological equality, and personal distinctiveness through functional subordination is present. He writes, "Tertullian's concepts of Divinity hold in dynamic interplay the idea of ontological equality, personal distinction, and functional temporal subordination."[121] Because there is a hierarchy in the African concept, Ogbonnaya employs such ideas to argue for functional subordinationism.[122]

Ogbonnaya employs the community concept of Africa to formulate the Trinity as a divine community that resonates with the social trinitarianism of Boff, and Moltmann, albeit Ogbonnaya's work struggles to undo the confusion of subordinationism. His argument that God's unity does not contradict God's socially oriented community speaks the social trinitarian language. Ogbonnaya's emphasis on interconnectedness as a vital characteristic of the divine community strengthens God's social trinitarian argument.

---

117. Birtus, *Community and Trinity in Africa*, ebook.

118. Manganyi and Buitendag, "A Critical Analysis on African Traditional Religion and the Trinity," 5.

119. Manganyi and Buitendag, "African Traditional Religion and Trinity," 6.

120. Ogbonnaya, *On Communitarian Divinity*, 27–28.

121. Ogbonnaya, *On Communitarian Divinity*, xii.

122. Kärkkäinen, *Trinity*, 378. Argues that Ogbonnaya's way of relating diversity in the Trinity to African culture speaks more of the hierarchy rather than equality.

The Trinitarian Dharma

Nyamiti, a Tanzanian Catholic theologian, intends to make a theology for the masses of Africa, leading the traditional way of life. He believes that not doing theology in the African way is the opposite of pastoral concern and rejects the theological attempts that neglect African cultures.[123] In his theology, Nyamiti is initiating a dialogue between traditional Christianity and African concepts of God. He believes that "God reveals himself to all people through their conscience and religious experiences, through creation, and even through supernatural revelation in faith."[124] When Christianity seeks to grow in Africa, it cannot avoid taking the African color and adopting the African way of thinking in the process. As Nyamiti writes, "As Christianity surpasses the African religions, one will have to search in the Christian doctrine for the Christianized African religious and moral doctrines' missing elements. The missing elements should then be organically integrated into African theology."[125] The link between Christianity and African tradition is built on the African concept of the relationship between living relatives and those already dead.[126] Nyamiti explains the trinitarian relationship as follows, "The Father is the Ancestor of the Son, the Son is the Descendant of the Father. These two persons live their ancestral kinship through the Spirit whom they mutually communicate to as their ancestral Oblation and Eucharist. The Spirit is reciprocally donated not only as a token of their mutual love as a Gift but also on behalf of the homage to their reciprocal holiness and gratitude for their beneficence to each other."[127]

For Nyamiti, Christ stands as the brother ancestor whose ancestorship is derived from his incarnation or divine-human nature. There are two established relationships, one is concerning people and the other is the relationship within Trinity.[128] These relationships are interconnected in Christ. Nayamiti argues that "Christ is our brother-Ancestor," who has become "trinitarian ancestral communication" toward the creation through the incarnation.[129] Similar to what Ogbonnaya speaks of, in Nyamiti's

---

123. Nyamiti, "The Theological Value of African Tradition," 103–4.

124. Nyamiti, *African Tradition and the Christian God*, 4.

125. Nyamiti, *Way to Christian Theology for Africa*, 55; Parrat, *Reinventing Christianity*, 39.

126. Manganyi, and Buitendag, "A critical analysis on African Traditional Religion and the Trinity," 7.

127. Nyamiti, "African Christologies Today," 11.

128. Nnamani, *The Paradox of a Suffering God*, 342–45.

129. Nyamiti, "African Christologies Today," 12.

theology, the Trinity is a community. Nyamiti emphasizes the significance of the trinitarian community for us. "Christ functions ancestrally towards us through the Holy Spirit under the salvific mission he received from the Father. Nyamiti looks to integrate the ideas of liberation with the inculturation that he is advocating so that his theology becomes sociologically relevant in the present history.[130] Though Nyamiti approached trinitarian theology from an African perspective, his emphasis on the Trinity's ancestral community shares many aspects of the social Trinity. As the community of ancestors, the Trinity matches with the perichoretic relationship of divine life for divine unity. The relationship between the divine community and human society through the brother ancestor Jesus Christ resonates with trinitarian involvement in the social Trinity history.

The relational and openness of the Trinity can function as a model for interfaith dialogue. The observation shows the interaction of trinitarian theology with various contextual symbols like *Advaita* of India, *Yin-yang* of East Asia, and Ancestor worship and community concept in the African context. Since Social trinitarianism seeks to speak in human relational terms, one can pair trinitarian relationships and community with contextual symbols that Nepali *dharma* carries. Such paring would initiate an interchange of ideas between the context and the theology. It will be easy to communicate the Christian message of God's love, justice, and hope to the context. At the same time, the contextual symbol can bring a newer meaning and significance to the trinitarian understanding of God.

TOWARDS THE IMPLICATION FOR A CONTEXTUAL THEOLOGY

This chapter has dealt with the various possibilities of integrating social trinitarianism in contextual theologies, where social and cultural elements come to play a vital role in making Christian theology. Firstly, by observing liberation theologies, though we find that not all liberation theologies have utilized social trinitarianism, social trinitarianism does not contradict any of these liberation theologies. Instead, social trinitarianism provides a language to express social justice issues. The avoidance of liberation theologies such as Minjung theology and Dalit theology is because of the avoidance of classical trinitarianism, which is rigid in its attitude toward making the social experience a theological subject. Social Trinity

---

130. Nyamiti, "African Christologies Today," 17.

The Trinitarian Dharma

provides a platform to develop a theology that uses the context's social issues in theological construction. Secondly, from the observation of social trinitarian elements in various contextual theology, it is argued that social trinitarianism is an appropriate platform for interreligious dialogue. Social trinitarianism advocates trinitarian God's openness toward the world and opens itself to it. For this research, the social Trinity provides the best for all the needs of both the cultural as well as the social issues. The following six implications have been drawn from paring social Trinity with liberation theologies and contextual theologies.

First, God's trinitarian community provides a basis for the human community, especially particularly the Church. The church is a community called to fulfill God's mission to reflect the trinitarian communion of love and be involved in social transformation. Trinity encourages a social order, a communitarian social order where all individual rights of the persons are respected and preserved.[131] Second, participation in God's liberating work is the prime task of the church. Trinity is not the possession of the church rather it is the task of the church.[132] Third, the trinitarian God calls for a mutual relationship in human beings. As a result, Christian theology can get rid of the oppressive symbols associated with the traditional understanding of God. Trinitarian features such as self-giving love, equality, and infinite generosity are there to be imitated by societies.[133] Fourth, the Trinity's communitarian concept places God in history and actively participates in human suffering and liberation. Trinity is a criticism against all injustices and suffering.[134] Fifth, social trinitarianism stands as a bridge to overcome Western dualism making Christianity relatable to non-Western thoughts. Trinitarian life, especially, opens up for intercultural friendship. Trinitarian communion and fellowship are extended to the believers and ultimately to all humanity.[135] Sixth, the openness of the trinitarian God can be made a platform for interreligious dialogue. The language of relationship and community can be developed into a common understanding between Christianity and other religions.

---

131. Collin, *Father, Son and Holy Spirit*, 25.
132. Sarot, "Trinity and Church," 33.
133. Deetlefs, "Political Implications of the Trinity: Two Approaches," para 3.
134. Boff, *Trinity and Society*, 13.
135. Ilo, "Crosscurrents in African Christianity," 192.

SUMMARY

This chapter has dealt with various social trinitarian features and examined different liberation theologies to determine social trinitarianism's possible role in different contexts. Various contextual theologies that brought contextual concepts into theological reflections were also studied to see their similarities with the social Trinity and potential collaboration.

There is a considerable possibility of making social trinitarian language to give voices to various social issues. Though many liberation theologies have not adopted social trinitarian language to formulate their theological voice for the social problems of the relative context, this chapter has demonstrated that social trinitarianism does not obstruct liberation theology. Somewhat, social trinitarianism can be modeled to speak about various social concerns. The social Trinity can be paired with the various indigenous depictions of Christian theology. A dialogue between the Hindu interpretation of Christian theology is that the social Trinity seems productive while an interpretation of the Trinity in the Yin-Yang concept can enlighten God's perichoretic relationship. As a divine community of social trinitarianism, the Trinity can be a platform to build a bridge between traditional African veneration of ancestors and Christianity. It testifies to a clear possibility that the social Trinity can be paired with Nepali *dharma*, which is the Nepali community's foundation.

7

Dharma and the Social Trinity

A Transformative Encounter

WE KNOW THAT NEPALI *dharma* and social trinitarianism do not have equivalent concepts and frameworks to conduct a straightforward dialogue. Social Trinity is a doctrine that attempts to be relevant for a believer and the church's practical life, whereas *dharma* is anything but a doctrine.[1] It is a practical living of life in Nepali society, not about Nepali people's beliefs.[2] Though it is peculiar to make a head-to-head comparison and analysis between *dharma* and social trinitarianism, the assumption is that both can be complementary and help Nepali Christianity take part in society. Social trinitarian doctrine can bring ethical, spiritual, and political implications[3] to the dialogue, while Nepali *dharma* can bring the Nepali social context's relational framework to make this conversation possible. The import of social trinitarianism can add Christian meaning to the practice of *dharma* for Nepali Christians.

To add a reference to the task of this chapter, I would like to bring Hans-Georg Gadamer's model of the "fusion of horizons." "The comparison and analysis" are a hermeneutical task where two different horizons are in the process of fusion of horizon. Social trinitarianism represents the

---

1. Gibson, *Suffering and Hope*, 51.

2. Sharma, "Theological Education in Nepal," 194. Sharma writes, "According to these traditions, all religious rituals and practices do not need to be comprehended; they need to be simply obeyed and performed."

3. Scoff, "Practicing the Trinity in the Local Church," 439.

Dharma and the Social Trinity

horizon of the Nepali church, which is fused to the historical horizon of Nepali *dharma*. However, this hermeneutical task is not completed by assimilating the Nepali church into the past or Nepali *dharma*, but the past is overhauled by the new horizon of the social Trinity through its ethical and political participation in *dharma*.[4] This thesis brings *dharma* and social Trinity to bridge the distance between Christianity and Nepali society by assisting the Nepali church to overcome its alienation.[5]

This chapter utilizes the synthetic model of contextual theology proposed in the research methodology to facilitate the fusion of *dharma* and Trinity into a new horizon of Nepali Christian theology. The synthetic model combines various contextual models such as translation, anthropological, and praxis models. Therefore, this chapter incorporates the issue of inculturation as well as praxis. Since the synthetic model gives equal value to the culture of the context and the tradition, here *dharma* and social Trinity are in two spectra where they will be put in the conversation for a mutual transformation of both sides. Nepali *dharma* enhances the understanding of the Trinity for Christianity in Nepal, while *dharma* is challenged by mutuality and egalitarianism of the social Trinity.[6]

The conversation between Nepali *dharma* and social trinitarianism happens on the following four fronts. First, the practical religiosity of Nepali *dharma* and praxis of Social trinitarianism are paired together to initiate a dialogue between Nepali culture and Christianity. Secondly, *dharma* and social trinitarianism can be used as a foundation for Nepali indigenous theology, contributing to Nepali society. Thirdly, the Nepali church can be modeled after Nepali *dharma* giving Nepali color while making the social Trinity as the divine community as its underlying foundation. Lastly, Nepali Christians can face social problems as the trinitarian task and fulfillment of Nepali *dharma*.

NEPALI CHRISTIAN *DHARMA* AND ITS PRAXIS

Though the study of religion seeks to contemplate a higher reality, such as God, eternal life, salvation, or life after death, the study of Nepali religion, which is *dharma*, diverts the question to its practicality. This is not to say that it rejects the discussion on God and eternal life, but such is not the question of religious quest in Nepal. While doing his ethnographic study

---

4. Gadamer, *Truth and Method*, 305–6.
5. Gadamer, *Truth and Method*, 310.
6. Bevans, *Models of Contextual Theology*, 91.

The Trinitarian Dharma

on *dharma* among the *Newar* people of Bharkapur, a city within the Kathmandu valley, Gregory Price Grieve discovers that ordinary Nepali people can only answer about religion by saying what they do. As he states, "While the discipline of religious studies tends to interpret religious phenomena as reflections of an unseen reality—from ideology to the sacred, in Bhaktapur *dharma* is used to describe world-generating acts. That is, rather than asking the elite question 'what is religion,' people in Bhaktapur tend to ask the more pragmatic question of 'what can religion do.'"[7] Forcing the Nepali religion to be defined into theological terms diverts the discussion to scriptural Hinduism, which is limited in academic literature, not so much in the concept of ordinary people's *dharma*. Grieve calls for serious consideration of "prosaic religious practices," or simply the *dharma* of ordinary people present in Nepali people's contemporary life.[8]

People refer to both this life and the next to come as a reason for their dharmic action. People give alms and serve others. People seek to earn their merits of *dharma* by doing good deeds to others. Though there is an association of *dharma* to the after-life concept, it is never divorced from its relationship with the present life, here and now. Even the hope of after-life makes Nepali people practical about their *dharma*.[9] The various beliefs on karma, good actions of the present life, salvation, or hopes of the future make them active in their current lives and society. *Karma's* concept is that good works of this life ensure better for the coming life, while the desire for salvation makes them even more concerned about their present life activities.[10]

Rituals are the most favored act of *dharma* by Nepali people because they can associate with their deity while being practical in their social relationships. Though rituals are the demand of *dharma*, they are/supposed to be the intentional act of the performer. Rituals may contain meaning, but the meaning is not the focus, but the change that these rituals deliver is always highlighted.[11] For example, rituals of marriage ceremonies do contain some specific meaning, but the focus is always put on the consequence of the ritual that after the rituals, two are a married couple. The meanings behind the rituals are not given consideration. Thereby, Nepali

---

7. Grieve, *Retheorizing Religion in Nepal*, 136.
8. Grieve, *Retheorizing Religion in Nepal*, 137.
9. Kunwar, "Paganism and Spiritism," 7–8.
10. Grieve, *Retheorizing Religion in Nepal*, 137.
11. Michaels, *Homo Ritualis*, 57.

Dharma and the Social Trinity

dharma is more about practicality and action than theory and teachings. Rituals regarding the funeral of dead parents are a significant part of Nepali *dharma*. It is the *dharma* of the living offspring to fulfill the ritual for the dead.[12] The belief in the good settlement of the spirit of the dead is behind these funeral rituals. These rituals are very practical oriented in that "the series of rituals ease the transition for survivors and symbolize the powerful connection between individuals and families, the living and the dead, the past and the present."[13]

Through rituals and their performance, the sacred and divine are interconnected, and simple non-sacred items are turned into something sacred. Michael points out how rituals turn ordinary water, *pani* into sacred water, *jala*.[14] The rituals and ceremonies turn ordinary stone-carved images into gods. With further rituals and ceremonies offered to these stone gods, they gain their pragmatic value and become effective in Nepali people's day-to-day lives.[15] The gap between the ordinary and the sacred or divine is bridged with *dharma* rituals in Nepali society. As shown in figure 1, *dharma*, action as religiosity is the departure point that searches for social significance and theology. However, developing the concept of God as the result of religious action is not emphasized in *dharma*. Therefore, *dharma* mostly revolves around religiosity, as the action of *dharma* and its social significance.

---

12. Michaels, *Homo Ritualis*, 95.

13. Acharya, "From Spirit to Ancestor," para 3.

14. Michaels, *Homo Ritualis*, 57. *Pani* is the Nepali word for water, and *jala* is the Sanskrit word, which is mostly used in religious occasions.

15. Grieve, *Retheorizing Religion in Nepal*, 137.

The Trinitarian Dharma

Figure 2—Relationship of Action to Theology in *Dharma*

Unlike *dharma*, trinitarian theology deals mostly with theoretical issues. The practical aspect of trinitarianism is always secondary in comparison to its theory. However, one of the distinguishing features of social trinitarianism is that it seeks to be relevant to human society. As Miroslav Volf says, "trinitarian concepts such as a person, relation, or *perichoresis* can be applied to the human community only . . ."[16] The social Trinity is based on the concept of God's involvement in history, which is human society. Therefore, it is considered that it is easily tied up with the praxis of the faith.[17] In the social Trinity, orthopraxis, the right practice, or right acts in response to God's life with us, is inseparably associated with orthodoxy, the right knowledge on the subject of God. Therefore, the trinitarian praxis always corresponds to the belief while advocating the practicality of such belief.[18] Unlike Nepali *dharma*, where actions are not always bound to the content of the belief behind such actions, a person's trinitarian actions can never be divorced from the scope of belief in God as a relational Trinity. Instead, the actions are a result of the belief.

As demonstrated in chapter 5, the social Trinity is an open and inviting system that God himself desires to participate in the creation's history. In other words, the praxis of the social Trinity springs out of the divine desire to be involved in the lives of his creation. Humans become part of

---

16. Volf, "Trinity is Our Social Program," 405.
17. Lacugna, *God for Us*, 381.
18. Lacugna, *God for Us*, 383.

Dharma and the Social Trinity

trinitarian involvement in society.[19] Unlike in Nepali *dharma*, the relationship is extended from human action to the concept of the divine, the social Trinity brings God into the realm of human action. For the one practicing *dharma*, because their *dharma* responsibility has a societal implication, the action is not linked with the divine subject. In contrast, trinitarian praxis reaches toward both directions to the world for action and to the Trinity God for meaning and significance of the praxis in the society. In social trinitarianism, a person receives inspiration and direction for the praxis from his/her trinitarian relationship.[20]

Figure 3—Flow of Theology and Praxis in Social Trinity

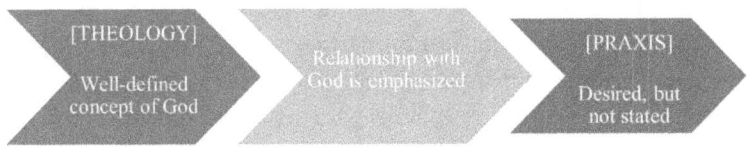

The church is another dimension with which the social Trinity communicates its praxis in society. Church called and identified by the trinitarian God, is in the world for the trinitarian purpose. The main action of the church, according to Moltmann, is to hold to the presence of Christ in the poor, weak, and oppressed of this world.[21] There is a special place for the world in the social Trinity, and the trinitarian universal plan for the whole creation is extended to the world by the church and people who confess their relationship to the Trinity.[22] Trinitarian plan for the world and its praxis is no other than God's work in the history of Jesus Christ. The social Trinity states that God's works in history are not abstract or metaphysical.[23] Therefore, the Trinity is significant for people's daily experience, their struggle, and living in the world and the Trinity's efforts to build a more human form of society, with the sacrifices and involvement in society.[24] Same

---

19. McDougall, "Trinitarian Praxis?," 187.
20. Boff, *Trinity and Society*, 149.
21. Moltmann, *History and the Triune Go*, 121–22.
22. Moltmann, *History and the Triune God*, 87, 114
23. Boff, *Trinity and Society*, 32.
24. Boff, *Trinity and Society*, 157.

The Trinitarian Dharma

way, the trinitarian relationship becomes a guideline for praxis for human beings they are called to take part in the transpersonal and structural relationship. Though human life in the Trinity is spoken in an individualistic term, the social Trinity stands against such personalized spirituality. It calls for a participatory relationship in the world.[25]

Though praxis is essential in social trinitarianism, it mostly invokes participation in society rather than providing a practical guideline for human living as we find in Nepali *dharma*. Ted Peters writes that though the Trinity cannot be translated into human society, the trinitarian vision of God's kingdom inspires us to seek the transformation of society.[26] Figure 2 illustrates the relationship between the social Trinity and praxis. Social Trinity is a theology that inspires or invokes social participation rather than giving straightforward direction regarding the Christian life.[27] As LaCugna writes, "The practical nature of the doctrine of the Trinity does not mean it is a pragmatic principle that furnishes an easy solution to war and violence, or yields the blueprint for a catechetical program, or settles vexing disagreements over the church's public prayer. Rather, the theoretical framework of trinitarian theology yields a wisdom, a discernment, a guide for seeing the two hands of God at work in our salvation."[28] Each step of human life in society can be inspired by the social Trinity, but it still lacks the concreteness of practicality we find in the Nepali *dharma*.

While putting Nepali *dharma* and social Trinity side by side, we can see that both emphasize the practicality one way or the other. Nepali *dharma* speaks of religious practicality and attempts to create meaning of the divine and such through participation. *Dharma*'s focus lies in its usefulness and its significance in society, which may or may not convey the transcendent meaning behind it. Social Trinity is theology in a Western fashion, which revolves around a theory though it emphasizes and calls for praxis in the society. However, trinitarian praxis is limited to the call for participation, but the specific practical guideline is found in the Nepali *dharma* to derive meaning from it. Trinitarian praxis finds its significance in the trinitarian meaning of such participation. The practical religiosity of Nepali *dharma* enjoys its presence and importance in society and

---

25. Boff, *Trinity and Society*, 157
26. Ted Peters, *God as Trinity*, 184.
27. McDougall, *Pilgrimage of Love*, 138.
28. Lacugna, *God for Us*, 379.

Dharma and the Social Trinity

aspects of having theological meaning in it. Therefore, trinitarian praxis is a theory that expects social participation.

In the Nepali context of *dharma*, the social Trinity lacks the concreteness of practicality, and for Nepali people, it becomes vague and insignificant to society. Likewise, *dharma* from the Christian perspective lacks the definite meaning of their religious participation called *dharma*. Giving Nepali Christians only the theory of the social Trinity keeps them at bay in Nepali society. Since this research is constructive work to help Nepali Christians be involved in Nepali society, rather than concluding the similarities and differences between trinitarian praxis and *dharma*, it aims to bring these two together.

The possible coalition of *dharma* and the social Trinity is demonstrated in Figure 4. *Dharma* complements the social Trinity to call for the praxis with the practicality that is significant in society. By incorporating *dharma* as a part of the social Trinity for the context of Nepal, Nepali Christianity can find a way to be part of a larger Nepali society. Social Trinity contextualized in Nepal can make *dharma* its theological subject. *Dharma* as a present history of Nepali society can be made part of the Trinity of Nepali context.

Figure 4—Cooperation between *Dharma* and Social Trinity in the Context of Nepal

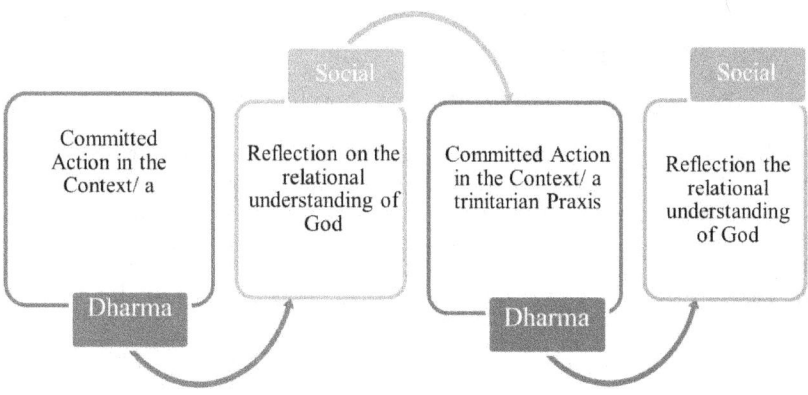

The Trinitarian Dharma

COMMUNITY-ORIENTED NEPALI CHRISTIAN *DHARMA*

The term social Trinity points out the eternal community of three persons and has implications for human societies. At the same time, Nepali *dharma* has a profound relationship with the community, and it is unimaginable to envision *dharma* outside of its community. Observing the concepts of community in *dharma* and social Trinity provides the possible alliance between these two.

With its rituals and requirements, *dharma* binds people in a community and is committed to the welfare of all members of society. When people are gathered for ceremonies such as a funeral and wedding, they are not just for ritual sake but also to take care of the immediate family's needs. People come forward as a community to assist, and they consider it their social *dharma*.[29] Ritual ceremonies consist of personal and community dimensions one is fulfilling his/her *dharma* by following the rituals of funerals, weddings, and more. At the same time, it includes the whole community to function and complete.[30] In some communities in Nepal, the ceremonies are done collectively to minimize the cost.[31] In some Nepali people groups, the community plays an even greater role in initiating and completing the so-called private aspect of one's life. A community decides whom one can or cannot marry. Their own *dharma* outlines such guidelines. The community can also pronounce punishments in case of going against the *dharma*.[32] In other words, while *dharma* forms a community, it is the community that ensures the fulfillment of *dharma*. Nepali people's personal, social, and religious life is bound by *dharma* in a community.

---

29. Ranjeet, "At the Crossroads of Religions," 84f. being lived in United States for years, Bidya Ranjeet narrates her own experiences of two funerals that she had to experience in weeks apart. One is of her mother in Nepal, and other is of her brother in States. She explains how she missed the Nepali community in back home despite her effort to replicate the rituals of Nepali funeral during she was mourning for her brother in the United States.

30. Regmi, *Dimensions of Nepali Society*, 84. Regmi shows how a wedding ceremony which is the fulfillment of familial *dharma* by a person includes the community called *janti*.

31. Regmi, *Dimensions of Nepali Society*, 94.

32. Gautam and Thapa-Magar, *Tribal Ethnography of Nepal*, Vol. 2, 1–11. For example, the Ethnography of *Limbu* people group, who mostly live in Eastern mountainous reason of Nepal, has customs that dictate the arrange marriage done by the community. Community also can excommunicate some in case they do not follow the *dharma* of their community.

Dharma and the Social Trinity

Nepal is a land of various people groups who have different languages and *dharmas*. Some people's *dharma* is more inclined to Hindu traditions, while others show Buddhist characters. In all communities, their *dharma* is the key to their identity and social functions. The main distinguishing characteristic of these different people groups is their *dharma*.[33] Nepali communities get their identity from their *dharma*, and *dharma* is kept alive in the community. In other words, both *dharma* and communities are in a complementary relationship but exist for each other.

Dharma with rituals and festivals makes their gods part of society and makes them active in it. Materially speaking, some of the gods that Nepali people worship do not look more than mere stones or wood; however, it is not the material that is focused during the rituals. Grieve's ethnographic study on Nepali *dharma* showed that in the Nepali community "god-images are brought to life by being enmeshed in a net of social practices." He adds further, "The ceremony indicates that worship is a type of recipe that brings together materials and methods that furnish the divine with 'eyes and ears' by treating god-images as if they were extraordinary persons."[34] Rituals, the practical aspects of *dharma*, turn "a simple stone," "the seat of the gods," and place in the society.[35] Eventually, the divine presence is felt in the community and people's lives and becomes an essential part of *dharma*.[36]

Quite different from Nepali *dharma*, the social Trinity stands for the divine relationship of the persons within the Trinity than the human society. Most of the theologians borrow the Greek term *Perichoresis*, the mutual indwelling, and co-inherence of three divine persons, to express the social nature of triune God.[37] However, perichoresis does not stand for the intra-divine relationship alone; instead, it opens to human society and all the creation of God. As Moltmann says, "This *perichoretic* unity of Jesus with God the Father is not an exclusive unity; it is a community

---

33. Gautam and Thapa-Magar, *Tribal Ethnography of Nepal*, 264, 304. Among various people groups mentioned by the authors, *Tamangs* are the Buddhist people, who have their own deities, priest, festivals and Life cycle rituals. These *dharma* related features give them their identity and distinguish them from other people groups in Nepal. Similarly, *Thakuri* people group who claim to be Hindus, but their traditions and rituals are different from other Hindus of the society.

34. Grieve, *Retheorizing Religion in Nepal*, 23.

35. Michaels, *Homo Ritualis*, 57.

36. Michaels, *Homo Ritualis*, 125. Points out that all gods become part of *dharma* when people perform annual memorial ritual of ancestors.

37. Kinnison, "The Social Trinity and the Southwest," 4.

The Trinitarian Dharma

so open, inviting, and embracing that the community of the disciples can exist in the triune God: that they also may be in us."[38] While the community that *dharma* stands for is entirely a human community where gods and belief in gods find their role and significance for the community, the social Trinity speaks of a divine community that projects the ideal community for a human being in the world.

Similarly, Boff says that "if God means three divine persons in eternal communion among themselves, then we must conclude that we also, sons and daughters are called to communion. We are the image and likeness of the Trinity. Hence, we are community beings."[39] The human community exists as the reflection of the trinitarian community, from which the human community receives its characteristics.[40] In other words, like *dharma* dictating the Nepali communities, the social Trinity influences the communities it envisions.

The concretizing of the Trinity-envisioned human community happens with the church as the trinitarian community. Here just like *dharma* becomes the identity of a particular community in Nepal, a church as a Christian community constructs its identity from the trinitarian community of God. As for John D. Zizioulas, the churches are to be modeled after the Trinity, he argues, "There is no model for the proper relation between communion and otherness either for the Church or for the human being other than the trinitarian God. If the Church wants to be faithful to her true self, she must try to mirror the communion and otherness that exists in the triune God. The same is true of the human being as the 'image of God'. The relation between communion and otherness in God is the model both for ecclesiology and for anthropology."[41]

As the importance of community in the Nepali context is not limited to religious matters or every aspect of the community is made into *dharma* affairs, the trinitarian church is also called to be inclusive of all matters religious and social.[42] Leonardo Boff's idea of the trinitarian church reflects the *dharma* community to some extent. He says, "The church's communion is not expressed merely in the religious field. It also takes place in a social project

---

38. Moltmann, *A Broad Place: An autobiography*, 289.

39. Boff, *Holy Trinity, Perfect Community*, 2. Boff speaks for the importance of relations and communion over individual merit and beliefs.

40. Moltmann, *A Broad Place*, 289.

41. Zizioulas, *Communion and Otherness*, 4.

42. Moltmann, *The Source of Life*, 95.

Dharma and the Social Trinity

of the communion of goods, sharing of life, and the creation of kinship."[43] Though it is identified according to the *dharma* of the particular community, Nepali communities are not only concerned regarding their religious matter. As a trinitarian community, the church is called to maintain its distinctive features, especially in its local context. Plurality within the churches as well as among the churches is also desired. However, cooperation among local churches and their oneness is maintained by the local churches' relationship with the trinitarian community.[44] The trinitarian community calls for openness toward the like and unlike.[45]

While Nepali communities maintain their differences and distinctness, they lack the openness of the social Trinity. In Nepal, certain aspects of *dharma* are transcultural and trans-clans that constitute the collective identity of Nepal. Certain festivals act as a force of unity in the whole country of Nepal.[46] For example, *Dashain* is the most significant part of Nepali *dharma*, and it is trans-culturally celebrated throughout Nepal. At the same, the *Dashain* festival is also celebrated at the national level from the part of Nepal's government. Such a trans-cultural aspect of *dharma* brings Nepali communities into one.[47] Unlike Nepali communities built around *dharma*, which tends to focus on the lives of the people who belong to the particular community, the church as a Trinitarian community is called to be part of the life of all. As Boff says, "The more the church imbibes from its eternal fountain, the trinitarian communion by which the three distinct Ones are unified and are one God, the more it will overcome its internal divisions. It will cease being clerical and lay and will become a space of equal relationships in a single people of God, of true brothers and sisters serving the reign of the Trinity."[48]

Social Trinity and Nepali *Dharma* are both committed to community building and service. While Trinity is speaking of the community in a universal term, the community of *dharma* is anything but contextual. The local church, as a trinitarian community, can adapt to its specific context. In Nepal, the specific contexts are the communities defined by *dharma*. In the

---

43. Boff, *Holy Trinity*, 43.

44. Zizioulas, *Being as Communion*, 254.

45. Jürgen Moltmann, *A Broad Place*, 284.

46. Majpuria and Gupta, *Nepal: the Land of Festivals*, 7.

47. Gellner and Letizia, "Introduction: Religion and Identities in Post-Panchayat Nepal," 12.

48. Boff, *Holy Trinity, Perfect Community*, 44.

The Trinitarian Dharma

Nepali context, local churches have their trinitarian mission to participate in the communities defined by *dharma*.

NEPALI CHRISTIAN *DHARMA* AS *DHARMA* OF AND FROM THE MARGINS

Both Social Trinity and Nepali *Dharma* are committed to community building. While *dharma* is making a more closed community and deals mostly with inner-community matters, trinitarian communities tend to be more open to outsiders. Since Nepali communities are closed, they reject others as foreigners without giving a second thought to their potential. Anyone crossing the line of community is named as a *dharma* destroyer.[49] It is a task to transform a closed system into an open and willing community.

The meaning of *dharma* is also a service to the community and humanity. Everyone related to *dharma* is expected to assist and contribute to the community. *Dharma* becomes an ethical principle for individuals to be involved in the community.[50] *Dharma* defines society differently regarding ethics than the Western language of the rights of individuals. From the *dharma* perspective, the language of human rights is empty and is not grounded in society's principle, the *dharma*. For Nepali people, evaluating *dharma* based on the human rights perspective is not a fair comparison, because human right is not committed to the community for which *dharma* is a binding principle.[51] Dharmic society speaks in terms of the community's collectivity and harmony rather than an individual's rights apart from the community.

One cannot deny that, in Nepal, though *dharma* is committed to society's harmony, many people are suffering due to discrimination and oppression. With its emphasis on community harmony over people's individual rights, *dharma* cannot tackle social problems and provide relief to the individuals and people groups suffering in the community.[52] This section explores if the import of the trinitarian community concept helps Nepali

---

49. Ghimire, "Religious Conversion in Nepal: from Superstition to Liberation," 82. In this article, Ghimire has done case study of religious conversion of Nepali people who leave their traditional *dharma* to Christianity, and he cites in one of the case the converts are called *dharma chhada*, meaning a degratory term *dharma* rejecter.

50. Rai, *Human Rights in the Hindu-Buddhist Tradition*, 60.

51. Rai, *Human Rights in the Hindu-Buddhist Tradition*, 61.

52. Dhungana, "Nepali Hindu Women's Thorny Path to Liberation," 39–57. This article shows how *dharma* has been the cause of the suffering of Nepali women, and difficult path to their liberation.

Dharma and the Social Trinity

dharma be effective toward people's suffering. As previously mentioned in the earlier chapter, the problems in Nepali society can be outlined in three main categories: the caste system, the suffering of women, and poverty.

Dharma *from and of the Margins Resists Caste Discrimination*

Nepali society is segregated into many castes and sub-castes; many people blame the ancient Hindu caste system[53] for such chaos. Today such a caste system and segregation have been made part of Nepali *dharma*. In the past, such segregation and imposing of the same system were done for political purposes. However, in the present time, the system has been internalized by the Nepali people. Now there are some privileged people while others are suffering from discrimination. Even after Nepal's constitution has made it illegal to make caste-based discrimination against any in society, caste discrimination is not eradicated.[54] Many Nepali low-caste people continue to suffer discrimination and other tortures related to the caste system at the community level.[55]

The caste system is the biggest black lash against the Nepali *dharma* and it still protects and promotes such discriminatory policy in the society. Many admirers of such a system point to the functionality of the caste system. They believe that the caste system provides *dharmic* moral education to the people regarding their caste's manners and customs. They also point out the cooperation within the caste.[56] Though these people agree that the caste system has some defects, their concerns are more about economic development and national integration at risk, not the discriminated low caste people's rights.[57] People who advocate *dharma*'s integrity still insist that the caste system in Nepal is about social harmony and cooperation.[58] Those people who seek to disregard the caste system and cross the boundary to make relationships with other castes are considered the ones who

---

53. Johnson, "Caste," 80. Verna system indicates traditional Brahmanically established, idealized hierarchy based on social function. It is a very complex system which is divided into castes, subcastes, and sub-subcastes. Now this caste system has infiltrated every part of Nepali society.

54. *Constitution of Nepal*, 2072, Part 3.23, p. 11.

55. Rajopadhyaya, "History of Dalit movements in Nepal," para 5–7.

56. Regmi, *Dimensions of Nepali Society and Culture*, 106.

57. Regmi, *Dimensions of Nepali Society and Culture*, 108.

58. Rai, *Human Rights in the Hindu-Buddhist Tradition*, 65.

The Trinitarian Dharma

have interrupted the rhythm of society's *dharma*.[59] This way, *dharma* as a social system is incapable of understanding the suffering of low-caste people because its prime focus is social harmony and preservation of tradition rather than uplifting people's lives.

In contrast to Nepali *dharma*, which is determined to preserve community harmony rather than helping the people suffering caste discrimination, the social Trinity is known for its egalitarianism. In trinitarian social language, even within the divine community, there is no superiority of any sort because the Trinity stands for radical equality.[60] The social trinitarian relationship of God is the source of inspiration for achieving equality. Unlike *dharma*, which focuses on the function of society, trinitarian theology speaks of the religious community, which represents equality, life, love, and communion, that there is no superiority and inferiority to others. Though the trinitarian community respects and maintains the difference, it refuses to relate the differences with inequality.[61] Leonardo Boff ties divine equality to human society, that "The trinitarian mystery beckons us toward social forms in which all relations between persons and institutions are valued, in an egalitarian way, one of kinship and respect for differences. Only thus will oppression be overcome and life and freedom triumph."[62] The equality, respect, and cooperation between three persons of the trinitarian community are expressed through humans in the community. Here again, the church, which is the trinitarian divine community's image, forms the context for human equality in society. Church then draws people of all sides toward the trinitarian community of God.[63]

In the Nepali context, where *dharma* strives to maintain harmony in the community can partner with the social Trinity to make the society a harmonious inequality. While *dharma* is useful in Nepali society for its identity, the social Trinity prevents *dharma* from making certain people's groups superior. *Dharma* does allocate the role for each individual and people group in the society, but segregating people based on the roles and opportunities

---

59. Acharya, *Nepal Culture Shift*, 263–66. Acharya is documenting the changes occurring in Nepali society, but he laments on the rise of inter-caste marriage as the interruption of the rituals and culture. This is the prime example, how people cannot view caste discrimination as the problem of the society.

60. Kinnison, "Social Trinity and South West," 7.

61. Boff, *Holy Trinity, Perfect Community*, 64.

62. Boff, *Holy Trinity, Perfect Community*, 64.

63. Grenz, *Social God and Relational Self*, 303.

Dharma and the Social Trinity

to make an oppressive society. Here looking to the perfect, holy community of Trinity can be an inspiration for the Nepali community.

Dharma *from and of the Margins Struggle for Gender Justice*

Nepali is a country where *dharma* incorporates the worship of many female goddesses. As part of Nepali *dharma*, many virgin girls are established as the living goddesses named *Kumari*, from whom even the heads of government seek a blessing in national rituals.[64] Yet, unfortunately, a certain aspect of *dharma* makes Nepal a difficult place for women to live. Women are regarding lesser important than men in the family and society because *dharma* gives the importance of males in society. This research seeks to find out if Trinity is better positioned to help Nepali *dharma* find solutions to women's plight in society.

Nepali *dharma* puts men over women, just like the caste system's hierarchy is supported by it. Especially in family *dharma*, men are considered the gods of women, whose role is to serve their husbands and be under their authority at all costs. Women are not supposed to have the right to family property.[65] *Dharma* plays a significant role in forming such a social ideology that makes women lesser than men. Women are never free in society. Before their marriage, women are under the control of their parents, especially the Father, and after the marriage, they are put under the realm of their husbands and sons.[66] During the menstrual period of a woman, she is considered unclean and forbidden from entering her home or touching household holy items or people. She must purify herself after the menstrual period ends and resume her regular life as a normal woman.[67]

Regarding the family *dharma*, men are supposed to fulfill their duty to provide male offspring to continue the family lineage. Women are not considered as partners to fulfill this *dharma* but as vehicles to achieve male children. In the past, many men got more than one wife because their first wives could not give birth to a male child. The *dharmic* preference of the Son is so high that the daughter is neglected in the home. When a son is born in a family, there is rejoicing and celebration, but no one gives care in

---

64. Demaury, *Kumari Living Goddess Nepal*, 3.

65. Holmelin, "Competing Gender Norms and Social Practice in Himalayan Farm management," 85–95.

66. Vaidya, Manandhar, and Joshi, *Social History of Nepal*, 96.

67. Keshar Lall, *Nepali Customs and Manners*, 17.

The Trinitarian Dharma

the case of a daughter.[68] Today's advanced technology made it possible to detect the gender of the child before birth, and some parents take extreme measures to discard the baby if it is a girl.[69]

Nepali women are generally very religious and faithfully fulfill their *dharma* requirement to earn salvation for the next life. No matter how devoted they are to the *dharma*, it does not grant liberation from the suffering of the present life.[70] The *dharma* path also ends if a woman is a widow because she is deprived of religious ceremonies and activities to perform her *dharma*.[71] A widow's *dharmic* doors are closed for her unless she is from a wealthy family who can indulge in expensive *dharma* such as constructing temples etc.[72]

From the perspective of women's suffering, Trinity is not a women-friendly concept. Trinity has been understood as supportive of the images that subordinate women in society. Well-known feminist theologian Elizabeth Johnson is critical of using the male language of the Trinity and calls for a new way to conceptualize the Trinity. She says, "Giving rise to the uncritically held assumption that maleness is of the essence of the triune God, it has the sociological effect of casting men into the role of God while women stand as dependent and sinful humanity."[73] Trinity that siding with the male supremacy would not fare better than *Dharma* in Nepali society. However, Johnson is critical of the Trinity, which does not recognize its relational characters but rather speaks in terms of divine modes with no inner trinitarian life. Johnson is searching for a reciprocal trinitarian symbol, and only such a symbol can represent life and love.[74] Social Trinity, which inherently speaks of a relational Triune God, is favored by those who like to address women's subordination in society. Nepali *dharma*, which is entangled in the social issues of women's suffering but cannot find its way out because it is committed to the preservation and continuation of the *dharma*, can adopt social trinitarianism to make way for women's liberation in society.

---

68. Vaidya et al., *Social History of Nepal*, 96.
69. Adhikari, "Son preference over daughter high among Nepalis," para 1–3.
70. Dhungana, "Nepali Hindu Women's Thorny Path to Liberation," 41.
71. Yadav, "White Sari—Transforming Widowhood in Nepal" 1–24.
72. Vaidya et al., *Social History of Nepal*, 106.
73. Johnson, *She Who Is*, 203.
74. Johnson, *She Who Is*, 206.

Social trinitarianism speaks of God in terms of his participation in the world, which is to heal, redeem, and liberate by bringing the world into trinitarian life.[75] Women are made part of the Nepali society with many relations terms such as mother, sister, daughter, and friend, the relational God of the social Trinity, conveys the message of women's liberation. It does this by incarnating God's power in human agents, such as the church, to reflect the relational image of the triune God.[76] While in Nepal, the women's relationships have not been reciprocal but subordinated by their male relatives, the connections are not equal. The trinitarian relationship represents an authentic self-giving relationship characterized by the preservation of freedom and liberation.[77] Thereby, Trinity provides the resource for Nepali *dharma* to uplift women in society by promoting the genuine relationship of self-giving and preserving others' freedom.

Dharma *from and of the Margins* Search for the Fullness of Life for All

In Nepal, *dharma* means to be responsible in society with one's resources and capacity. Nepali people are committed to charity to earn the merits of *dharma* for their lives to come.[78] However, Nepal is among the least developed countries in the world[79], and the poor people in the community are neglected and fall into the vicious cycle of poverty, never to be free from it. *Dharma* may not be entirely at fault because it does call for the life of sharing.[80] The effectiveness of *dharma*'s call for a sharing in life needs to be examined because the chronic poverty of certain people groups in society indicates the social system's systemic faults.

---

75. Johnson, *Quest for the Living God*, 214.
76. Carr, *Transforming Grace*, 152.
77. Bacon, "Thinking the Trinity as Resource for Feminist Theology Today?" 460.
78. Rai, *Human Rights in the Hindu-Buddhist Tradition*, 60.
79. "South Asia: Nepal," *World Fact Book*, (CIA: August 4, 2020), accessed August 29, 2020, World fact book states that per capita income of Nepali people ranks 195 in the world, which is among the poorest of the poor.
80. Acharya, "Measuring and Analyzing Poverty: With a Particular reference to the Case of Nepal," 195–215. The Author points out that certain people groups are more vulnerable economically, and caste system makes it even more difficult some people group to lift themselves from their economic poverty.

The Trinitarian Dharma

Another aspect of *dharma* is believed to be directly related to the cause of poverty in the country, which is called *karma*.[81] Karma means work or one's deed in life for the sake of *dharma*, but mostly in Nepal, it is understood as fate. *Karma*, as good work, is done for the betterment of your next life, and if your present life is not satisfactory, it has to result from the bad *karma* of the previous life.[82] Since this is the consequence of a previous life's deeds, people think nothing can be done about it. As a result, Nepali people resign to fate rather than seeking a way out of their dreadful condition, which includes their caste, economic status, marital, and family life. People in the low caste, women and poor, all blame their fate or karma for the plight of their lives. *Dharmic* teachings in Nepal also focus on helping people accept their lives rather than encouraging them to liberate themselves from their suffering.[83]

Dharma, which has been the reason for the retention of Nepal's caste system, traditionally allocated certain privileges to the higher caste people, especially the Brahmans, the priestly class. Such provisions from the government of the past put certain people groups above others in society in terms of financial and educational capacity.[84] Lack of change in society and reluctance from *dharma* and its protector to change their traditional way of doing things has pushed certain people group into the bottom.[85] Though reducing poverty, is probably the government's jurisdiction to work on, *dharma* as the basic principle still lacks the direction to lead people to share and uplift life.

Dharma does demand ethical participation in society, but it has shown certain ambiguities against public participation in sharing and economic and social equality.[86] Unlike *dharma*, the commonality of social trinitarianism speaks in terms of the economy, politics, and social aspects

---

81. Majpurias, *Religions in Nepal*, 66. "Action or *Karma* must be in conformity with *dharma*." It shows that *karma* is integral to the concept of Nepal

82. Regmi, *Dimensions of Nepali Society*, 118.

83. Bista, "Structure of Nepali Society," 110. Bista is a renowned anthropologist from Nepal. Regarding the Fatalistic philosophy among people he writes, "Fatalism does not encourage people to work hard or to believe in self-promotion of personal industry . . . . Preaching have no promise or hope for the poor and the deprived except in the life after. Therefore, the enterprising people of the society, including the individuals who are paid to preach, neglect those moral injunctions completely."

84. Vaidya et al., *Social History of Nepal*, 42.

85. Tiwari, "Horizontal Inequalities and Violent Conflict in Nepal," 34.

86. Boff, *Trinity and Society*, 151.

Dharma and the Social Trinity

of human life. Communal life that Trinity calls is not to be equated with the socialist vision of the society, which speaks of communalism and egalitarianism, but it leaves out to foster an individual's differences. Simultaneously, the Trinity does not stand with the powerful in the name of the majority but makes self-giving love the basis for social decisions.[87] Trinitarian calls for social life in the Nepali context speak of social participation, making self-giving the part of *dharma*.

From a social trinitarian perspective, fate has no place in society because it seeks to make a community based on love. From the standpoint of love, fate cannot be an excuse for anyone's suffering.[88] While *dharma* calls for good karma as ethical participation in society is directed toward self-promotion in the life to come, the trinitarian call, which is based on love, is directed outward, promoting the receiver of love. Our love in the trinitarian realm is about God's love toward the world. As Moltmann puts it, "Our neighbor too- even our enemy- belongs as an object to God himself in the movement of our love for God. Neighbor, sinner, and enemy will be loved because they are the image of God, and so that they may be led to God and belong to God."[89] From the standpoint of God's love, fate cannot be an excuse for anyone's suffering, let it be the financial one. The trinitarian community cannot ignore others' suffering in the community because of the love that is fundamental to the community.

Social Trinity, in its eschatological orientation, calls all individuals of society to be involved in life from God's Kingdom's perspective. The trinitarian history of God moves toward the final consummation in the eschatological kingdom of God. In its movement toward the final course to the *eschaton*, God does not overpass human lives here on earth, but God's history takes place in the human lives to unite his creation to himself.[90] The trinitarian history in Nepali people's lives, which is eschatological in direction, does not leave them in the hand of the fate of *karma*, which is the consequence of supposedly past life. Instead, it involves them from the perspective of God's future and its open possibilities for all. *Dharma*, though, incorporates religious and non-religious aspects of human life. It is shy on the subject of social injustices and leaves *karma* to define it. However, the Trinity calls for a communion life that embraces the whole

87. Boff, Trinity and Society, 150–51.
88. Moltmann, *The Spirit of Life: A Universal Affirmation*, 248.
89. Moltmann, *The Spirit of Life*, 249.
90. Moltmann, *Trinity and Kingdom*, 94–96.

The Trinitarian Dharma

being. The trinitarian communion is to be manifested in the social, political, and economic lives of people.[91]

Dharmic community includes social and religious functions, but it does not necessarily take responsibility for all people's needs. The church, as the trinitarian community, has its mission among the human being and their need. A trinitarian community cannot overlook people's economic depravity because the trinitarian communion is expressed beyond the religious field by sharing life and goods.[92] As a trinitarian community in Nepal, the Nepali Church can be part of Nepali *dharma*, adding such an eschatological participating perspective of trinitarian vision.

NEPAL CHRISTIAN *DHARMA* DIALOGUES WITH OTHER RELIGIONS

In the historical analysis of Nepali society and Nepal's religion, Chapter 2 argued that Nepali *dharma* is a unique religious system that collaborates with many traditions such as Hinduism, and Buddhism, and indigenous practices such as animism and shamanism. Nepali *dharma* has adopted all these features to make the society, and different *dharma* practices within Nepali are never a problem. However, when Nepali *dharma* encountered Christianity, the relationship between the two has not been very cooperative.[93] Christianity in Nepal has faced numerous challenges due to its presence in the society that is defined by *dharma*.

Dharma has taken a confrontational stance against Nepali Christians in the community. Christianity has been understood as a foreign *dharma*. It means Christians are the ones who follow foreign gods and ways of living in society.[94] They are the ones who disturb the social harmony that *dharma* is attempting to maintain in society.[95] Norma Kehberg's ethnographic research on Christian presence in the Nepali Society shows several cases of conflict between *dharma* and Christianity. According to her findings, 66% of the hatred toward Christianity came from family, community, and neighbors. The confrontation is Nepali Christians' rejection of *dharma* as the way of life, such as not following the funeral of dead parents as defined by their

91. Boff, *Holy Trinity, Perfect Community*, chapter 22, Kindle.
92. Boff, *Holy Trinity, Perfect Community*, chapter 23, Kindle.
93. Letizia, "Ideas of Secularism in Contemporay Nepal," 53–55.
94. Kehrberg, *The Cross in the Land of the Khukuri*, 156.
95. Sharma, *From this World to the Next: Christian Identiy and Funerary Rites in Nepal*, 179.

Dharma and the Social Trinity

community and family *dharma*.⁹⁶ Converting to the Christian faith is synonymous with rejecting the *dharma*. Even Nepali people who converted to Christianity think that rejecting the traditional cultural way of life is essential to their belief. Their rejection of *dharma* includes the religious or ritual aspect of *dharma* and the social life in the community.⁹⁷

The rift between Nepali society in general, and the Christians exists because Nepali Christianity has not made itself open toward the Nepali culture, the concept of *dharma*, and more. Mangal Man Maharjan, a renowned Christian leader from Nepal, published a book titled 'A Comparative Study of Hinduism and Christianity,' in which he brought Western dogmatic theology to compare with the philosophical teachings of Hinduism. He neither tried to relate to society's *dharma* nor sought to interpret Christian theology in the Nepali concept.⁹⁸ Recently, the call for a new Nepali contextual theology has been growing—however, the main focus is to defend the Christian faith in the larger non-Christian society.⁹⁹ Nepali Christians need to be involved in issues like the caste system and other social problems. If Nepali Christianity seeks to be the problem solver of Nepali society without opening itself for and toward *dharma*, it will always remain an outsider. Moreover, their goodwill gesture toward Nepali society is considered an attack on their *dharma* from outsiders.

Nepali Christianity has adopted an attitude of non-involvement regarding anything religious nature in Nepali social life. *Dharma* is intertwined into all aspects of Nepali life. Nepali people's attempt to find a line between religious and non-religious in Nepali society creates further rifts between Christianity and Nepali culture.¹⁰⁰ A genuine effort from Nepali Christianity is needed to mend the separation between Nepali society and the Christian presence in Nepal. Bal Krishna Sharma, who has done extensive research on a social issue raised by Christian refusal to cremate the deceased body because it is considered a Hindu practice,

---

96. Kehrberg, *The Cross in the Land of the Khukuri*, 156.

97. Kehrberg, *The Cross in the Land of the Khukuri*, 159. Sharma, *From this World to the Next*, 180. Sharma writes that Nepali Christians are reluctant to participate in social aspect of *dharma* activities, such as the funeral rites.

98. Maharjan, *Comparative Study of Hinduism and Christianity*, 59.

99. Bakkavemana, "Toward a Nepal Christian Theology: A Proposal," 135–39. The writer puts syncretism as possible distortion to the Christian message.

100. Kirchheiner, "The Challenge of Tika between Christian Traditional Nepalis," 104–7. Kirchheiner points out that Nepali Chrsitian make abstract distinction between what is religious, *(sanskar* in Nepali), and what is non-religious (*sanskriti* in Nepali).

The Trinitarian Dharma

calls for a broader perspective from the side of Nepali Christians.[101] In the words of Kehrberg, the issue is that "for the church in Nepal is how to be a good citizen of Nepal, in a society which is Hindu, and remain faithful to the Gospel."[102] Christianity in Nepal needs to find a model to develop a relationship with society and be part of it.

Social trinitarian theology stands for the view that trinitarian God is a community, a model for the relationship between themselves and others. The church takes its root in the Trinity, where fellowship with otherness is complete.[103] John Zizioulas says that social trinitarianism is a model for developing a relationship between the world and the church, but it is the only way to remain a true church. He says, "There is no model for the proper relation between communion and otherness either for the Church or for the human being other than the trinitarian God. If the Church wants to be faithful to her true self, she must try to mirror the communion and otherness that exists in the triune God. The same is true of the human being as the 'image of God.'"[104] The church's relationship with God is not exclusive or limited between God and the church. Just as through the incarnation of Jesus, the trinitarian God extends His relationship to outside of himself, a church which is the image of trinitarian communion is called to extend its relationship to outside the Church.[105] The incarnation of Jesus opens the Trinity to the world and is united with it. Through the act of incarnation, two opposites, the world, and God, are joined. In other words, God is in the world, and the world is in God.[106]

---

101. Sharma, *From this World to the Next*, 198.
102. Kehrberg, *The Cross in the Land of the Khukuri*, 120.
103. Zizioulas, *Communion and Otherness*, 6.
104. Zizioulas, *Communion and Otherness*, 4.
105. Moltmann, *Trinity and Kingdom*, 120.
106. Moltmann, *Trinity and Kingdom*, 121–22.

Dharma and the Social Trinity

Figure 5—Proposed Relation between *Dharma*, Trinity, and Nepali Church

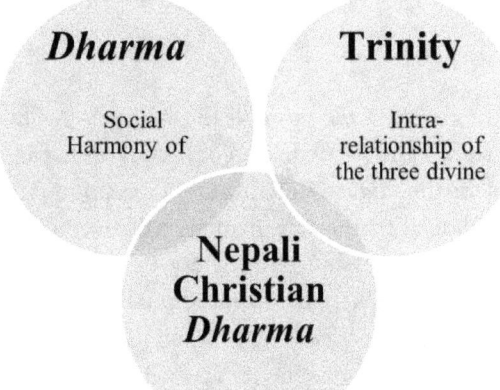

From the social Trinity side, there is a strong criticism of the Nepali church that seeks to be outside of the context and maintain its difference from Nepali society because it is ruled by *dharma*. Zizioulas states, "[A Church] is the most disincarnate entity there is; this is precisely why its content is usually borrowed from one or other of the existing cultures and is not a locality which critically embraces all cultures."[107]

In other words, the Nepali church, with its approach of relating to Nepal with not its own native culture but the one borrowed from outside, makes it an improbable trinitarian image. Nepali church cannot incarnate into Nepali society unless it adopts its culture of *dharma*. Incarnation is about the church repeating what Jesus did, and the chasm between God and history was conquered through the incarnation.[108] The Nepali church cannot be the bridge between Nepali society and the Trinity without its incarnation in the community.

Nepali church's trinitarian living is embracing a living revealed in trinitarian participation in events of Jesus and the Holy Spirit. It includes embracing the Nepali people despite their rejection. Nepali church is to seek harmony with the *dharma* and society. It also cannot ignore the problems of the suffering that this research has pointed out previously.

---

107. Zizioulas, *Being as Community*, 260.
108. Zizioulas, *Communion and Otherness*, 28.

The Trinitarian Dharma

Trinity does not allow the Nepali church to adopt a path of non-relational approach to Nepali society.[109]

SUMMARY

In Nepali *dharma*, practical religiosity is the expression of belief expressed in and through rituals and participation in society. Belief and theology are not expressed as the theological statement, but it is undoubtedly embodied in their practice. Social trinitarian theology also seems to be relevant to public life and seeks to be involved in society. Praxis is a common ground for both social Trinity and Nepali *dharma*. Social trinitarian praxis begins from divine participation in history. In Nepali *dharma*, practical religiosity is more about people's involvement in the ritual and making their god/essence part of human history. Due to the immanent divinity concept, it is more prevalent in Nepali society than Western theology's transcendentalism. Though human involvement is a prevalent priority in Nepali *dharma*, it is never the absence of the idea of the divine. Social trinitarian praxis is divine involvement in the history of humankind, which occurs through the church. Practical religiosity and the trinitarian praxis arrive simultaneously though social trinitarian praxis emphasizes the divine initiation more than Nepali *dharma*.

While the term "social" represents the trinitarian divine community, *dharma* is the building block of Nepali society though it does not claim the divine community of any sort. *Dharma* forms the Nepali community and realizes its fulfillment in society. Through the practice of *dharma*, people realize the divine presence in the community from which they derive their identity and direction in life. Social Trinity speaks of the trinitarian divine community, which has relevance for human life and society. *Dharma* marks that an individual life is impossible to be separated from the community, and divine presence is made active in people's social and personal lives. The Social Trinity also arrives at the human community level from a different perspective to the inside approach, reflecting God's incarnation into human history from the outside. In a dharmic community, the divine presence is within it, and people are joined to the divinity by practicing their *dharma*. While the community envisioned by Trinity is an open society that welcomes outsiders and provides space in it, Nepali dharmic society tends to be a closed one that does not have any space for outsiders.

109. LaCugna, *God for Us*, 401.

Dharma and the Social Trinity

Nepali *dharma* intends to maintain social harmony in society—many social problems are ignored in being functional in the community. Unlike *dharma*, the trinitarian community attempts to reflect the divine community in human history; therefore, equality and egalitarianism are prime. *Dharma* is entangled in social problems like the caste system and women suffering from its intention to maintain harmony and social function, which ignores suffering and discrimination. *Dharma* itself is bound by its commitment to social harmony and particularity that it does not function as a critical tool against repressive structures built in the name of maintaining *dharma*. Trinity, on the other hand, can also be associated with hierarchy and male supremacy over women. However, social trinitarianism can be taken as a tool to promote egalitarianism and reject any legitimacy of male superiority over women.

Dharma creates and seeks to maintain a community from within, and it becomes a closed society of certain people in a particular location. Such a stance of *dharma* puts Nepali Christians in an outsider position. Converting to Christianity is stepping outside of the *dharma* community. Nepali churches left outside of the Nepali community defined by *dharma* have taken a non-involvement attitude toward Nepali *dharma* and society. By distancing itself from Nepal's religious practices, the Nepali church makes itself ineffective regarding the social problems. However, the social Trinity can be a useful tool to make the Nepali church involved in society. The open trinitarian community toward the human history and incarnation of the Son to be part of human life can be a model for the Nepali church to eliminate its non-involvement approach and be part of Nepali society. The following chapter outlines the possible outcomes of partnering with social Trinity in the Nepali church and Nepali community.

8

Dharma Unveiled

The Trinitarian Praxis of a Global Church

FROM THE NEPALI PERSPECTIVE of *dharma*, gods are related to people's daily lives in the community, whether it be Hindu, Buddhist, or traditional animistic and shamanistic beliefs. Since *dharma* rarely expresses any theological statements other than practices in the society as part of their faith, we cannot conclude that Nepali understanding of the divine is communal or relational. However, from the Nepali way of practicing their religion, we are confirmed that in Nepal, the faith is associated with the community, and through their participation in practical religiosity, people take part in divinity. Therefore, *dharma* and Nepali people are in an inseparable bond that through *dharma*, various people groups get their identity and place in society. *Dharma*, as the religious concept of Nepali people, is relational in every aspect.

Since this study aims to provide the Nepali church a way to be part of Nepali society, because it has been outside of the Nepali dharmic community, it needs a theology that can make it open for Nepali culture within itself as well as push the church into the Nepali society for relationship. Social trinitarianism, which speaks of divine communion, demands a church to reflect the community's trinitarian image in its context by opening itself to the world and the context and making space for the world within it. The Nepali church, as the icon of the trinitarian community in the Nepali context, is required to dialogue with *dharma* for its mission and theology. Implications of such conversation between social Trinity

Dharma Unveiled

and Nepali *dharma* are drawn for the Nepali Church in the following two areas, a restatement of Trinity from the Nepali Context and Nepali Church and its trinitarian praxis of *dharma*.

TRINITY IN NEPALI CONTEXT

As an abstract philosophy, Trinity cannot relate to the Nepali context in which *dharma* as a religious system plays the role of making community and guiding community life. Trinitarian theology, which advocates the divine and world relationship, can develop a relationship with *dharma* and relate to Nepali society. God in social trinitarianism is relational and seeks to develop a relationship with his creation through the incarnation of the Son and the work of the Holy Spirit. Trinitarian God opens Himself to the creation and takes part in history, and at the same time, God invites the world and history into his own trinitarian life and makes it part of the trinitarian history. The trinitarian community is open to the history of the world, especially opening itself to the context of Nepali *dharma*. Trinitarian God seeks to be part of Nepali *dharma* and invites Nepali *dharma* in the trinitarian life.

Considering *dharma*, the Trinity is a divine community that has practical relevance for Nepali people's lives in their community. In its openness toward the world, Trinity takes part in Nepali society, giving them meaning and identity in life in the community. Trinity involves every aspect of Nepali life, their social, personal, and family life, guiding them to the right action and making them an essential member of society. Since *dharma* is not expressed in the concept or theory but by participating in it, the Trinity in the Nepali concept is more than a theory. Trinity is the participation in the divine life, and this participation is fulfilled by the daily practice of trinitarian life in society. Participation in the *dharma* derives a trinitarian understanding of God that the Trinity invites the *dharma*, and *dharma* becomes part of trinitarian life.

While the Trinity opens itself to *dharma* and makes it part of trinitarian history, *dharma* is subjected to trinitarian transformation. The *dharma* community finds an eschatological orientation to participate in *dharma* for the people. Nepali religiosity finds new eschatological goals and purpose in society. Since *dharma* becomes part of the Trinity, love, and communion add trinitarian meaning and purpose to the *dharma*. As *dharma* encounters the Trinity, people act *dharma*, but the Trinity acts among them, transforming people's lives with trinitarian love and communion. Especially, the Holy

The Trinitarian Dharma

Spirit is active in the Nepali context. Because of the Holy Spirit's presence, Nepali life and their *dharma* in society become a 'majestic sacrament of the Trinity.'[1] The Nepali community is to be a model after the communion, equality, and mutual surrender characteristics of the Trinity.

Trinitarian openness and its presence in Nepali society are as much as to appreciate the *dharma* and its contribution to the Nepali community; it is also to challenge the social injustices overlooked by *dharma*. The triune love, equality, mutual sacrificial relationship, and inclusiveness challenge the *dharma* to seek liberation and justice for caste discrimination, women, and poor people in Nepal. In Nepali society, the Trinity incarnates with the trinitarian love between father, son, and the Holy Spirit and begins the redemption and liberation works in the community. The presence is not limited to religious affairs, but it makes a holistic presence in society.

The trinitarian presence is possible by positioning the Nepali church in its context. The church represents the trinitarian characteristics in Nepali society because the church results from trinitarian work in history. Nepali church embodies the trinitarian characteristics in its life and mission in the community and makes the Trinity effective in the Nepali context.

TRINITARIAN PRAXIS OF NEPALI CHURCH

It is the Nepali church's trinitarian calling to imitate the trinitarian openness and willingness to reach the world. Nepali church cannot isolate itself from Nepali society with its non-participation and non-involvement in the community. As the trinitarian God, through the incarnation of the Son, took the first step to building a relationship with the world outside of himself, the Nepali church as a trinitarian community is to initiate reaching Nepali society and *dharma*. Through the incarnation, Jesus took the body of creation and became part of it to build the trinitarian community. Similarly, the Nepali church has a trinitarian invitation as an image of the Trinity to adopt the body of Nepali society given by Nepali *dharma*. Nepali church's incarnation into the Nepali dharmic community calls to participate in their lives and live like one of them while representing the transformation that the Trinity seeks to bring in. Nepali church becomes the trinitarian agent to infuse God's love, redemption, equality, justice, and freedom. As a trinitarian community, the Nepali church represents the mutuality and egalitarianism in Nepali society. By doing so, the Nepali church becomes the actual representation of the Trinity.

1. Boff, *Trinity and Society*, 223.

Dharma Unveiled

Nepali church, with its attitude of non-involvement in Nepali religious affairs, cannot incarnate into the society. To cross the gulf of different religious lines, Jürgen Moltmann suggests dialogue as the method.² The purpose of the conversation of Nepali Christianity with *dharma* is not to make Nepali people's religious conversions; instead, it is a call to participate, in a trinitarian fellowship that the Nepali church demonstrates in society. From the dialogue with Nepali *dharma*, the Nepali church discovers the valuable elements for a trinitarian life in the Society. The Nepali church's openness directs it to appreciate Nepali *dharma*'s practical religiosity, such as festivals and rituals that help form the community. Nepali churches can use such aspects of practical religiosity to participate in society and be witnesses of trinitarian love, equality, justice, and liberation in society. The dialogue with *dharma* is valuable for the church to find a location to live out the trinitarian calling within Nepali society. However, the dialogue Nepali church can offer Nepali people an invitation to participate in trinitarian life. By implementing trinitarian openness and dialogue, the Nepali church can expand its relationship with the wider Nepali community.

Nepali churches must invent a new way to relate to Nepali society. The traditional approach that all humans are sinners can be very counterproductive to establish a fruitful dialogue. Such a system blocks any possibility of cooperation and relation. God's willingness to approach Nepali people in their society must be a new approach. To do so, the Nepali church is not judgmental towards Nepali *dharma* but seeks to establish a relationship. Though the Nepali church holds the position of society's sinfulness, God plans to liberate it from, not to condemn the Nepali way of life. Sin should represent the suffering of people's caste system, women's oppression, and poverty.³

Dharma, as a duty of Nepali people, provides ethics for the community. Nepali church is for its fulfillment, but not to avoid due to religious differences. The trinitarian mission is to fulfill the *dharma*s as the responsibility. Therefore, church life is to be incarnated in the family as the responsibility of fathers, children, husbands, wives, brothers, and sisters, society as the individual and community responsibility, and the politics of Nepal government and citizen responsibility. While Nepali *dharma* provides the Nepali church's ethical category, it is in the mission of a trinitarian God

---

2. Moltmann, *God for a Secular Society*, 227.

3. Mangany and Buitendag, "A critical analysis on African Traditional Religion and the Trinity," 13,

The Trinitarian Dharma

that it finds its direction. Therefore, the Nepali church's dealing with Nepali *dharma* is not for conformation to it. Instead, it is for the transformation of *dharma* according to God's mission for human beings. As the trinitarian community, the church stands against *Dharma*'s attitude regarding the caste system's problem, women suffering in families and society, and poverty in the country. Nepali church must deal with Nepal's social reality as the criticism by the self-giving love of the Trinity.[4]

Perichoresis vs. Caste System and Women Suffering

Trinitarian theology imparts to the Nepali church the dignity of each human being, and therefore, it becomes a synonym for equality of people of all castes, genders, and stages of life. Nepali church does not view people with the labels given by the society in *dharma* but brings a new definition of humanity in light of the trinitarian image. Perichoresis, which stands for the trinitarian community to express the relatedness of three divine persons, is the foundation for building a Nepali church as an inclusive community where all members are equal.[5] Perichoresis is the underlining principle of the Nepali church, and it stands against all forces that bring division and rifts in the community, such as the caste system and women's oppression in society. Through the perichoresis Nepali church stands for others in society; in other words, the church involves action for the people under caste discrimination and oppressed women.[6]

Human as the trinitarian image of God is another notion that underlies the Nepali church's stance against caste discrimination and women's oppression in society. Only by acknowledging the full humanity of all people, men, and women together, the Nepali church can speak itself as an image of society's Trinity. Nepali church's solidarity with people under caste discrimination and suffering women starts from acknowledging that they are created in God's image. Being created in the image of God is the essence and destiny of all people. When the Nepali church attributes the suffering and oppressed people the title of being made in God's image, it becomes a criticism against those higher caste people who discriminate

---

4. Volf, *Exclusion and Embrace*, Introduction, ebook.

5. LaCugna, *God for Us*, 272–73.

6. Boff writes that *Perichoresis* means one person's action of involvement with the other two, and it can be principle for Nepali church to stand for the oppressed ones in the society. Boff, *Holy Trinity, Perfect Community*, Chapter 8, Kindle.

Dharma Unveiled

against the lower caste people and men who despise and oppress women in their homes and communities.[7]

Genuine friendship is what the Trinity demands from the Nepali church as its praxis and its incarnation in the society.[8] Open friendship is the principle that causes the Nepali church to initiate a relationship with the Nepali society with their self-sacrificing love and mutual uplifting. Open fellowship as the Nepali church's trinitarian praxis widens the church community to include all persons because it stands on the self-giving love that knows no boundaries and conditions. Friendship breaks the social and economic boundaries and limitations of hierarchy, difference, and hatred with boundless hospitality and society's transformation. In this sincere friendship, the Nepali church does not stand for a unitary life practice, erasing different people groups' cultural particularity. The individual characteristics and gifts of each person and cultural particularities enabled them to flourish. With the open friendship praxis, the Nepali church brings all Nepali society's particularities to celebrate every culture and particularities. The differences are not the categories to make hierarchy or separation; they are gifts to beautify the diverse Nepali society. Nepal, which is declared as 'the garden of four castes and thirty-six subcastes,'[9] shines in its beauty in the Nepali church where caste differences are not the category for hierarchy, oppression, hatred, and rejection. Nepali church, with its open friendship, stands against all divisiveness of the society because it sides with those on the margins.[10]

Open friendship crosses the barriers caused by a biological relationship such as family and clan. The trinitarian praxis of open friendship is based on free will and self-sacrifice of loving God and is not tempered and broken by any human standards.[11] Nepali church's open friendship

---

7. Moltmann, *On Human Dignity*, 23.

8. Mcdougall, "Return of Trinitarian Praxis?," 196.

9. "Nepali is the garden of four castes and thirty-six subcastes" is a famous quote of Late Great King of Nepal, Prithvi Narayan Shah, who is admired for his vision of inclusiveness of Nepali society of various people group. However, such division of castes and subcaste does not represent the social inclusiveness today rather it is the basis for hatred and discrimination. This research envisions that Nepali church truly can be transformed into a place in Nepali society where the beauty of diversity shines and has no place for hatred and discrimination. Baral, *Life and Writings of Prithvinarayan Shah*, 28.

10. Mcdougall, "Return of Trinitarian Praxis?," 200.

11. KotzeI and Noeth, "Friendship as a Theological Model: Bonhoeffer, Moltmann and the Trinity," 1–7.

The Trinitarian Dharma

attitude toward Nepali people helps society bypass any castes, gender, and other artificial divisions in Nepali society. The open friendship between the Nepali people is not temporal, but it is based on the eschatological orientation of salvation in Christ. In the open trinitarian friendship between the Nepali church and the Nepali people, God is in solidarity. Trinitarian God is among his creation.[12] In this friendship of God, no division or discrimination can exist among the Nepali community of the Nepali church. With its trinitarian praxis, the Nepali church brings Nepali society into the trinitarian divine community.

Trinitarian Love vs. the Poverty of Nepali Society

Trinitarian God sides with the poor people in society. Trinitarian God who enters the world to take part in and make it part of trinitarian life does not watch people's suffering impassively but engages in the liberation of the suffering. Trinitarian involvement in the world does not separate the religious and non-religious experience but takes life with a holistic approach.[13] The eschatological hope of God's kingdom is a must to lead Nepali society into liberation because poverty is stuck in the past with their concept of *karma* and fatalistic view of life. With its message of God's eschatological kingdom, the Nepali church does not let people resign in fate due to past *karma* but opens the possibility of God's future. The Future of God has begun with the redemption work of the Son and the liberating work of the Spirit, leading the people to the eschatological glory. Though liberation from poverty is not the absolute freedom promised by God's kingdom, it is one of its projects in society.[14]

With historical openness, God's eschatological kingdom begins a project among the poor and oppressed in Nepal, where he partners with the Nepali church. Nepali church is called to rise above to live its vocation of communion with the poor in society and help them reject the mechanisms that are the causes of their poverty. It is the Nepali church's trinitarian sacrament to be involved in the cause of poor people in Society.[15] Trinitarian self-giving love becomes a model for the Nepali church to imitate. Nepali churches should provide more than their message of hope to people. In the Nepali context, religious understanding is derived from the practice in the

---

12. Moltmann, *God in Creation*, 95–97.
13. Leonardo Boff and Clodovis Boff, *Introducing Liberation Theology*, 50–51.
14. Moltmann, *Trinity and Kingdom*, 213.
15. Boff, *Trinity and Society*, 237.

society. Love of God is not just a message of the Nepali church for the Nepali people. It is their praxis.[16] Nepali church becomes the witness of divine love by loving their neighbor themselves. Nepali churches transform themselves into a trinitarian image by living a life of trinitarian love. The recipients of the action of the Nepali church are not others but themselves. They give and live for others because it is their existence. The love and sacrifice of the Nepali church reflect God's love and sacrifice in Nepali society. By the action of love, providing for the needy, the Nepali church announces God's love in the community. For the Nepali church, not being for the poor and suffering people in the society is being in disharmony with the Trinity.

However, confronting the inequality and oppression in Nepali *dharma* as practiced in Nepali society is only possible and appropriate by being inside the Nepali community as one of them. Nepali Church should participate in Nepali social life as part of their incarnation as demanded by Nepali *dharma* to become one of them and show the trinitarian vision for Nepali society. No oppression and discrimination exist in trinitarian liberation it is the transformation brought within. Incarnation into the Nepali society and aiming for its transformation must be done simultaneously. Trinitarian inclusivity does not allow the injustices within the Nepali church. Trinitarian God who, in the incarnation of Son, stepped outside of himself to engage in history and make the creation part of himself, should instruct the Nepali church to step outside its territory to engage in the society and be hospitable enough to welcome others who is not themselves in them. The engagement and relationship in the society open the possibility of the transformation of Nepali society in Trinity's likeness. The Nepali church's social involvement is not the transformation of the Nepali society alone, but it is an essential part of its spiritual formation. It is living a trinitarian life.[17]

---

16. Lin, "Appropriating the Trinity for an Inclusive Christian Vision: 38–60.
17. David Thang Moe, "Identity and Otherness," 283.

9

Bridging Nepali *Dharma* and the Social Trinity for the Transformation of the Church

SUMMARY OF THE STUDY

THIS STUDY, AS OUTLINED in the first chapter, endeavors to foster a constructive dialogue between Nepali *dharma* and the Social Trinity. The objective is to formulate a contextual trinitarian praxis model tailored for the Nepali Church. While the analysis of *dharma* establishes the contextual groundwork, the Social Trinity is embraced to craft a trinitarian praxis for the Nepali Church.

To achieve these goals, the study follows four key steps. Firstly, it delves into the analysis of the Nepali context, revealing how the current religious landscape is shaped by various events in Nepali political history. Despite Nepal's designation as a Hindu country, its religious landscape is a fusion of Hinduism, Buddhism, and traditional folk and shamanistic practices. *Dharma*, as a comprehensive religious concept, represents the Nepali religious panorama more holistically than specific labels such as Hinduism or Buddhism. The second task involves scrutinizing the development and features of the Social Trinity. Chapter four explores the evolution of the Social Trinity, distinct from the ontological Trinity that has been a primary doctrine for centuries. Chapter five examines key features such as God's perichoretic relationship and the Trinity as a religious community open and responsive to history. The Social Trinity is contextualized alongside various expressions globally, underscoring its suitability for contextual theological dialogue, even within Nepal. The third task, covered in chapters seven and

The Transformation of the Church

eight, constitutes a dialogue between Nepali *dharma* and the Social Trinity, connecting themes such as *dharma* as practical religiosity versus trinitarian praxis. *Dharma* necessitates the Nepali church to embody its beliefs practically, intertwined with the Nepali community. Social issues like the caste system, women's oppression, and poverty are approached from a trinitarian perspective. Chapter eight outlines the significance of the Trinity in the Nepali church, emphasizing its transformative role within Nepali society.

The research concludes that both Nepali *dharma* and trinitarian theology are indispensable for shaping an authentic Nepali church. The active participation of the Nepali church in society, rooted in practical religiosity and engagement with Nepali *dharma*, is crucial for fulfilling the trinitarian mission in Nepal. Ultimately, the mission of a trinitarian God is realized through the active involvement of the Nepali church in the liberation and transformation of the Nepali community.

THE IMPLICATION FOR FURTHER STUDIES

This research endeavors to pave the way for the active involvement of the Nepali church in Nepali society by establishing a meaningful dialogue between Nepali *dharma* and the Social Trinity. While this work represents a contextual initiative, it falls short of constituting a comprehensive contextual theology for the Nepali church. Rather, it serves as an initial step toward constructing a distinctive Nepali contextual theology, emphasizing the imperative for the Nepali church to integrate itself into Nepali society. By engaging with Nepali *dharma*, this study serves as a starting point, urging the Nepali church to immerse itself in the diverse religious and social facets that can shape its theology.

While this research identifies certain social issues in Nepali society, each topic can evolve into a comprehensive theology, such as "Theology of the Nepali Caste System," "Nepali Feminist Theology," and "Theology of Nepal's Poverty." The development of these theological perspectives hinges on the willingness of the Nepali church to actively participate in these social issues from within. As the Nepali church enters Nepali society and engages with Nepali *dharma* as an active participant, numerous other theological considerations can emerge for future reflection.

Glossary

Advaita—According to Hindu philosophy, *Advaita* speaks of the existence of distinction without differentiation. Sankara was a leading figure in speaking of *Advaita* philosophy. *Brahman* is the Absolute, the truth, the ground of all existence, and human life's goal.[1]

Brahmin—A person from a Priestly caste. Or the highest caste people in Nepali society. Most Brahmins live on the western hill, and form about eighty percent of the area's total population. Nepali is their mother tongue. The primary religion of Brahmins is Hinduism.[2]

Chhetri—are the people of the second-highest caste in Nepali society. Like Brahmins, most *Chhetris* live on the western hill. Together with Brahmins, they form about eighty percent of the area's total population. Nepali is their mother tongue. Most *Chhetries* are Hindus.[3]

Christianity in Nepal and Nepali Church—Christianity in Nepal is a relatively new minority religion. Most Nepali Christians converted from their traditional religions such as Hinduism, Buddhism, or other folk practices such as animism and shamanism. Despite its short history, Christianity is the fastest-growing religion in Nepal, and it has recorded an annual 10 -20 percent growth of Christian populations.[4] Now,

---

1. "Advaita Vedānta," *The Concise Oxford Dictionary of World Religions*,.
2. Bista, *People of Nepal*, 1-11
3. Bista, *People of Nepal*, 1-11.
4. Shellnutt, "Nepal Criminalizes Christian Conversion and Evangelism,"

1

Glossary

after 60 years of Christian penetration, there are 375,699 Christians in Nepal.[5]

Dashain—*Dashain* is the most important religious festival in Nepal. It falls in September or October. It is celebrated for fifteen days. The celebration of this festival consists of various rituals, animal sacrifice, tika ceremony, and more. *Dashain* centers on worshiping Durga or Shakti, a Hindu mother goddess.[6]

Gopala—Cow herding people who once were the rulers of the land where Nepal presently is.[7]

Guthi—A Traditional Nepali Religious organization mainly involved in social work from religious perspectives. *Guthis* comprise members who celebrate the feast and festival communally. Sometimes, such *guthis* are composed of the same caste people.[8]

Hinduism and Nepali *Dharma* —Etymologically, Hinduism came from the word Hindu which is of geographical origin and the name of the inhabitants that settled near the river *Shindu* (Sanskrit name of the river Indus). Hinduism is an English word that refers to a Brahmanical faith that originated within the Indus civilization.[9] Hinduism in Nepal is its Brahmanical form, which carries a high value in social and ritual practices.[10] The concept of *dharma* characterizes Nepali Hinduism as more than a religion. It is a socio-cultural life of Nepali people. Festivals and social customs replace the creeds and dogmas of religion in Nepal.[11] Participating in the celebrations and performing the social customs characterizes the Hindu faith in Nepal. Their belief is expressed in the *dharma* (acts) of such participation and performing duties.

Christianity Today.

5. Government of Nepal, *Population Monograph of Nepal*, 18.
6. Deep, *The Nepali Festivals*, 71-78.
7. Shrestha and Bhattarai, *Historical Dictionary of Nepal*, 149.
8. Fürer-Haimendorf, "Elements of Newar Social Structure," 24-27.
9. Majpuriya, *Religions in Nepal*, 45.
10. Dastider, *Religious Minorities in Nepal*, 24.
11. Majpuriya, *Religions in Nepal*, 47.

Glossary

Kirat—Kirat is a traditional Nepali religion of *Kirat* people groups such as Rai and Limbu. Most Kirat people are initially from the eastern mountainous part of Nepal. Previously Kirat religion is also considered part of the Nepali Hindu religion. In the Kirat religion, rituals for the dead ancestor, spirit, and the land are essential. The belief is mostly based on oral traditions, but they also have their scripture called Mundhums.[12]

Mahispala—water-buffalo herding people who once were the rulers of the land where Nepal presently is.[13]

Nepali Church—Nepali Church is a body of Christian believers who converted to Christianity. Nepali churches are mostly independent churches without the direct supervision of western denominations.[14] However, some Christian churches maintain their ministry relationship with their counterparts in India. In Nepal, the Roman Catholic church has its native bishop while Pope universally heads it in the Vatican.[15] Churches in Nepal are a suffering community that faces the hurdles put forth by the Hindu majority. Christianity is seen as a foreign religion and is blamed for promoting their faith using money, and now it is made illegal to proselytize.[16] Hindu inclusivist tendency was also a challenge for Christianity to find a way to accommodate or prevent the Hindu elements in Christianity.[17]

Newar—Nepali indigenous people group originally resided in the Kathmandu valley. Most Newari people are Hindus and Buddhists and use Newari *bhasa* or Newari language. There are also well-structured social divisions (caste system) within the Newar community.[18]

Parivar—a family

---

12. Gaenszle, "Redefining Kiranti religion in contemporary Nepal,", 326-352.
13. Shrestha and Bhattarai, *Historical Dictionary of Nepal*, 17.
14. T. C. Majupuria and R. K. Majpuriya, *Religions in Nepal*, 331.
15. Sharma, "Nepal's first bishop Mgr Anthony Francis Sharma passes away," *Asianews*, (November 12, 2015.
16. Pattisson, "They use money to promote Christianity," *The Guardian* 15 August 2017,
17. Pant, "Religion, Society and State in Nepal," 47-57.
18. Gautam, and Thapa-Magar, *Tribal Ethnography of Nepal*, 115-120

Glossary

Praxis—Praxis is understood as mere practice, and it speaks more than an application of an interpretation that is independent of its practice. Praxis means that all practice is derived from a particular theory, and theory is tested by the practice it serves.[19] In praxis hermeneutics, the application is not just related to a theory or truth; instead, the interpreter correlates the interpretation task to the context to make the interpretation possible.[20] As Gadamer says, " . . . [K]nowledge must arise from praxis and . . . must relate itself to praxis."[21] Theologically, praxis speaks of a constructive task to do theology related to the reality of people's lives in a particular context. "Christian identity does not come in the form of doctrinal deliberation but in the form of liberating praxis." To be Christian is to be identified in a real context of life by participation and involvement.[22]

Rana—Rana is the ruling dynasty of Nepal, who snatched the Shah Kings' ruling power and ruled the country from AD 1846 to 1951.[23]

Saccidannanda—is a three-fold characterization of reality in philosophy. It is also a word used by Christian theologians who reflect on Hindu philosophy to express the Trinity. Sat- truth or being, cit-consciousness of the reality or truth, and Ananda-is the bliss or experience of the truth or reality.[24]

Sanskritization—refers to the influence of Sanskritic Hinduism on regional or tribal culture.[25] In the Nepali context, the term is used by scholars to denote the political attempt to make Nepal a purely Hindu nation.

Sherpa—Sherpa are a tribal people group of Nepal who mostly live in Nepal's eastern high mountainous region. Sherpa people speak their own Sherpa language. They practice a form of Buddhism and animistic religion.[26]

---

19. Tracy, *Plurality and Ambiguity*, 10.
20. Dallmayr, "Hermeneutics and inter-cultural dialogue", 29.
21. Gadamer, "Hermeneutics as Practical Philosophy," 102.
22. Gockel, "Constructive Theology, the Cross of Christ, and the Praxis of Liberation," 230.
23. Kharel, *A Brief History of Nepal*, 145.
24. Raju, *The Philosophical Traditions of India*, 228.
25. Stall, "Sanskrit and Sanskritization," 261–75,
26. Gautam, and Thapa-Magar, *Tribal Ethnography of Nepal*, 239–49.

Glossary

Sudra — are the people of the lowest caste according to the Nepali caste system. There are many occupational castes regarded as *Sudra*. Nepali is their mother tongue, and Hinduism is their religion.[27]

Tamang — One of the indigenous people groups that mostly lives in the lower mountains of Nepal. Most *Tamang* people follow Buddhism as their religion. However, many Tamang people converted to Christianity. *Tamang* people have their own language, which is Tibetan in origin. *Tamang* people have their own priest called Lama to facilitate the religious rituals and ceremonies.[28]

Trinity — Trinity speaks of the mystery of God's unity in diversity.[29] Confession of Trinity generally means the affirmation that "God is one in essence and three in-person". However, one has to confess that Trinity is "beyond human capacity to understand it in its fullness".[30] Many attempts to define Trinity has ended up being abstract and detached from human experience and life. Knowing God cannot be separated from our actions according to knowledge and faith.[31] With the Greek term *perichoresis,* Trinity can be understood as a union of person. "The Father begets the Son in the bosom of the Spirit or the Father breathes out the Spirit together with the Son, or the Spirit reveals the Father through the Son, or the Son loves the father in the Spirit, or the Son and the Spirit see each other in the Father."[32] This way, the Trinitarian community becomes the human community prototype for those who seek to build a society in the image and likeness of God.

Vaishya — is the Second lowest cast of Nepali People. Traditionally, these people were considered merchants.[33]

---

27. Bista, *People of Nepal*, 1-16.
28. Gautam and Thapa Magar, *Tribal Ethnography*, 258-80.
29. L. Boff, *Trinity and Society*, 3.
30. Sproul, *What is the Trinity,* kindle.
31. Gutiérrez and Shaull, *Liberation and Change*, 82.
32. L. Boff, *Trinity and Society*, 6.
33. Subedi, "Caste System: Theories and Practices in Nepal," 134–59..

Glossary

Yin-Yang—two opposite complementary principles in Confucian traditions. The human being lives at the intersection of the *yin* and *yang* or heaven and earth.[34]

---

34. Wang, *Yinyang: The Way of Heaven and Earth in Chinese Thought and Culture*, 1–6.

APPENDIX

Timeline of Political And Religious Development in Nepal[1]

Period	Key Political Events	Religious Development
Early history (before AD 400)	Period of *Gopala* and *Mahispala* in Nepal	Birth of Buddha in Lumbini Construction of *Swayambhunath* Stupa
Lichhavi Period in Nepal (400–879)	The flourishing of diplomacy between Tibet and Nepal after the marriage between Nepali Princess Bhrikuti and Tibetan King Strong-Tsen Gampo This period marks the economic and cultural prosperity of Nepal.	Hinduism and Buddhism had equal influence in the country. Hindu temple Changu Narayan and Buddhist stupa *Buddhanath* were constructed.

---

1. This table is made by consulting the key events timeline made by John Whelpton, and religious development provided in the work of Mollica Dastider and Narendra Shrestha and Keshav Bhattarai's compilation of Dictionary of Nepal History. Dastider, *Religious Minorities in Nepal,* xii–xiv; Whelpton, *A History of Nepal,* x–xviii; Shrestha and Bhattarai, *Historical Dictionary of Nepal.*

Appendix: Timeline of Political And Religious Development in Nepal

Period	Key Political Events	Religious Development
The Medieval Period to Malla Rule (880–1769)	Establishment of Khasa Empire in Western Nepal, many principalities under various kings were established in Nepal	Many important religious festivals such as *Intrajatra*, and Matsyendranath chariot festivals were introduced.
	Within the Kathmandu valley, there were three kingdoms frequently at war with each other.	Many religiously important temples, Taleju Bhawani, in Kathmandu were established.
	Legal codes for instituting the caste system were given	Capuchin missionaries were granted to stay in Kathmandu.
		Kings were made the protector of *dharma*
Early Shah Rule, Rana Regime (1770–1951)	King Prithvi began the formation of present-day Nepal by unification	Hinduism was made the national religion of Nepal.
	Nepal faced war with Tibet, China, and East India (British Empire)	Many Hindu systems were enforced upon people who initially followed Buddhism and other traditional folk practices.
	Nepal's ruling dynasties were in constant quarrel.	Capuchin missionaries and a small number of Nepali converts were expelled from the country.
	Rana family took power into their own hands	
		The state law was made based on the Hindu varna system. Hindu priests were in prominent government positions.

Appendix: Timeline of Political And Religious Development in Nepal

Period	Key Political Events	Religious Development
Return of Shah rule Panchayat System (1951–1990)	Formation of the Nepali Congress Party and Nepali communist party to agitate against Rana's rule. King Tribhuvan's flees to India Establishment of multiparty democracy in Nepal King Mahendra's overtake of state affairs under his direct rule (Panchayat System)	Continuation of the Hindu monarchy system in the country Policy against proselytization targeting Nepali Converts to Christianity Laws to prohibit caste discrimination promogulated. Continuation of a state sponsor of Hindu religious events Persecution of Christianity under *Panchayat* system
Democratic Kingdom & Republic of Nepal (1990–present)	People's uprising against *Panchayat* system The establishment of a multiparty democracy under the Shah Monarchy Maoist revolt has begun. King Gyanendra's dissolution of Parliament People's mass movement against Monarchy Establishment of Secular Republic of Nepal	Continuation of designating Nepal as the official Hindu country, which was changed after 2006. End of the rule of Hindu Kingship in Nepal The restriction against religious conversion Continuation of a state sponsor of Hindu rituals and state participation in such Hinduism is the de facto national religion.

Bibliography

Abhishiktananda, Swami. *Saccidananda: A Christian Experience of Advaita*. Delhi: ISPCK, 1984.
Acharya, Madhu Raman. *Nepal Culture Shift! Reinventing Culture in the Himalayan Kingdom*. Delhi: Adroit, 2002.
Adams, Marilyn McCord. "Anselm on Faith and Reason." In *Cambridge Companion to Anselm*, edited by Brian Davies and Brian Leftow, 32–60. Cambridge Companions to Philosophy. Cambridge: Cambridge University Press, 2004.
Adhikari, Ankit. "Burial Ground Row: Hopeless, Christians to Protest afresh." *Kathmandu Post,* July 24, 2013. http://kathmandupost.ekantipur.com/news/2013-07-24/burial-ground-row-hopeless-christians-to-protest-afresh-375256.html.
Ahn, Byung-Mu. *Stories of Minjung Theology: The Theological Journey of Ahn Byung-Mu in His Own Words*. Translated by Hanna In. Edited by Wongi Park Atlanta: SBL Press, 2019.
———. "Jesus and Ochlos in the Context of His Galilean Ministry." In *Asian Contextual Theology for the Third Millennium: Theology of Minjung in Fourth-Eye Formation*, edited by Paul S. Chung et al., 33–50. Cambridge: James Clarke, 2010.
Allison, Gregg R. *Historical Theology: An Introduction to Christian Doctrine: A Companion to Wayne Grudem's Systematic Theology*. Grand Rapids: Zondervan, 2011.
Anatolios, Khaled. "Discourse on Trinity." In *The Cambridge History of Christianity: Constantine to c. 600*, edited by Augustine Casiday and Frederick W. Norris, 2:431–59. Cambridge: Cambridge University Press, 2007.
Anderson, Mary. *Festivals of Nepal*. London: Allen & Unwin, 1971.
Anselm. *Monologion*. Translated by Simon Harrison. In *Anselm of Canterbury: The Major Works*. Edited by Brian Davis and G. R Evans. Oxford: Oxford University Press, 1998.
———. *On the Incarnation of the Word*. Translated by Richard Regan. In *Anselm of Canterbury: The Major Works*. edited by Brian Davis and G.R Evans. Oxford: Oxford University Press, 1998.
———. *On the Procession of the Holy Spirit*. Translated by Richard Regan. In *Anselm of Canterbury: The Major Works*. Edited by Brian Davis and G. R Evans. Oxford: Oxford University Press, 1998.

Bibliography

Aquinas, Thomas. "Theology, Faith and Reason: On Boethius On the Trinity, 1–2 (1257)." In *Selective Writings*. London: Penguin, 1998.

———. "Thomas Aquinas on Divine Omnipotence." In *Christian Theology Reader*, edited by Alister E. McGrath, 181–82. 5th ed. West Sussex, UK: Wiley-Blackwell, 2017.

———. *Summa Theologica*. New York: Benziger, 1947.

Arius. "The Letter of Arius of Eusebius, Bishop of Nicomedia." In *Documents of the Christian Church*, edited by Henry Bettenson and Chris Maunder. 3rd ed. Oxford: Oxford University Press, 1999.

Arockiadoss, P. "The Spirit of New Creation an Exploration into Dalit pneumatology." In *Frontiers of Dalit Theology*. Edited by V. Devashayam. Madras: Gurukul, 1997.

Ashwin-Siejkowski, Piotr. *The Apostles' Creed: The Apostles' Creed and Its Early Christian Context*. London: T. & T. Clark, 2009.

Athanasius of Alexandria. "Athanasius of Alexandria on the Holy Spirit and The Trinity." In *Christian Theology Reader*. Edited by Alister E. McGrath. 5th ed. West Sussex, UK: Wiley-Blackwell, 2017.

Augustine of Hippo. "Augustine of Hippo on The Trinity." In *Christian Theology Reader* 5th edition. Edited by Alister E. McGrath. West Sussex, UK: Wiley-Blackwell, 2017.

Bacon, Hannah. "Thinking the Trinity as Resource for Feminist Theology Today." *Crosscurrents* 62 (2012) 442–64.

Barnes, René Michel. "Latin Trinitarian Theology." In *Cambridge Companion to the Trinity*, edited by Peter C. Phan, 70–84. Cambridge Companions to Religion. Cambridge: Cambridge University Press, 2011.

Barth, Karl. *Church Dogmatics*. Vol. 1, *The Doctrine of the Word of God*, Part 1. Edited by G. W. Bromiley and T. F. Torrance. Edinburgh: T. & T. Clark, 1975.

———. *Church Dogmatics*. Vol. 4, *The Doctrine of Reconciliation*, Part 2. Edited by G. W. Bromiley and T. F. Torrance. Edinburgh: T. & T. Clark, 1975.

Basil of Caesarea. "Basil of Caesarea on the Work of the Holy Spirit." In *The Christian Theology Reader*. Edited by Alister McGrath. West Sussex, UK: Wiley-Blackwell, 2017.

Beeley, Christopher A. *Gregory of Nazianzus on the Trinity and the Knowledge of God: In Your Light We Shall See Light*. Oxford: Oxford University Press, 2008.

Bernard, David K. *History of Christian Doctrine: The Post-Apostolic Age to the Middle Ages, A.D. 100–1500*. Hazlewood: Word Aflame, 1995.

Bethune-Baker, J. F. *Introduction to the Early History of Christian Doctrine to the Time of the Council of Chalcedon*. London: Methuen, 1903.

Bettenson, Henry, and Chris Maunder, eds. "Nicene Creed." In *Documents of the Christian Church*. 3rd ed. Oxford: Oxford University Press, 1999.

Bevans, Stephen B. *Models of Contextual Theology*. Rev. and exp. ed. Faith and Cultures Series. Maryknoll, NY: Orbis, 2002.

Bhandari, Lok Mani. "The Role of Power Encounter in the Growth of Christianity in Nepal." PhD diss., Fuller Theological Seminary, 1999.

Bharati, Dayanand. "Conversion Is the Confusion." *Voice of Bhakti: Text and Context in Dialogue* 1.1 (Feb. 2002). http://www.bhaktivani.com/volume1/number1/conversion.html.

Birken Holtz, and Jessica Vantine. *Reciting the Goddess: Narratives of Place and the Making of Hinduism in Nepal*. Oxford: Oxford University Press, 2018.

Birtus, Ibrahim S. *Community and Trinity in Africa*. London: Routledge, 2017, ebook.

Bibliography

Boff, Leonardo, and Clodovis Boff. *Introducing Liberation Theology.* Translated by Paul Burns. Maryknoll, NY: Orbis, 1989.

Boff, Leonardo. *Jesus Christ Liberator: A Critical Christology for Our Time.* Translated by Patrick Hughes. Maryknoll, NY: Orbis, 1978.

———. *The Cry of the Earth, Cry of the Poor.* Ecology and Justice. Maryknoll, NY: Orbis, 1997.

———. *Trinity and Society.* Theology and Liberation Series. Maryknoll, NY: Orbis, 1988.

Bucur, Bogdan G. "Is Binitarian Monotheism a First Step toward Trinitarian Theology?" in *The Bible and Early Trinitarian Theology.* Edited by Christopher A. Beeley and Mark E. Weedman. Washington, DC: Catholic University of America Press, 2018.

Calvin, John. *Institutes of Christian Religions.* Book 1. 2. 4. Edited by John T. McNeill. Translated by Ford Lewis Battles. Louisville: Westminster John Knox, 1960, 243, ebook.

Canterbury, Anselm of. "Anselm of Canterbury on the Compassion of God." In *Christian Theology Reader.* Edited by Alister E. McGrath. 5th ed. West Sussex, UK: Wiley-Blackwell, 2017.

Carr, Anne E. "Anne Carr on Feminism and the Maleness of God." In *The Christian Theology Reader.* Edited by Alister E. McGrath. West Sussex, UK: Wiley-Blackwell, 2017.

———. *Transforming Grace: Christian Tradition and Women Experience.* San Francisco: HarperSanFrancisco, 1990.

Casaldaliga Pedro, and Jose Maria Vigil. *The Spirituality of Liberation.* Translated by Paul Burns and Francis McDonagh. Liberation and Theology 12. Maryknoll, NY: Orbis, 1994.

Central Bureau of Statistics. "Nepal Living Standards Survey 2003/04." http://www.cbs.gov.np/nada/index.php/catalog/9.

———. *Population Monograph of Nepal.* Vol. 2: *Social Demographics.* Kathmandu, Nepal: National Planning Commission, Government of Nepal, 2014.

Central Intelligence Agency. "Nepal: Economy." In *World Fact Book.* https://www.cia.gov/library/publications/the-world-factbook/geos/in.html.

Chaulagain, Nawaraj. "Hindu Kingship: Ritual, Power and History." PhD diss., Harvard University, 2013.

Choi Hee An. "Minjung Theology." In *The Hope of Liberation in World Religions.* edited by Miguel A De La Torre. Waco, Texas: Baylor University Press, 2008.

Chun, Young-Ho. "The Trinity in the Protestant Reformation." In *Cambridge Companion to the Trinity,* edited by Peter C. Phan, 128–48. Cambridge Companions to Religion. Cam-bridge: Cambridge University Press, 2011.

Chung, Paul S. "Introduction: Asian Contextual Theology of Minjung and Beyond." In *Asian Contextual Theology for the Third Millennium: Theology of Minjung in Fourth-Eye Formation,* edited by Paul S. Chung et al., 1–14. Cambridge: James Clarke, 2010.

———. *Constructing Irregular Theology: Bamboo and Minjung in East Asian Perspectives.* Studies in Systematic Theology 1. Leiden: Brill, 2009.

———. "The Asian Pursuit of Trinitarian Theology in a Multireligious Context." *Journal of Reformed Theology* 3 (2009) 144–56.

Clooney, Francis X. SJ. "Trinity and Hinduism." In *Cambridge Companion to the Trinity,* edited by Peter C. Phan, 309–24. Cambridge Companions to Religion. Cambridge: Cam-bridge University Press, 2011.

Bibliography

Coffey, David. "Trinity." In *Cambridge Companion to Karl Rahner*, edited by Declan Marmion and Mary E. Hines, 98–111. Cambridge Companions to Religion. Cambridge: Cambridge University Press, 2005.

Collins, Paul M. *Christian Inculturation in India*. London: Routledge, 2007. http://ebookcentral.proquest.com.ssl.access.yonsei.ac.kr:8080/lib/yonsei/detail.action?docID=438599.

Cone, James H. "Biblical Revelation and Social Existence." In *Black Theology: A Documentary History*. Vol. 1, *1966–1979*. Edited by James H. Cone and Gayraud S. Wilmore. Maryknoll, NY: Orbis, 1993.

———. *A Black Theology of Liberation*. Philadelphia: Lippincott, 1970.

Crisp, Oliver D. *Divinity and Humanity: The Incarnation Reconsidered*. Current Issues in Theology. Cambridge: Cambridge University Press, 2007.

Dallmayr, Fred. "Hermeneutics and Inter-cultural Dialogue: Linking Theory and Practice." *Ethics and Global Politics* 2 (2009) 23–39.

Dastider, Mollica. *Religious Minorities in Nepal*. New Delhi: Niraja, 1995.

D'Costa, Gavin. "The Pluralist Paradigm in The Christian Theology of Religions." *Scottish Journal of Theology* 39 (1986) 211–24. Doi:10.1017/S0036930600030568.

———. *Christianity and World Religions: Disputed Questions in the Theology of Religions*. West Sussex, UK: Wiley-Blackwell, 2009.

Deep, Dhruba K. *Popular Deities, Emblems, and Images of Nepal*. Delhi: Nirala, 1994.

Deep, Dhruba K. *The Nepal Festivals: Articles on Nepali Art, Culture and Deities*. Kathmandu: Ratna Pustak Bhandar, 2007.

Deetlefs, J. P. "Political Implications of the Trinity: Two Approaches." *HTS Teologiese Studies/Theological Studies* 75.1 (2019) 8pp. https://doi.org/10.4102/hts.v75i1.5396.

Devasahayam, V., ed. *Frontiers of Dalit Theology*. Madras: Gurukul, 1997.

Díaz, Miguel H. "The Life-Giving Reality of God from Black, Latin American, and US Hispanic Perspective." In *Cambridge Companion to the Trinity*, edited by Peter C. Phan, 259–73. Cambridge Companions to Religion. Cambridge: Cambridge University Press, 2011.

DiNoia, J.A. "Knowing and Naming the Triune God: The Grammar of Trinitarian Confession." In *Speaking the Christian God: The Holy Trinity and the Challenge of Feminism*. Edited by Alvin F. Kimel. Grand Rapids: Eerdmans, 1992.

Doig, Desmond and Dubby Bhagat. *Down History's Narrow Lanes: Sketches and Myths of the Kathmandu Valley*. Denmark, Braaten Books, 2009.

Donnell, John O.' "Trinity as Divine Community: A Critical Reflection upon Recent Theological Developments." *Gregorianum* 69.1 (1988) 25–34. https//: www.jstor.org/stable/23577819.

Dowman, Keith. *Power-Places of Central Tibet: The Pilgrim's Guide*. London: routledge & Kegan Paul, 1988.

Dünzl, Franz. *Brief History of the Doctrine of the Trinity*. Translated by John Bowden. London: Continuum, 2007.

Evans, G. R. "St. Anselm's Analogies." *Vivarium* 14.2 (1976) 81–93.

———. "Anselm's Life, Works and Immediate Influence." In *Cambridge Companion to Anselm*. Edited by Brian Davies and Brian Leftow. Cambridge Companions to Philosophy. Cambridge: Cambridge University Press, 2004.

Fiorenza, Francis Schüssler. "Schleiermacher's Understanding of God as Triune." In *Cambridge Companion to Friedrich Schleiermacher*. Edited by Jacqueline Mariña. Cambridge Companions to Religion. Cambridge: Cambridge University Press, 2006.

Bibliography

Forbes, William P., and V. K. Chaube. *The Glory of Nepal.* Kathmandu: Pilgrim, 2000.

Ford David F., and Rachel Muers, editors, *Modern Theologians: An Introduction to Christian Theology since 1918.* Oxford: Blackwell, 2005.

Fricke, Tom. "Tamang Conversions: Culture, Politics and the Christian Conversion Narrative in Nepal." *Contributions to Nepali Studies* 35.1 (2008) 35–62.

Friedman, Russell L. *Medieval Trinitarian Thought from Aquinas to Ockham.* Cambridge: Cambridge University Press, 2010.

Fulkerson, Mary McClintock. *Places of Redemption Theology for a Worldly Church.* Oxford: Oxford University Press, 2007.

Gadamer, Hans-Georg. "Hermeneutics as Practical Philosophy" (1972). In *Reason in the Age of Science.* Translated by Frederick G. Lawrence. Cambridge: MIT Press, 1981.

Gaenszle, Martin. "Redefining Kiranti Religion in Contemporary Nepal." In *Religion, Secularism, and Ethnicity in Contemporary Nepal.* Edited by David N. Gellner, Sondra S. Hausner, and Chiara Letizia. New Delhi: Oxford University Press, 2016.

Gilman, Christine. "Hinduism in Nepal." *Mahavidhya* (March 2013). http://www.mahavidya.ca/2015/03/10/hinduism-in-nepal-2/.

Gockel, Matthias. "Constructive Theology, the Cross of Christ, and the Praxis of Liberation." *Dialogue: A Journal of Theology* 56 (2017) 228–32.

Gonzales, Justo L. *Manana: Christian Theology from a Hispanic Perspective.* Nashville: Abingdon, 1990.

Goodman, Jim. *Guide to Enjoying Nepali Festivals: An Introductory Survey of Religious Celebration in Kathmandu Valley.* Kathmandu: Pilgrims, 1992.

Gregory of Nazianzus. "Gregory of Nazianzus on the Gradual Revelation of The Trinity." In *The Christian Theology Reader.* Edited by Alister E. McGrath. West Sussex, UK: Wiley-Blackwell, 2017.

Gregory of Nazianzus. *On God and Christ: The Five Theological Orations and Two Letters to Cledonius.* Crestwood, NY: St. Vladmir's Seminary Press, 2002.

Gregory of Nyssa. "Gregory of Nyssa on Human Analogies of The Trinity." In *Christian Theology Reader.* 5th ed. Edited by Alister E. McGrath. West Sussex, UK: Wiley-Blackwell, 2017.

———. "Gregory of Nyssa on Human Analogies of the Trinity." In *The Christian Theology Reader.* 5th ed. Edited by Alister E. McGrath. West Sussex, UK: Wiley-Blackwell, 2017.

Gregory Price Grieve. *Retheorizing Religion in Nepal.* New York: Palgrave Macmillan, 2006.

Grenz, Stanjey J. *The Social God and the Relational Self: A Trinitarian Theology of the Imago Dei.* Louisville: Westminster John Knox, 2001.

Grenz, Stanley and Roger E. Olson. *20th Century Theology: God and the World in a transitional Age.* Downers Grove, IL: InterVarsity, 1992.

Grey, Mary. "Feminist Theology." In *Cambridge Companion to Liberation Theology.* Edited by Christopher Rowland. 2nd ed. Cambridge Companions to Religion. Cambridge: Cambridge University Press, 2007.

Groppe, Elizabeth T. "Catherine Mowry LaCugna's Contribution to Trinitarian Theology." *Theological Studies* 63 (2002) 730–31.

Gunton, Collin. *Father, Son and Holy Spirit: Essay toward a Fully Trinitarian Theology.* London: T. & T. Clark, 2003.

———. *The One, the Three and the Many: God, Creation and the Culture of Modernity the Bampton Lectures 199.* Cambridge: Cambridge University Press, 1993.

Bibliography

Gutierrez, Gustavo. *A Theology of Liberation: History, Politics, and Salvation*. Translated and edited by Sister Caridad Inda and John Eagleson. Maryknoll, NY: Orbis, 1988.

Hale, Thomas. *Don't Let the Goats eat the Loquat Tree: Adventures of an American Surgeon in Nepal*. Grand Rapids: Zondervan, 1986.

———. *Living Stones of the Himalayas: Adventures of an American Couples in Nepal*. Grand Rapids: Zondervan, 1993.

Hall, Gerard. "Radicalizing the Trinity: A Christian Theological Reflection on Panikkar's Radical Trinity." *CIRPIT Review* 3 (2012). https://gerardhallsm.wordpress.com/wp-content/uploads/2018/08/hall-panikkars-radical-trinity.pdf.

Hasker, William. "Objection to Social Trinitarianism," *Religious Studies* 46 (2010) 421-39. Doi: 10.1017/S0034412510000107.

———. *Metaphysics and the Tri-personal God*. Oxford: Oxford University Press, 2013. DOI: 10.1093/acprof:oso/9780199681518.001.0001.

Hebden, Keith. *Dalit Theology and Christian Anarchism*. Surrey: Ashgate, 2011.

Hegel, Georg Wilhelm Friedrich. *Lectures on the Philosophy of Religion*. Vol. 1, *Introduction and Concept of Religion*. Edited by Peter C. Hodgson. Translated by R.F. Brown, P. C. Hodgson, and J. M. Stewart. Berkeley: University of California Press, 1984.

———. *Lectures on the Philosophy of Religion*. Vol. 2, *Determinate Religion*. Edited by Peter C. Hodgson. Translated by R. F. Brown, P. C. Hodgson, and J. M. Stewart. Berkeley: University of California Press, 1987.

Helmer, Christine. "Christian Trinitarian Thinking after the Reformation." In *Cambridge Companion to the Trinity*. edited by Peter C. Phan. Cambridge Companions to Religion. Cambridge: Cambridge University Press, 2011.

Hick, John. *The Metaphor of God Incarnate: Christology in a Pluralistic Age*. Louiseville, Kentucky: Westminster John Knox, 1993.

Holmberg, David H. *Order in Paradox: Myth, Ritual, and Exchange among Nepali Tamang*. New York: Cornel University Press, 1989.

Holmes, Stephen R. "Three Versus One? Some Problems of Social Trinitarianism." *Journal of Reformed Theology* 3 (2009) 77–89.

Hurtado, Larry W. "Observation on the 'Monotheism' affirmed in the New Testament." In *The Bible and Early Trinitarian Theology*. Edited by Christopher A. Beeley and Mark E. Weedman. Washington, DC: Catholic University of America Press, 2018.

Hypollytus. "Against Beron and Helix." In *Earlychristianwritings.com;* Internet; accessed: February 26, 2020. http://www.earlychristianwritings.com/text/hippolytus-dogmatical.html.

Iltis, Linda Louise. "The Swasthani Vrata: Newar Women and Ritual in Nepal." Doctoral diss., University of Wisconsin—Madison, 1985.

Ilo, Stan Chu. (2016). "Crosscurrents in African Christianity." In *Pathways for Interreligious Dialogue in the Twenty-First Century*. Edited by V. Latinovic et al. Pathways for Ecumenical and Interreligious Dialogue. New York: Palgrave Macmillan, 2016. https://doi.org/10.1057/9781137507303_14.

Ina Zharkevich. "When Gods Return to Their Homeland in the Himalayas." In *Religion, Secularism, and Ethnicity in Contemporary Nepal*. Edited by David N. Gellner, Sondra L. Hausner and Chiara Letizia. New Delhi: Oxford University Press, 2016.

Inchley, Valerie M. *the Nepali Diaspora: Migrants, Ministry and Mission*. Kathmandu, Nepal: Ekta, 2014.

Bibliography

Ingles, Andrew W. "Religious Beliefs and Rituals in Nepal." *Conserving Biodiversity Outside Protected Areas: The Role of Traditional Agro-ecosystems*. Gland, Switzerland: IUCN, 1995.
Irvin, Dale T. "The Trinity and Socio-Political Ethics." In *Cambridge Companion to the Trinity*. edited by Peter C. Phan. Cambridge Companions to Religion. Cambridge: Cambridge University Press, 2011.
Jerkins, Phili.p *The Next Christendom: The Coming of Global Christianity*. Oxford: Oxford University, 2002.
Jeyaharan, John. "A Dalit Reading of Lord's Prayer." In *Frontiers of Dalit Theology*. Edited by V. Devashayam. Madras: Gurukul, 1997.
Jha, Hemanta K. *Hindu-Buddhist Festivals of Nepal*. New Delhi: Nirala, 1996.
Johnson, Elizabeth A. *She Who Is: The Mystery of God in Feminist Theological Discourse*. New York: Crossroad, 2002.
———. *Quest for the Living God: Mapping Frontiers in the Theology of God*. New York: Continuum, 2007.
Johnson, Mark. "Lifting the Yoke: Why the *Bhakta* of Christ Should Take *Tika*." Voice of Bhakti 3.3 (2004). https://www.bhaktivani.com/volume3/number3/yoke.html.
Jones, Major J. *The Color of God: The Concept of God in Afro-American Thought*. Georgia: Mercer University Press, 1987.
Joseph, P. V. *An Indian Trinitarian Theology of Missio Dei: Insights from St. Augustine and Brahmbandhab Upadhyay*. Eugene, OR: Pickwick Publications, 2019.
Kant, Emmanuel. *The Conflict of Faculties* translated by Mary J. Gregor, New York: Abiras, 1979.
———. *The Philosophical Theory of Religion*, in *Complete Works of Emmanuel Kant*. East Sussex, UK: Delphi Classics, 2016. Kindle edition.
Kärkkäinen, Veli-Matti. "Trinity, Triune God." *Global Dictionary of Theology: A Resource for the Worldwide Church*. Edited by William A. Dyrness, and Veli-Matti Kärkkäinen. Downers Grove, IL: IVP Academic, 2008.
———. *A Constructive Christian Theology for the Pluralistic*, vol. 1 *Christ and Reconciliation*. Grand Rapids: Eerdmans, 2013, eBook.
———. *A Constructive Christian Theology for the Pluralistic*, vol. 2 *Trinity and Revelation*. Grand Rapids: Eerdmans, 2014, eBook.
Kehrberg, Norma. *The Cross in the Land of the Khukuri*. Kathmandu, Nepal: Ekta, 2000.
Kelly, J.N.D. *Early Christian Doctrines*. London: Adams & Charles Black, 1960.
Kharel, Laxmi Prasad. *A Brief History of Nepal*. Kathmandu: Pairavi Prakashan, 2019.
Khatry, Ramesh. "Christology for Everest Land". *Dharma Deepika*, 11 no 2 (Feb. 2007): 7-23.
———. "Church and Mission Relationship in Nepal—Forty Years Ahead." *International Review of Mission* 86.342 (1997) 301-5.
———. "The Authenticity of the Parable of the Wheat and the Tares and Its Interpretation." Doctoral Dissertation, Oxford University, 1991.
Kilby, Karen, "Perichoresis and Projection: Problems with Social Doctrines of the Trinity." *New Blackfriars* 81.957 (2000) 432-45.
Kim, Andrew Eungi. "Minjung Theology in Contemporary Korea: Liberation Theology and a Reconsideration of Secularization Theory." *Religions* Vol. 9 no 12. (December 2018): 415f. https://doi.org/10.3390/rel9120415.
Kim, Han Sung. "A Missiological Assessment of the State and Christianity in Nepal." *The Journal of Korean Evangelical Missiological Society* Vol. 27 (2014): 213-55.

Bibliography

Kim, Heup Young. *A Theology of Dao*. MaryKnoll, Maryknoll, NY: Orbis, 2017.

Kinnison, Quentin P. "The Social Trinity and the Southwest: Toward a Local Theology in the Borderlands." *Perspectives on Religious Studies* Vol. 35. No 3 (Fall 2008): 1-20.

Kirchheiner, Ole. Culture and Christianity Negotiated in Hindu Society: A Case Study of a Church in Central and Western Nepal. PhD Thesis, Middlesex University, 2016.

Knitter, Paul F. *Without Buddha I Could not be a Christian*. London: One World, 2009, ebook.

Kombo, James Henry Owino. *The Doctrine of God in African Christian Thought: The Holy Trinity, Theological Hermeneutics and the African Intellectual Culture*. Leiden: Brill, 2007.

Krohn, J.B. "The Triune God who Speaks: Calvin's Theological Hermeneutics." *Koers: Bulletin for Christian Scholarship* Vol. 66 (August 2001): 54-56.

Kuruvila, Kadakkal P. "The Incarnation and the Cross: The Inseparable Paradigms for An Indian Christian Theology of Inculturation and Liberation." PhD Diss., Lutheran School of Theology at Chicago, 1999.

LaCugna, Catherine Mowry. "The Practical Trinity." *Christian Century*, 109 no. 22 (1992) 678. http://search.proquest.com.ssl.access.yonsei.ac.kr:8080/docview/217196950?accountid=15179.

———. "The Baptismal Formula, Feminist Objections, and Trinitarian Theology." *Journal of Ecumenical Studies* 26.2 (1989) 235-50.

———. *God for Us: The Trinity and Christian Life*. San Francisco: HarperSanFranscisco, 1973.

Lane, D. A, "Praxis", *Encyclopedia.com*; Internet; accessed: December 5, 2019; available: https://www.encyclopedia.com/social-sciences-and-law/sociology-and-social-reform/sociology-general-terms-and-concepts/praxis.

Larbeer, P. Mohan. "Dalit Identiy—A Theological Reflection." In *Frontiers of Dalit Theology*. Edited by V. Devashayam. Madras: Gurukul, 1997.

Lawler, Michael G. "*Perichoresis*: New Theological Wine in an Old Theological Wineskin." *Horizons* 22.1 (1995) 49-66. DOI: https://doi.org/10.1017/S0360966900028930.

Lee, Archie Chi Chung. "Contextual Theology in Asia." In *The Modern Theologians: An Introduction to Christian Theology Since 1918*. Edited by David F. Ford and Rachel Muers. Oxford: Blackwell, 2005.

Lee, Jung Young. *The Trinity in Asian Perspective*. Nashville: Abingdon, 1996.

Lee, Seung Goo. "The Relationship between the Ontological Trinity and the Economic Trinity." *Journal of Reformed Theology* 3 (2009) 90-107. DOI: 10.1163/156973109X403741.

Letizia, Chiara. "Shaping Secularism in Nepal." *European Bulletin of Himalayan Research*, 39 (2011) 66-104. http://himalaya.socanth.cam.ac.uk/collections/journals/ebhr/pdf/EBHR_39_full.pdf#page=67.

Lindell, Jonathan. *Nepal and the Gospel of God*. Kathmandu: Pilgrims, 1997.

Locke, John. *A Second Vindication of the Reasonableness of Christianity, &c.* London: Churchill, 1697, 99. https://quod.lib.umich.edu/e/eebo/A48892.0001.001?rgn=main;view=fulltext.

Locke, John. *Reasonableness of Christianity: as Delivered in the Scriptures*. Chicago: Regnery, 1969.

Louth, Andrew. "Review Essay: The Orthodox Dogmatic Theology of Dumitru Staniloae." *Modern Theology* 13.2 (1997) 253–67.

Bibliography

Luther, Martin. *Creed*. Translated by C. M. Jacobs in *Works of Martin Luther* Vol. 2. Albany: Books for Ages, 1997.

———. *Disputation against Scholastic Theology*. In *Martin Luther's Basic Theological Writings*, edited by Timothy F. Lull and William R. Russell, no. 48-50. Minneapolis, Fortress, 2012, ebook.

———. *Heidelberg Disputation*, 21 in *Martin Luther's Basic Theological Writings*, edited by Timothy F. Lull and William R. Russell, no. 21. Minneapolis, Fortress, 2012.

———. *Sermon in Castle Pleissenburg, Leipzig (1539)*. In *Martin Luther's Basic Theological Writings*. Edited by Timothy F. Lull and William R. Russell. Minneapolis, Fortress, 2012,

Maharjan, Mangal Man. *Comparative study of Hinduism and Christianity*. Kathmandu, Nepal: Ekta, 2002.

Majupuria Trilok Chandra, and Rohit Kumar Majupuria. *Religions in Nepal*. Lashkar, India: Devi, 2008.

Majupuria, Trilok Chandar, and S. P. Gupta. *Nepal: The Land of Festivals*. New Delhi: Chand, 1981.

Manandhar, Jan Kaji. *Myths and Legends of Nepal*. Banepa, Nepal: Suhabeti Manandhar, 2010.

Manganyi, J.S. & J. Buitendag. "A critical analysis on African Traditional Religion and the Trinity." *HTS Theological Studies* 69 (2013) 227-40. http://dx.doi.org/10.4102/hts.v69i1.1934.

Marmion, Declan, and Rik Van Nieuwenhove. *An Introduction to the Trinity*. Introduction to Religion. Cambridge: Cambridge University Press, 2011.

Matthews, Gareth. "Anselm, Augustine, and Platonism." In *Cambridge Companion to Anselm*. Edited by Brian Davies and Brian Leftow. Cambridge Companions to Philosophy. Cambridge: Cambridge University Press, 2004.

McDermott Gerald R., and Harold A. Netland. *A Trinitarian Theology of Religions: An Evangelical Proposal*. Oxford: Oxford University Press, 2014.

McDougall, Joy Ann. *Pilgrimage of Love: Moltmann on the Trinity and Christian Life*. Oxford: Oxford University Press, 2005.

McGrath, Alister E. *Historical Theology: Introduction to the History of Christian Thought*. Malden, MA: Wiley-Blackwell, 2013.

———. "Richard of St. Victor on Love within the Trinity." In *The Christian Theology Reader*, Edited by Alister E. McGrath. West Sussex, UK: Wiley-Blackwell, 2017.

Merkle, Benjamin R. *Defending the Trinity in the Reformed Palatinate: The Elohistae*. Oxford: Oxford University Press, 2015.

Metzler, Norman. "The Trinity in Contemporary Theology: Questing the Social Trinity." *Concordia Theological Quarterly* 64.3/4 (2003) 270-87.

Mocko, Anne T. *Demoting Vishnu: Ritual, Politics and the Unraveling of Nepal's Hindu Monarchy*. Oxford: Oxford University Press, 2016.

Moe, David Thang. "A Trinitarian Theology of Religions: Themes and Issues in Evangelical Approaches." *Evangelical Review of Theology* 41.3 (2017) 234–253.

———. "From a Trinitarian Theology of Religion to a Trinitarian Theology of Religions: Bridging First theology and Second Theology." *Expository Times* 130.7 (2019) 285-304.

Moltmann, Jürgen. *Sun of Righteousness, Arise! God's Future for Humanity and the Earth*. Translated by Margaret Kohl. Minneapolis: Fortress, 2010.

Bibliography

———. *History and the Triune God: Contributions to Trinitarian Theology*. New York: Crossroad, 1991.

———. *The Crucified God: The Cross of Christ as the Foundation and Criticism of Christian Theology*. Translated by R. A. Wilson and John Bowden. Minneapolis: Fortress, 1993.

———. *The Trinity and the Kingdom: The Doctrine of God*. Translated by Margaret Kohl. London: SCM, 1981.

———. *Trinity and Doctrine of God*. Translated by Margaret Kohl. Minneapolis: Fortress, 1993.

Munteanu, Daniel. "Dumitru Staniloae's Influence on Jürgen Moltmann's Trinitarian and Ecological Theology." *International Journal of Orthodox Theology* 6.4 (2015) 24–52.

Nnamani, Amuluche Gregory. *The Paradox of a Suffering God: On the Classical, Modern Wester and Third World Struggles to Harmonise the Incompatible Attributes of the Trinitarian God*. Frankfurt: Lang, 1995.

Norman, Ralph V. "Problems for the 'Social Trinity'-Counting God." *Modern Believing* 41.3 (2000) 3-13. http://online.liverpooluniversitypress.co.uk/loi/mb.

Northey, W. Brook, and C. J. Morris. *The Gurkhas: Their Manners, Customs, and Country*. Delhi: Cosmo, 1974.

Nyamiti, Charles. "African Christologies Today." In *Faces of Jesus in Africa*. Edited by Robert J. Schreiter. Faith and Cultures Series. Maryknoll, NY: Orbis, 1997.

———. "The Theological Value of African Tradition." In *African Christian Spirituality*. Edited by Aylward Shorter. Maryknoll, NY: Orbis, 1978.

———. *African Tradition and the Christian God*. Eldoret: Gaba, 1978.

Ochab, Ewelina U. "Nepal's Protection of Religious Freedom on Downward Spiral." *Forbes*, February 7, 2018. https://www.forbes.com/sites/ewelinaochab/2018/02/07/nepals-protection-of-religious-freedom-on-downward-spiral/#3e47a34bc87b.

Ogbonnaya, A. Okechukwu. *On Communitarian Divinity: An African Interpretation of the Trinity*. St. Paul: Paragon, 1998.

Oldmeadow, Harry. *A Christian Pilgrimage in India: The Spiritual Journey of Swami Abhishiktananda (Henri Le Saux)*. Bloomington, IN: World Wisdom, 2008.

Olson, Roger E. *The Journey of Modern Theology: From Reconstruction to Deconstruction*. Downers Grove, IL: IVP Academic, 2013.

Ortner, Sherry B. *High Religion: A Cultural and Political Hisoty of Sherpa Buddhism*. Princeton: Princeton University Press, 1989.

Panikkar, Raimon. *The Interreligious Dialogue*. Mahwah, NJ: Paulist, 1999.

———. *The Rhythm of Being: The Unbroken Trinity—the Gifford Lectures*. Maryknoll, Maryknoll, NY: Orbis, 2010.

Pannenberg, Wolfhart. *Systematic Theology*. Vol. 1. Translated by Geofery W. Bromiley. London: T. & T. Clark, 1992.

Pant, Deepak Raj. "Religion, Society and State in Nepal." *Occasional Papers in Sociology and Anthropology* 3 (1993) 47-57.

Papanikolaou, Aristotle. *Being with God: Trinity, Apophaticism, and Divine-Human Communion*. Notre Dame, IN: University of Notre Dame Press, 2006.

Parrat, John, ed. *An Introduction to Third World Theologies*. Cambridge: Cambridge University Press, 2004.

———. *Reinventing Christianity: African Theology Today*. Grand Rapids: Eerdmans, 1995.

Pattisson, Pete. "They Use Money to Promote Christianity: Nepal's Battle for Souls." *The Guardian* 15 August 2017. https://www.theguardian.com/global-development/2017/aug/15/they-use-money-to-promote-christianity-nepal-battle-for-souls.

Bibliography

Perkins, Pheme. "Gnostics." In *Encyclopedia of Early Christianity*. Edited by Everett Ferguson. London: Routledge, 1999.
Perry, Cindy. *A Bibliographical History of the Church in Nepal*. Kahmandu, Nepal: Nepal Church History Project, 1990.
———. *Nepalis Around the World: Emphasizing Nepali Christians of the Himalayas*. Kathmandu, Nepal: Ekta, 1997.
Peters, Ted. *God as Trinity: Relationality and Temporality in Divine Life*. Louisville: Westminster John Knox, 1993.
Phan, Peter C., ed. *Cambridge Companion to the Trinity*. Cambridge Companions to Religion. Cambridge: Cambridge University Press, 2011.
———. *Christianities in Asia*. Oxford: Blackwell, 2011.
———. "Systematic Issues in Trinitarian Theology." In *Cambridge Companion to the Trinity*, edited by Peter C. Phan, 13-30. Cambridge Companions to Religion. Cambridge: Cambridge University Press, 2011.
Plantinga, Cornelius, Jr. "Gregory of Nyssa and the Social Analogy of the Trinity." *The Thomist* 50 (1986) 325-54. DOI: https://doi.org/10.1353/tho.1986.0017.
Platter, Jonathan. "The Trinity, Social Justice, and the Missio Dei: A Trinitarian Construal of Agency, Treating Social Justice as Paradigmatic of Christian Action." *Didache: Faithful Teaching* 13.1 (2013) 1-15.
Ployd, Adam. *Augustine, the Trinity, and the Church: A Reading of the Anti-Donatist Sermons*. Oxford: Oxford University Press, 2015.
Rahner, Karl. *Foundations of Christian Faith: An Introduction to the Idea of Christianity*. Translated by William V. Dych. New York: Crossroad, 1987.
———. *The Trinity*. Translated by Joseph Donceel. London: Burns & Oates, 1970.
RajKumar, Peniel. *Dalit Theology and Dalit Liberation: Problems, Paradigms and Possibilities*. Surrey, UK: Asghate, 2010.
Richard of St. Victor. *On the Trinity*, Book 3. II. Translation and commentary by Ruben Angelici. Cambridge: James Clarke, 2012.
Rikheim, Lars Erik. "Johannes Zizioulas." In *Key Theological Thinkers: From Modern to Postmodern*. London: Routledge, 2013.
Roberson, Ronald G. "Dumitru Staniloae on Christian Unity." In *Dumitru Staniloae: Tradition and Modernity in Theology*. Edited by Lucian Turcescu. Oxford: The Center for Romanian Studies, 2002.
Robinson, Bob. *Christian Meeting Hindus: An Analysis and Theological Critique of the Hindu-Christian Encounter in India*. Oxford: Regnum, 2005.
Rongong, Rajendra K. *Early Churches in Nepal: An Indigenous Christian Movement till*. Kathmandu, Nepal: Ekta, 2012.
Rowland, Christopher. "Introduction: The Liberation Theology." In *Cambridge Companion to Liberation Theology*. Cambridge: Cambridge University Press, 2007.
Russell, Heidi. *The Source of all Love: Catholicity and the Trinity*. Maryknoll: Orbis, 2017.
Sanders, Fred. "Entangled in the Trinity: Economic and Immanent Trinity in Recent Theology." *Dialogue: A Journal of Theology* 40.3 (2001) 175.
Sapkota, Deepak. *Ten Years of Upheaval*. Kathmandu: Revolutionary Journalist Association, 2010.
Sarot, Marcel. "Trinity and Church: Trinitarian Perspectives on the Identity of the Christian Community." *International Journal of Systematic Theology* 2.1 (2010) 33-42.

Bibliography

Savada, Andrea Matles, ed. *Nepal and Bhutan: Country Studies.* 3rd ed. Washington, DC: Federal Research Division, Library of Congress, 1993.

Schleiermacher, Friedrich. *The Christian Faith in Outline.* Translated by D.M. Baillie. Edinburgh: Henderson, 1922.

Schleirermacher, Friedrich. *The Christian Faith.* Edited by H.R Mackintosh and J.S. Stewart. Edinburgh: T. & T. Clark, 1928.

Schreiter, Robert J. *Constructing Local Theologies: 30th Anniversary Edition.* Maryknoll, NY: Orbis, 1985.

Scott, Peter. *Theology, Ideology and Liberation.* Cambridge Studies in Ideology and Religion 6. Cambridge: Cambridge University Press, 1994.

Serchan, Sanjaya. *Democracy, Pluralism and Change: An Inquiry in the Nepali Context.* Kathmandu: Chhye Pahuppe, 2001.

Sharma, Bal Krishna. *Christian Identity and Funerary Rites in Nepal,* Kathmandu, Nepal: Ekta, 2012.

Shaull, Gustavo Gutiérrez and Richard. *Liberation and Change.* Atlanta: John Knox, 1977.

Shellnutt, Kate. "Nepal Criminalizes Christian Conversion and Evangelism." *Christianity Today,* Oct. 25, 2017. https://www.christianitytoday.com/news/2017/october/nepal-criminalizes-conversion-christianity-evangelism-hindu.html.

Shin, Sung Im. "A Mission Strategy through the Contextualization of *Dashain* Festival in Nepal." Doctoral diss., Juan International University, South Korea, 2019.

Shrestha, Bal Gopal. *The Sacred Town of Sankhu: The Anthropology of Newar Ritual, Religion and Society in Nepal.* Newcastle, UK: Cambridge, 2012.

Shrestha, Manoj. "Contextual Expository Preaching: A Way of Forming Congregations that Is Faithful to Scripture and Relevant to the Lived Experience of the Nepali People." Doctoral diss., Princeton Theological Seminary, 2014.

Singh, Nagendra Kr. *Nepal: Refugee to Ruler: A Militant Race of Nepal.* New Dehli: APH, 1997.

Smith, Richard Travers. *St. Basil the Great.* London: SPCK, 1879.

Soskice, Janet Martin. "Trinity and Feminism." In *Cambridge Companion to Feminist Theology.* Edited by Susan Frank Parsons. Cambridge Companions to Religion. Cambridge: Cambridge University Press, 2004.

Sproul, R. C. *What Is the Trinity.* Orlando: Reformation Trust Publishing, 2011.

St. Augustine, *On the Trinity.* Book 5.6.7; Translated by Arthur West Haddan. *Nicene and Post-Nicene Fathers,* First Series, Vol. 3. Edited by Philip Schaff. Buffalo, NY: Christian Literature Publishing Co., 1887. http://www.newadvent.org/fathers/130105.htm.

Staniloae, Dumitru. *Orthodox Dogmatic Theology.* Vol 1, *Revelation and Knowledge of the Triune God: The Experience of God.* Translated and edited by Ioan Ionita and Robert Barringer. Brookline, MA: Holy Cross Orthodox, 1998.

———. *The Holy Trinity: In the Beginning There Was Love.* Translated by Roland Clark. Brookline, MA: Holy Cross Orthodox, 2012.

———. *Theology and the Church.* Translated by Robert Barringer. Crestwood, NY: St. Vladmir's Seminary Press, 1980.

Stead, Christopher. "Arius in Modern Research." In *Doctrinal Diversities: Varieties of Early Christianity.* Edited by Everett Ferguson. London: Garland. 1999.

Sunuwar, Olak Bahadur. 'Social Crisis and the Alien God: Pursuing Social Justice in the Land of Temples and Gods.' Doctoral Dissertation, Lutheran School of Theology, Chicago, 2019.

Swinburne, Richard. "Trinity." In *Philosophical and Theological Essays on the Trinity.* Oxford: Oxford University Press, 2009.

Bibliography

———. "A Posteriori Arguments for the Trinity." *Studia Neoaristotelica* 10.1 (2013) 13-27. DOI: 10.5840/studneoar20131012.
———. "The social theory of the Trinity." *Religious Studies* 54.3, (2018) 419–37.
Teasdale, Wayne. "Abhishiktananda's Contemplative Theology." *Monastic Studies* (1982) 194. Quoted in Oldmeadow, *A Christian Pilgrimage in India*, 143.
Tertullian. "Against Praxeas." *Early Christian Writings*. http://www.earlychristianwritings.com/text/tertullian17.html.
———. "The Incarnation of the Logos." In *Documents of the Christian Church*. edited by Henry Bettenson and Chris Maunder. Oxford: Oxford University Press, 1999.
———. *On the Flesh of Christ*. Translated by Homes, Earlychristianwritings.com. http://www.earlychristianwritings.com/text/tertullian15.html.
Tracy, David. *Plurality and Ambiguity: Hermeneutics, Religion, Hope*. Chicago: University of Chicago Press, 1994.
Upadhyaya, Brahmabandhaba. *The Writings of Brahmabandhab Upadhyay*. Vol. 1. Edited by G. Gispert-Sauch and Julius Lipner. Bangalore: United Theological College, 1991
Upreti, B. C. *Nepal: Transition to Democratic Republican State*. Delhi: Kalpaz, 2010.
Vaidya, Tulasi Rama, and Bajracharya. *Nepal: The People and the Culture*.
Vaidya, Tulasi Rama et al. *Social History of Nepal*. New Dehli: Anmoi, 1993.
Volf, Miroslav. *After our Likeness: The Church as the Image of the Trinity*. Grand Rapids: Eerdmans, 1998.
Wagner, Luke. "A Rumour of Empire: The Discourse of Contemporary Hindu Nationalism in Nepal." *Studies in Ethnicity and Nationalism* 18.2 (2018) 147-66.
Wainwright, Elaine. "Like a Finger Pointing to the Moon: Exploring the Trinity in/and the New Testament." In *The Cambridge Companion to the Trinity*, edited by Peter C. Phan, 33–48. Cambridge Companions to Religion. Cambridge: Cambridge University Press,
Walker, Theodore, Jr., "Theological Resources for a Black Neoclassical Social Ethics." In *Black Theology: A Documentary History* Vol. II *1980-1992*. Edited by James H. Cone and Gayraud S. Wilmore. Maryknoll, NY: Orbis, 1993.
Watters David E., with Steve & Daniel Watters, *At the foot of the snows: A Journey of Faith and Words among the Kham-speaking People of Nepal*. Seattle, Washington, DC: Engage Faith, 2011.
Wessels, Antonie. *Images of Jesus: How Jesus Is Perceived and Portrayed in Non-European Cultures*. Grand Rapid: Eerdmans, 1990.
Whelpton, John. *A History of Nepal*. Cambridge: Cambridge University Press, 2005.
Williams, Rowan. "Eastern Orthodox Theology." In *Modern Theologians: An Introduction to Christian Theology Since 1918*. Edited by David F. Ford and Rachel Muers. Oxford: Blackwell, 2005.
Williams, Thomas. "God who Sows the Seed and Give the Growth: Anselm's Theology of the Holy Spirit." *Anglican Theological Review* 89.4 (2007) 611–27.
Wright, Daniel, ed. *Nepal: History of the Country and the People*. Translated Munshi Shew Shunker Singh and Pandit Gunanand. 1877. Reprint, New Dehli: Cosmo, 1983.
Zimmdar GL-Rai. *Pre-Brahminic Nepal: A Brief Account of Sanskritization of Nepal*. Self-published, 2013.
Zizioulas, John D. *Being as Communion: Studies in Personhood and the Church*. Crestwood, NY: St. Vladimir's Seminary Press, 1985.
———. *Communion and Otherness: Further Studies in Personhood and the Church*. Edited by Paul Mcpartlan. London: T. & T. Clark, 2006.

www.ingramcontent.com/pod-product-compliance
Lightning Source LLC
Chambersburg PA
CBHW051742230426
43670CB00012B/2122